THE ASSIGNMENT:

WHY AM I WRITING THIS ESSAY?

Rebecca Goodman

Martin Nakell

FOUNTAINHEAD PRESS

As a textbook publisher, we are faced with enormous environmental issues due the large amount of paper contained in our print products. Since our inception in 2002, we have worked diligently to be as eco-friendly as possible.

Our "green" initiatives include:

Electronic Products
We deliver products in non-paper form whenever possible. This includes pdf downloadables, flash drives, & CD's.

Electronic Samples
We use a new electronic sampling system, called Xample. Instructor samples are sent via a personalized web page that links to pdf downloads.

FSC Certified Printers
All of our Printers are certified by the Forest Service Council which promotes environmentally and socially responsible management of the world's forests. This program allows consumer groups, individual consumers and businesses to work together hand in hand to promote responsible use of the world's forests as a renewable and sustainable resource.

Recycled Paper
Almost all of our products are printed on a minimum of 10-30% post consumer waste recycled paper.

Support of Green Causes
When we do print, we donate a portion of our revenue to Green causes. Listed below are a few of the organizations that have received donations from Fountainhead Press. We welcome your feedback and suggestions for contributions, as we are always searching for worthy initiatives.
Rainforest 2 Reef
Environmental Working Group

Cover design: Doris Bruey
Text design: Ellie Moore

Books may be purchased for educational purpose.

For information, please call or write:

1-800-586-0030

Fountainhead Press
Southlake, TX 76092

Web site: www.fountainheadpress.com
Email: customerservice@fountainheadpress.com

ISBN: 978-1-59871-374-9

Printed in the United States of America

The authors would like to thank the following friends and family who have offered support for *The Assignment:* Suzanne & Leonard Goodman, Ravi Kahn, Vahid Norouzalibeik, Prof. Anne Marie Pederson, and all of our students who have taught us how to teach them and given us advice.

CONTENTS

PART 03: The Origins of Language III: Greek Myth   85

PART 04: The Origins of Language IV: African Myth   129

Chapter 10: The Art of Language | The Ever-Changing Verb   131

Chapter 11: The Act of Reading | Dialogue with the Text   147

Chapter 12: The Act of Writing | Dialogue to Analysis to Essay   159

PART 05: The Origins of Language V: Australian Myth · 167

PART 06: The Origins of Language VI: Asian Myth · 203

INTRODUCTION
the assignment: introduction to the instructor

I. How It Came About

A writer draws on all of his or her faculties of intuition, inspiration, craft, thought, and spontaneity to express him or herself. Having observed our students in the classroom struggle to do the same, we have taken note of what stands in their way, and we have observed what serves them well. *The Assignment* teaches by following patterns of learning and the natural processes of imagination and integration.

Literacy is an active, living, ubiquitous part of our lives. Whether viewing a painting or watching a movie or listening to music or reading a book, we don't participate passively—we interact. We carry on a dialogue with the text. The painting, movie, music, or book speaks to us while we, in our own minds, speak with it. When we write, we carry on a dialogue with our reader. We see this, our book, *The Assignment*, as a dialogue with you, the instructor, and with our students.

We discuss this dialogic perspective within *The Assignment*. We provide examples of how this philosophy works in individual cases, and we give the students opportunities to practice this philosophy in their own writing. Just as the authors of paintings, movies, music, and books have something to say to us, our students have something to say to their readers about their thoughts, their experiences, their observations, and their imaginations.

To teach writing—which we prefer to call literacy—we have developed a holistic approach. The act of writing is only part of the game. Literacy is an activity that is a part of—not a study separate from—the world at large. Our students need to read well, to think critically, and we want them to come to a conscious appreciation of the significance of language in their lives.

We unify the text of *The Assignment* through the theme of silence and language. When the authors we study write, they break the silence of their lives to speak; when our students write, they break the silence of their own lives to speak. We teach our students to experience language.

We hope to inspire students with the idea that they write to express themselves. After every third Chapter in *The Assignment,* we add a short piece that we call "The Origins of Language." We begin with a primitive wall painting from the Cave at Lascaux in France. Those paintings represent a very early example of "writing," i.e., they communicate in a visual language. We then present, throughout *The Assignment,* seven myths of the origins of language from cultures around the world. We complete this cycle with a scientific explanation for the origin of language. Every culture in the world has created a language that arises from the urge to communicate. Every culture has developed a language that brings them from silence to expression. The invention of language is so central to every culture, and, in a sense, so enveloped in mystery, that every culture has developed a myth to give substance to this creative invention. Likewise, every essay in our book partakes of this urge. Every essay students write expresses this urge.

II. Design and Tone

We designed *The Assignment* for students to experience the pleasure of learning itself. Because we know that pleasure in learning will enhance the rigor necessary to learn, we want the professors and their students to enjoy this book. Maintaining a sense of respect for our students, we've used humor, fresh readings to excite and challenge the students, and a personal tone where we address the student directly.

III. The Signature Question

We begin by asking the student to write a brief essay, so you will have some of their writing to evaluate as you begin the term. We also introduce the student in this section to the signature question of our text: **Why Am I Writing This Essay**? If the student asks him/herself that question, the answer will lead them to a thesis. Once they have a thesis, of course, they have the basis for a coherent essay. We stress this throughout the book.

IV. Visual Literacy

Visual literacy has always been with us. What are the Caves at Lascaux but a form of visual literacy? With the explosion of technology in our age, visual literacy has now come to equal, if not surpass, language literacy. To take advantage of this phenomenon, it has become common in composition courses to study the visual image in the context of visual literacy.

Each of the seven "Origins of Language" contains a visual image from the culture it discusses. We also use a Salvador Dalí painting, *The Persistence of Memory,* in the book. These images provide opportunities to explore and teach visual literacy. You can certainly apply our signature question "Why am I Writing This Essay?" to these visual images, and ask your students, "Why did the artist make this image?"

V. The Stucture

The Assignment is made up of <u>eighteen</u> sections. Each section is made up of three Chapters in a recurring pattern.

- **THE ART OF LANGUAGE**
- **THE ACT OF READING**
- **THE ACT OF WRITING**

Thus, the first section of *The Assignment* looks like this:

PART01

the origins of language | the cave at lascaux

CHAPTER01

the art of language | language & identity | parts of speech

In the first Chapter of Part 1, we study the **Parts of Speech,** including nouns, pronouns, verbs, adjectives, and adverbs.

CHAPTER02

the act of reading | noun : verb : image

In Chapter 2 of Part 1, we read an excerpt from *The Way to Rainy Mountain,* by N. Scott Momaday, focusing in particular on Momaday's use of the Parts of Speech we just studied. We expand this to explore how we use nouns to create images, and later on, how we use those images as concrete evidence in support of the thesis.

CHAPTER03

the act of writing | what's the point? | all about thesis

In Chapter 3 of Part 1, we discuss thesis. We look at what makes a good thesis, then we look at the N. Scott Momaday essay we have just read in Chapter 2 to discover Momaday's thesis. We then assign an essay for the students to write in which they pay particular attention to creating a good thesis and using the Parts of Speech we studied in Chapter 1 of this section.

Each of *The Assignment's* eighteen Chapters follows this same pattern.

VI. Using the Structure

In the students' interest and for practical purposes, we have made *The Assignment* shorter than other texts in the field. We want the students to find an approachable book when they go to the bookstore. Yet, *The Assignment* is a dense book, foregoing nothing a developmental or freshman composition student might need to learn.

You can use *The Assignment* straight through from beginning to end. But you might want to break down the structure of the book. Depending on the level of your students or other considerations, you can approach *The Assignment* as a modular text, rearranging it according to your own design.

For example:
- You could teach the grammar all together, going from one grammar/structure Chapter to the next. (Chapters 1, 4, 7, 10, 13, 16.)
- You could do all the "Act of Writing" Chapters in sequence. (Chapters 2, 5, 8, 11, 14, 17.)
- You could teach all the Readings together. (Chapters 3, 6, 9, 12, 15, 18.)
- You could choose a particular grammar/structure to focus on, then pair that with a reading from any other Section.

The following chart may aid you by identifying all the **grammar** chapters, all the **reading** chapters, and all the **writing** chapters.

THE ART OF LANGUAGE:	Chapter 1:	Chapter 4:	Chapter 7:	Chapter 10:	Chapter 13:	Chapter 16:
	Parts of Speech	Parts of Speech 2	One Sentence: One Thought	The Ever-Changing Verb	Punctuation	Making the Sentence Work Right
GRAMMAR AND LANGUAGE STRUCTURE			Subject/Verb	Verb Conjugation		Independent Clauses Run-Ons Comma Splices
THE ACT OF READING:	Chapter 2:	Chapter 5:	Chapter 8:	Chapter 11:	Chapter 14:	Chapter 17:
	Noun, Verb, Image	The Image Is Evidence	A Community of Readers	Dialogue with the Text	Quote, Paraphrase, & Summary	Essay As Argument
ESSAY & FICTION READINGS	N. Scottt Momaday: "The Way to Rainy Mountain"	Jack London: "The Story of an Eyewitness: The San Francisco Earthquake"	Diane Ackerman: "Modern Love"	Lewis Carroll: "Alice's Adventures in Wonderland"	John Seabrook: "Renaissance Pears"	William Manchester: "Okinawa: The Bloodiest Battle of All"

THE ACT OF WRITING:	Chapter 3:	Chapter 6:	Chapter 9:	Chapter 12:	Chapter 15:	Chapter 18:
	What's the Point: All About Thesis	Develop It!	Develop It:	From Dialogue to Analysis to Essay	Dialogue with the Reader	Dialogue of Text With Text(s): Language Expresses Identity
ESSAY ASSIGNMENTS		Parts of an Essay	Paragraph Unity	Freewriting; Dialogue with the Text		

VII. Silence and Speech : An Interwoven Theme

Within our theme of silence and speech, we have chosen essays that interlock and echo and respond to each other. You may want to group essay readings by those interrelated issues. For example, *Alice's Adventures in Wonderland,* page **281**, works well with the Ursula LeGuin essays in the back of the book ("World Making" and "Hunger," page **311**). The Messerli essay, page **301**, contrasts urban life beautifully with the rural life of Momaday, while both pieces raise issues of racial harmony/ disharmony. The Jack London essay, "The Story of an Eyewitness: The San Francisco Earthquake," page **273**, portrays the power that nature exerts over civilization, while "Our Vanishing Night," page **307**, highlights how civilization has obscured nature to our detriment. Octavio Paz's "The Day of the Dead," page **327**, discusses cultural rituals, while "Renaissance Pears," page **285**, discusses culturally cohesive qualities of our natural environment.

VIII. Grammar

We can look at the acquisition of writing skills and literacy as the mastery of two equally important components: the micro and the macro. The micro focuses on the management of the sentence, while the macro focuses on the development of essay writing. In *The Assignment,* we concern ourselves with both of these essential studies.

Grammar is a logical system for organizing language. It performs an analysis of language and language structure. As students study grammar, they study analysis. They study critical thinking. And they come to learn, in our book, that grammar is a form of communication. To communicate their ideas and feelings, the students need grammar.

We begin the study of grammar in Chapter 1, the book's densest chapter. While there may be controversy in the field today about the efficacy of teaching grammar, we take from both sides of that argument. Students must know the components of language, sentences, and essays in order to analyze and discuss the readings we offer as well as their own and their colleagues' work, and to construct, analyze, and discuss their own work. We prepare the student to go on to more complex studies of grammar and writing.

We begin with the Parts of Speech. In studying these basic building blocks of language, our students will see how we break language down to organize it into comprehensible systems they can master. While this may look like only rote learning, it introduces the student to the genius inherent in the intelligence of the human brain, which has invented language.

With the power of this knowledge, the student has the primary tools he or she needs to engage with you in a productive critique of their writing. He or she can also move on to the next level to discover how we use the Parts of Speech to construct the Parts of a Sentence.

IX. Reading

Among the skills of literacy, we count analysis, interpretation, and discussion. We have chosen each essay in *The Assignment* with the following criteria in mind: (a) it must be exciting; (b) it must be well written; (c) it must be well organized; (d) it must be on a topic which grabs the students' interest; (e) it must demonstrate the art of language in the preceding chapter; (f) it must leave room for analysis, interpretation, and argument, and (g) it must lead to a discussion which becomes productive in forming theses for the students' own essays.

In the back of the book, we include the whole of each essay we excerpt in the "Act of Reading" Chapters. The other essays that we've chosen to include in the back of the book complement and expand on the discussions and the readings within the book. Each of these additional essays also addresses the idea of language and silence, covering such various disciplines as science, film, sociology, etc. These essays can show students who will go on to study in these and other fields just how expressive and effective writing can be for them.

X. Writing

We've had students come up to us mid-semester or later to comment that they finally get the importance of thesis in their writing. They finally see the whole picture, and they finally understand how to write an essay. They have discovered that it's not all that hard once you have created your own guide: a good thesis.

While the writers may present their thesis late in the work, or not necessarily even overtly state their thesis, students benefit from stating their thesis early on, in the first paragraph. Then they know that everything they write from then on must relate to and prove that thesis.

We integrate all the rhetorical modes into each essay. Rather than basing an essay on a given rhetorical mode—description, argument, comparison/contrast, etc.—we base it on the development of a thesis. When you work from a thesis to develop an essay, you incorporate all the rhetorical modes of writing into the essay, using each one of them in an integrated way.

If an instructor wishes to highlight one or more of the rhetorical modes, he or she may easily do so using our essays. For example, in the Momaday essay, you could highlight the <u>descriptive</u> passages, you could point out the <u>narrative</u> passages, you could analyze the passages that use <u>comparison/contrast</u>, and so on. Following this holistic approach, the students can still clearly identify the rhetorical modes in the essays they read, while they can write thesis-driven essays in which they *use* the rhetorical modes to support their thesis development.

We work on thesis development using our signature question: **Why Am I Writing This Essay?** Applying that question to Chapter 3, we ask: "Why Did N. Scott Momaday Write This Essay?" The answer to that question leads us to Momaday's thesis.

Our students, likewise, will pose this same question to themselves: **Why Am I Writing This Essay?** In answering it, they will discover their own motivations, their own passions. They will know why it is important for them to write that essay. They can then formulate a thesis to guide them. They will also know how the essay they write is important to them. They will write with more vigor, more passion, and more concentration. They have something to say. They can only say it in well-written language.

XI. Exercises

To help students absorb the skills of writing, we provide a number of exercises for them to practice the skills they have just studied. You, of course, can use all those exercises, or you can pick and choose among them. But we want the students to understand that they are not simply doing these excercises as a homework assignment to test what they know. In working through these exercises, they *develop* skills and they build habits they won't forget. They train their eye and their ear and their brain to write correctly.

XII. Some Notes on the Readings

We have found it useful at times to draw thematic correspondences among two or more essays. Here we will offer a few suggestions of how these essays fit together, drawing on both the essays within the text and those at the back of the text.

All of the essays in *The Assignment* address the issue of <u>language, culture, and identity</u>. Beyond that, we can suggest a few more thematic possibilities:

A. <u>Landscape, Nature, Environment, and the Relationship between Environment and Culture</u>
   1. N. Scott Momaday. "The Way to Rainy Mountain."
   2. John Seabrook. "Renaissance Pears."
   3. William Manchester. "Okinawa: The Bloodiest Battle."
      Manchester discusses the effects of war on the landscape.

    4. Verlyn Klinkenborg. "Our Vanishing Night."

    5. Jack London. "The Story of an Eyewitness: The San Francisco Earthquake."

B. <u>Time and Change</u>

    1. Salvador Dalí. *The Persistence of Memory.*

    2. Lewis Carroll. *Alice in Wonderland.*

    3. Ursula LeGuin. "World-Making."

    4. John Seabrook. "Renaissance Pears."

C. <u>War and Reflection</u>

    1. William Manchester. "Okinawa: The Bloodiest Battle of All."

    2. Steve Freidman. "A Moment of Silence."

    3. N. Scott Momaday. "The Way to Rainy Mountain."

D. <u>The Meetings of Cultures</u>

    1. N. Scott Momaday. "The Way to Rainy Mountain."

    2. Douglas Messerli. "20 Days in the City of Angels."

    3. Helen Barolini. "Buried Alive by Language."

    4. James Baldwin. "What It Means to be an American."

E. <u>Art</u>

    1. "Origins of Language I—VI" and the images that go with them.

    2. Salvador Dalí. "The Persistence of Memory."

    3. Pauline Kael. "Why are the Movies so Bad? or, The Numbers."

    4. John Seabrook. "Renaissance Pears."

PROLOGUE

the first day: why am i writing this essay?

begin writing

You come into class. It's your first day. You sit in the back of the room. The Professor calls the roll, mispronouncing your last name. Do you correct it? For now, you let it go.

The Professor passes out a syllabus. It lists all the subjects you'll cover and all the things you'll read and all the assignments you'll complete during this class. You have a lot of work ahead of you. You're up to it. You came to college to work, didn't you? You're serious about this. You're excited about it. You'll do well. The Professor asks you to write a short essay to evaluate your writing skills.

Imagine that one of your good friends, or someone special to you in your family, thinks you should not go to college. Maybe they think you're wasting your time. Write a short essay explaining to that person why you've chosen to go to college.

You look around the room. Other students have begun to write. You better get to work, but you have nothing to say. What can you write about? Your hands get clammy. The girl in front of you turns around because you're tapping your foot on the back leg of her chair. "I'm sorry," you whisper. You stop the tapping. You don't know what you're doing. You get frustrated. You ask yourself, "Why am I writing this essay?"

You've asked exactly the right question! Ask yourself that question—**"Why am I writing this essay?"**—before every essay you write.

Maybe you think to yourself, "I'm writing this essay only to pass this class." Now, ask yourself, "Why do I want to pass this class?" Perhaps you answer yourself, "I want to pass this class because I'm the first one in my family to go to college, and I want to succeed. I'm writing this essay to succeed in college."

Gather your thoughts. Write the essay. Put all of your desire to succeed in college into this essay.

After a while, the Professor asks you to turn in your papers. You were still going strong. You were in the middle of great ideas. You were writing about how going to college will make your whole future better. You were writing about how you're going to learn so many things. You're going to be somebody. But the time's up. As the Professor comes down your row, you hand in your paper.

"Sorry I was tapping on your chair before," you say to the girl in front of you as you both get up to leave.

"It's all right," she says. "How did you do?"

"I don't know. OK, I guess. I hope. We'll see."

"We'll see," she says. You walk out of the classroom together, then part ways as you head off toward your Math class.

what is language?
silence, language, and identity

On your second day of class, the Professor calls the roll, and he mispronounces your name again, a different mispronunciation from his mispronunciation on the first day. Should you say something?

The Professor passes your papers back, going up and down the rows. The guy two rows away gets his paper. He sighs, then scowls. When you finally get your paper, it's filled with red ink. Corrections! Mistakes! What's this all about? You know how to write. What's all this red ink? You got good grades in high school English.

So what do all the red marks mean?

VT	*P*	*FS*

When I work in your auto repair shop you told me I was a good mechanic I shouldn't go

CS	*FS*	*SP*

to college, I should stay and work with you I will own the auto repair shop one day and hav a lot

frag	*pr*	

of money. When I tell you I will go to college look at all the Mercedes in the shop. They came to

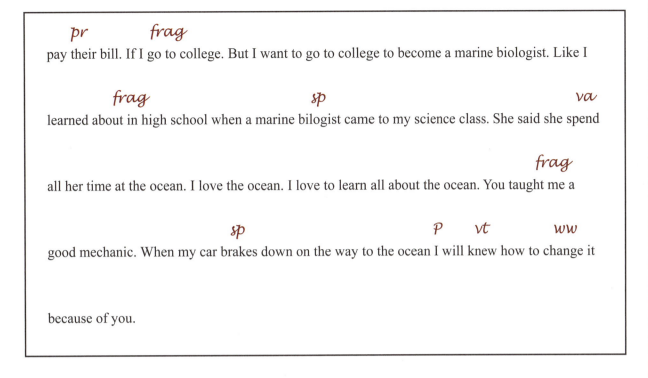

OK, so you have a lot of work to do. But just about everybody comes to college with writing problems. You're not alone. You'll have to work. Writing well doesn't come quickly. It takes time. You can do it.

As we move through this book, we'll explain the issues those red proofreading marks point out. For now:

what is language?

Imagine that we don't have language. Imagine that you're sitting with a friend in a public place, perhaps in a restaurant or café. In the whole place, no one speaks. You say to your friend, "How strange this silence is." But you can't say that because you, too, can't speak. You have no language. Imagine that quiet. How boring it would be. How frustrating it would be. You could never speak with anyone. You could have no conversations at all. You would have to live in complete silence.

But you do have language. You have words—thousands of them. We all do. Language, made up of those words, is a miracle of human intelligence.

We need to organize language into a form that allows us to communicate with each other, so that when we write, we use language that communicates our **THESIS** (our main point) and then proves that point with **EVIDENCE,** *developing* an essay.

what is grammar?

What do you want to do with your language? What do you want to say? Do you want to tell your mother on the phone that your college Math class is difficult?

You can't say, "Difficult why so math me always for." Your mother might understand you. After all, she's your mother. But no one else would understand. GRAMMAR organizes our sentences. LANGUAGE is a miracle of human intelligence. GRAMMAR is the genius that makes language work for us.

GRAMMAR organizes the chaos of words, words, words into sentences. Then we can use those words for anything we want. Would you tell your boyfriend or girlfriend, "Love you I"? You need LANGUAGE, but you also need GRAMMAR to organize the words for you into the sentence, "I love you." Would you tell your friend, "Salt please the pass"? You need both LANGUAGE and GRAMMAR to say "Please pass the salt." It's not a mystery. You use GRAMMAR all day long every day.

To create GRAMMAR, we use several different systems.

The Professor erases the whiteboard:

and writes instead:

parts of speech...

PART01

the origins of language: the cave at lascaux

On September 12, 1940, four French teenagers—Marcel, Jacques, Georges, and Simon—along with Simon's dog, Robot, hiked out into the woods. They climbed to the top of Lascaux Hill in Southwestern France, one of their favorite spots. Simon's dog, Robot, fell into a hole. The four boys went home, returning the next day with a rope and a lantern to rescue Robot. Lowering themselves into the dark hole, the boys found that the hole led them into what we now call the Cave at Lascaux, a system of 110 different caves branching off the main entrance. Those caves, dating from 17,000–13,000 B.C.E., contain 2,188 prehistoric, pre-literate wall paintings of animals.

Why did those pre-historic, pre-literate people of Lascaux make those wall paintings? Those people, from about 17,000–13,000 B.C.E., depended entirely on hunting. If the hunt failed, the people starved. We believe they made those paintings of deer, bison, bulls, etc. in order to ensure a good hunt. You could call the paintings a kind of magic. The artists made the paintings as a way of "capturing" the animals. Or, you could simply say the artists painted a successful hunt, practicing the art of positive thinking. However you phrase it, these pre-literate people, unable to write, sought a language to express themselves and their world. They found that language in painting. Today, we still have painting to express ourselves, but we also have written language.

We have asked why the people of Lascaux made those wall paintings. Ask yourself that same question about whatever you write: **"Why am I writing this essay?"** When you can answer it, you will write better.

1

CHAPTER 01

the art of language | language & identity | parts of speech

The grammar system that we call **PARTS OF SPEECH** organizes words for us into categories. We take words, just words, random words, and we organize them into systems we can use. The **PARTS OF SPEECH** make up the building blocks we use to understand language and to construct sentences.

> Some linguists organize language into eight Parts of Speech, while other linguists organize language into nine Parts of Speech.
>
> We will designate nine Parts of Speech. We believe that will make things more clear for you.

In this Chapter, we'll look at five **PARTS OF SPEECH**.

- Nouns
- Verbs
- Pronouns
- Adjectives
- Adverbs

> It's all about *nouns* and *verbs*. All the other **PARTS OF SPEECH** relate somehow to *nouns* and *verbs*.

You may already know some of these **PARTS OF SPEECH** well, perhaps all of them. In that case, you'll have a good review.

After we explain each **PART OF SPEECH** with examples, we'll give you one exercise for that **PART OF SPEECH,** so you get a little practice with it, a chance to get it into your memory. Then we'll give you more exercises at the end of this chapter. We'll go over the **PARTS OF SPEECH** throughout the book. In a short time, you'll know them all. Let's begin.

Parts of Speech I: Nouns

What kind of words are **NOUNS**? What do **NOUNS** do?

A **NOUN** names:

- persons
- places
- things
- ideas

Before we had language, nothing had a name. Nothing. Look around the room. Without language, you couldn't name one thing that you see. Now, we do have language. We have **NOUNS**. We can name the things that we see.

A **NOUN** names:

a **PERSON**,   a **PLACE**,   a **THING**,   an **IDEA**

Joey lives in **Chicago** in an apartment **building**. He loves to maintain his good **health**. He loves to play basketball.

NOUNS:
A *PERSON* : **JOEY**
A *PLACE*   : **CHICAGO**
A *THING*   : **BUILDING**
AN *IDEA*   : **HEALTH**

EXERCISES ON NOUNS

Fill in the missing **nouns**:

1. He rented an expensive _____ to drive up to San Francisco.
2. He played the _____ in the High School marching band.
3. The mother called her _____ in for dinner.
4. The _____ called the roll before beginning class.
5. Yesterday, we saw a great _____ at the zoo.

Parts of Speech II: Verbs

What kind of words are **VERBS**? What do **VERBS** do?

A **VERB** names an action, any action, every action, for example:

AN ACTION   **AN ACTION**   **AN ACTION**   **AN ACTION**

run   *talk*   *sing*   *write*

After Joey and his friends have **_run_** around the basketball court for an hour and have finished their game, they like to hang out together and **_talk_** for a while. Sometimes, they'll **_sing_** along with a song they play on an iPod. When Joey gets home, he **_writes_** down the names of everybody who played basketball that day and the final score of the game.

"Run," "talk," "sing," and *"writes"* are all **VERBS.** They all **name** actions that somebody or some thing does.

EXERCISES ON VERBS

Fill in the missing **verb**:

1. After running a mile, I _____ a half-gallon of water. {what **action** do you name?}
2. With my new iPhone, I _____ my grandmother in Hawaii. {what **action** do you name?}
3. Tonight, I will have to _____ my first paper for college. {what **action** do you name?}
4. I love to _____ soccer. {what **action** do you name?}
5. I _____ my boyfriend/girlfriend. {what **action** do you name?}

Now we know two **PARTS OF SPEECH**:
- A **NOUN** **names** persons, places, things, or ideas.
- A **VERB** **names** an action.

Parts of Speech III: Pronouns

What is a **PRONOUN**? What can a **PRONOUN** do? When your writing becomes awkward because you have used the same **noun** over and over, you can use a **PRONOUN** to take the place of that noun. That will make your language sound better. Writing should read well. When you read your work out loud to a friend or to yourself, see if it sounds right. As for pronouns, take the following paragraph, for example:

Joanne studies marine biology. Joanne's father wanted Joanne to become a lawyer, like Joanne's father is, but Joanne always loved the sea. Now, Joanne studies the sea and all the plants and all the creatures in it, large and small, from whales to starfish. Yesterday, Joanne spent the whole day sitting in a tide pool at the beach watching little sea creatures move about—starfish and crabs and anemones and barnacles. Joanne took a lot of notes about those sea creatures, including how they moved with the movement of the sea, how they ate, how they defended themselves against attack, and how they breathed. Tomorrow, Joanne will go out in a boat with her scuba gear so Joanne can dive into the sea to watch some larger fish. Joanne will take notes on those larger fish when she returns to her boat. In one more year, Joanne will graduate with a Bachelor of Science degree in Marine Biology.

That's an OK paragraph. It tells us about Joanne and her studies. But it gets a little boring because it always repeats Joanne's name: "Joanne does this; Joanne does that." We can use **PRONOUNS** to make it read better.

Joanne studies marine biology. Joanne's father wanted **HER** to become a lawyer, like **HE** is, but Joanne always loved the sea. Now, Joanne studies the sea and all the plants and all the creatures in it, large and small, from whales to starfish. Yesterday, **SHE** spent the whole day sitting in a tide pool at the beach watching little sea creatures—starfish and crabs and anemones and barnacles—move about. **SHE** took a lot of notes about those sea creatures, including how they moved with the movement of the sea, how they ate, how they defended themselves against attack, and how they breathed. Tomorrow, **SHE** will go out in a boat with **HER** scuba gear so **SHE** can dive into the sea to watch some larger fish. **SHE** will take notes on those larger fish when she returns to her boat. In one more year, Joanne will graduate with a Bachelor of Science degree in Marine Biology.

Some of the **PRONOUNS** in our English language are[1]:

I	we		me	us		my	our		mine	ours
you	you		you	you		your	your		yours	yours
he/she/it	they		him/her/it	them		his/her/its	their		his/her/its	theirs

We use **PRONOUNS** to make our writing sound better and flow more smoothly. But, when we use **PRONOUNS**, we can also cause confusion. We have to make sure our reader knows *who* or *what* the **PRONOUN** refers to.

Pronoun Reference

Every **PRONOUN** refers to a **noun.** In the paragraph above, both of the **PRONOUNS** "**HER**" and "**SHE**" refer to the **noun** "Joanne." The **PRONOUN** "**HE**" refers to the **noun** "father."

---

[1]See the **Index of Pronouns** at the back of the book for a list of the different types of **pronouns.**

You must be sure that your **pronoun reference** is clear; you must be sure that your reader knows to *which noun* your **pronoun** *refers*. In the following sentence, we don't know whether the **pronoun** "he" refers to Paul or to Sam.

Paul and Sam bought a computer together, agreeing that **he** would use it first.

While in the sentence below, the **pronoun reference** is clear:

When Paul and Sam bought a computer together, Sam said **HE** would use **IT** first.

EXERCISES ON PRONOUNS

Fill in the missing **PRONOUNS**:

1. _____ wash _____ car every Saturday afternoon.
2. After Ronnie washes _____ car, she waxes ____.
2. _____ walks _____ dog every afternoon.
3. When Latasha came home, _____ helped cook dinner.
4. Joe met _____ friend, Ronald, at the corner at 2:30.
5. Alice played _____ saxophone all night long.

Parts of Speech IV: Adjectives

What are **ADJECTIVES**? What can **ADJECTIVES** do?

ADJECTIVES *describe* ⟶ **NOUNS**

When you want to describe something—a **PERSON, PLACE, THING,** or **IDEA**—in more detail, adjectives do that for you. Let's say that, when you were young, your family moved from one state to another or from another country to the United States. You want to tell a friend about a tree that grew outside the house where you came from. Let's say you remember that tree from the summers, when green leaves filled its branches. Instead of just writing:

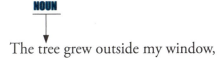

NOUN

The tree grew outside my window,

you might add an adjective:

The green tree grew outside my window.

When you complete the sentence, you have:

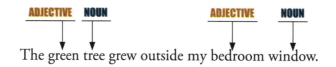

The green tree grew outside my bedroom window.

The **ADJECTIVE** "**green**" describes the **NOUN** "tree." The **ADJECTIVE** "**bedroom**" describes the **NOUN** "window."

EXERCISES ON ADJECTIVES

Fill in the missing **adjectives:**

1. I just saw that _____ car run a red light.
2. Maureen wore a _____ dress that I loved.
3. He was a very _____ basketball player.
4. He wore one _____ earring in his right ear.
5. Her new _____ tennis shoes look great on her.

Parts of Speech V: Adverbs

What are **ADVERBS**? What can **ADVERBS** do?

ADVERBS *describe* ⟶ **VERBS**.

How can you *describe* a verb?

A **VERB** *names* an action: *run, write, talk, sing.*

An **ADVERB** *describes* that action. An **ADVERB** *describes* the **VERB**.

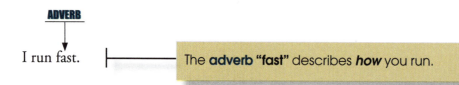

I run fast.   The **adverb "fast"** describes ***how*** you run.

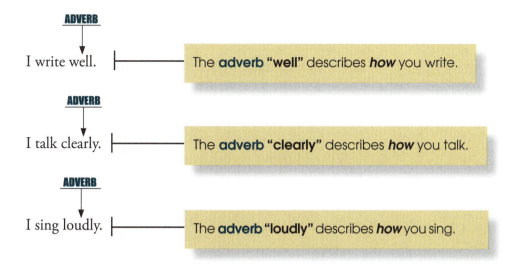

If we use the **VERB** "waved" we could use the **ADVERB** "**gently**" to describe *how* the leaves waved in the tree outside my bedroom window.

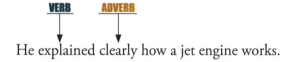

The green tree, whose leaves waved gently in the wind, grew outside my bedroom window.

The **ADVERB** "**gently**" *describes* the action of the **VERB** "waved."

If we were to say the **VERB** "**explained**" and ask you to *describe* it further, you might use the **ADVERB** "clearly," to describe the **VERB** "explained."

He explained clearly how a jet engine works.

The **ADVERB** "**clearly**" describes the action of the **VERB** "explained."

If we were to give you the **VERB** "text" and ask you to describe it further, you might give us this sentence:

She quickly texts her boyfriend.

The **ADVERB** "**quickly**" describes the **VERB** "texts."

ADVERBS can change the <u>meaning</u> of a sentence.

He walked **quickly** to work.

He walked **slowly** to work.

When you *describe* the *action* (**walk**) with an ADVERB (**quickly** or **slowly**), you change the meaning of what you say, and you communicate more vividly. In the following example, notice how the ADVERB changes the meaning of the sentence.

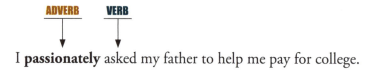

I **passionately** asked my father to help me pay for college.

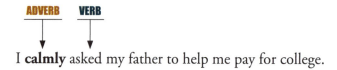

I **calmly** asked my father to help me pay for college.

Let's look at one more example. Let's try the VERB "dance."

He dances wildly.

As you can see, an ADVERB comes *either* before or after the VERB.

EXERCISES ON ADVERBS

Fill in the missing **adverb:**

1. I ran home _____.

2. Yesterday, he spoke _____ in favor of civil rights.

3. The sign was big, so he could read it _____.

4. I _____ ate my lunch.

5. The sea roared _____.

TRICKY:

"Good" is an **ADJECTIVE**; it describes **nouns**:

> We won the game. It was a **good** day.

"Well" is an **ADVERB**; it describes a **verb**:

> We won because we played **well**.

Chapter Review: Parts of Speech

NOUNS: Name a person, place, thing, or idea.
ADJECTIVES: Describe a person, place, thing or idea.
PRONOUNS: Take the place of (and refer to) nouns.
VERBS: Name actions, any action, every action.
ADVERBS: Describe verbs. They describe the action.

Exercises for Chapter 01

I. NOUNS

a. Go for a walk. Take a notebook with you. Write down ten nouns that name things you see.

1. _____   6. _____

2. _____   7. _____

3. _____   8. _____

4. _____   9. _____

5. _____   10. _____

b. In the following sentences, write **noun** above each **noun**.
    Example:

    noun   noun noun
    Johnny named his dog, Max.

1. Sally saw her Dad on the street.

2. The fire truck blared its sirens.

3. Roger asked Sally out to a movie.

4. The waitress brought us our tacos.

5. The big airplane landed noisily.

6. Rodrigo checked his iPhone for messages.

7. The balloons flew in the wind.

8. The band played all night long.

9. Judy made millions in the stock market.

10. The earthquake rattled everybody's nerves.

c. Fill in the missing noun in the following sentences:

1. Alicia served us _____

2. Jessica bought _____

3. Tyrone wanted _____

4. Mark cleaned _____

5. Miguel built _____

6. Susanna wrote _____

7. Francesco played _____

8. Marguerite wore _____

9. Kevin owned _____

10. Janet liked _____

II. VERBS

a. Watch a sports game. Write down ten **verbs** that name the actions in that game.

1. _____ 6. _____

2. _____ 7. _____

3. _____ 8. _____

4. _____ 9. _____

5. _____ 10. _____

b. In the following sentences, write **verb** above each verb.
   Example:

   verb
Johnny named his dog Max.

1. Sally saw her Dad on the street.

2. The fire truck blared its sirens.

3. Roger asked Sally out to a movie.

4. The waitress brought us our tacos.

5. The big airplane landed noisily.

6. Rodrigo checked his Blackberry for messages.

7. The balloons flew in the wind.

8. The band played all night long.

9. Alice made millions in the stock market.

10. The earthquake rattled everybody's nerves.

11. The wind carried the umbrellas into the sky.

c. Fill in the missing **verb** in the following sentences:

1. Joanne _____ cookies.

2. Luis _____ a book.

3. I _____ dinner.

4. Charles _____a motorcycle.

5. Rosa _____ the table.

6. Eric _____ his dog.

7. Sarah _____ the movie.

8. Justin _____ his name.

9. Tracy _____ New York.

10. Lucy _____ the guitar.

III. Nouns & Verbs

In the following sentences, replace each missing NOUN with a *different* NOUN and each missing VERB with a *different* VERB. Your new sentences can make sense or not. They can be normal or silly. Feel free to be playful if you like.

Example:

Johnny named his dog Max.   *Billy* *loved* his *elephant, George.*

1. Sally saw her Dad on the street.   _____ _____ her _____ on the _____.

2. The ambulance blared its sirens.   The _____ _____ its _____.

3. Roger asked Sally out to a movie.   _____ _____ _____ out to a _____.

4. The waitress brought us our tacos.   The _____ _____ us our _____.

5. The big airplane landed noisily.   The big _____ _____ noisily.

6. Rodrigo checked his iPhone for messages.   _____ _____ his _____ for _____.

7. The balloons flew in the wind.   The _____ _____ in the _____.

8. The band played all night long.

The _____ _____ all

_____ long.

9. Alicia made millions in the stock market.

_____ _____ _____ in the

stock _____.

10. The earthquake rattled everybody's nerves.

The _____ _____ _____

_____.

IV. PRONOUNS

Here's a paragraph with no **pronouns**. Where appropriate, cross out the **noun** and write the **pronoun** above it.

Roger and Roger's friend, Samantha, went to a concert last night. Roger bought the tickets

for the concert last week when Roger heard about the concert on the radio. Samantha wanted

to go because Samantha loved the group that was playing. Samantha listened to their music

all the time. When Roger told Samantha about the concert, Samantha said immediately that

Samantha wanted to go.

V. ADJECTIVES

a. We'll pick a noun, any noun, then think of **adjectives** that might describe that noun.

Young woman
Old woman
Skinny woman
Funny woman

Pick a noun of your own, any noun. Think of ten **adjectives** that might describe that noun.

1. _____   6. _____

2. _____   7. _____

3. _____   8. _____

4. _____   9. _____

5. _____   10. _____

b. Fill in the missing **adjective:**

1. I went to a _____ soccer game last night.

2. We had _____ seats.

3. My brother's new girlfriend is really _____.

4. My friend Juliet wore _____ jeans.

5. The goalies were both extremely _____.

6. One coach wore a _____ jacket; the other coach wore no jacket at all.

7. I had a _____ hot dog and a _____ soda.

8. Although it was a _____ night, the stadium lights showed everything well.

9. We were all _____ when we left.

10. In that _____ weather, we walked almost half a mile to our car.

c. Choose your favorite **adjective** for each sentence. It doesn't matter which one you choose, as either one may work well. Cross out the **adjective** you wouldn't use.

1. My new computer is extremely (fast, slow).

2. The (loud, harsh) sirens blared through the city.

3. My Professor is very (interesting, short).

4. The (beautiful, exciting) painting hangs in the entryway now.

5. All five (big, smart) guys came into the meeting at once.

6. Last October was the (hottest, coldest) October in 20 years.

7. The (blue, green) bird flew in through the window.

8. The city was (busy, quiet) today.

9. I bought the most (expensive, gorgeous) shirt this afternoon.

10. This summer, even the sea was (hot, wild).

VI. ADVERBS

a. We'll pick a verb, any verb, then think of **adverbs** that might describe that verb.
   He runs **fast**.
   He runs **slowly**.
   He runs **hard**.
   He runs **awkwardly**.
   He runs **beautifully**.

   Pick a verb, any verb, then choose ten **adverbs** to describe that verb.

   1. _____

   2. _____

   3. _____

   4. _____

5. _____

6. _____

7. _____

8. _____

9. _____

10. _____

b. Fill in an **adverb** wherever we have left a space.

When I hired Johnny, I thought he worked _____. One morning, we went

_____ to work together on that project I had on Delancy Street. All morning,

Johnny worked _____. At lunchtime, I bought Johnny something down at the

corner. He ate _____. He talked _____. When we got back to work,

Johnny worked _____ all afternoon. Had I hired the right guy?

c. Think of ten **adverbs** that describe some *action* that you do regularly.

1. _____

2. _____

3. _____

4. _____

5. _____

6. _____

7. _____

8. _____

9. _____

10. _____

CHAPTER02

the act of reading | noun : verb : image

Coming into the classroom, you take your usual seat. "Did you ever wonder," the Professor asks the class, "why we all take the same seat every time we come into a classroom? Your seat becomes your place, your home, someplace you're comfortable."

In the following excerpt from the narrative essay[1], "The Way to Rainy Mountain," the Native American writer N. Scott Momaday discusses a journey he takes to his native land in Southwestern Oklahoma. This becomes a journey of self-discovery for Momaday. He investigates his cultural roots to discover himself; he examines the "handprint" his people have left on the world, made up of their landscape, their religion, their history, and their myths.

Throughout this book, we give you different myths of the origins of language. Here, Momaday describes the Kiowas' myth of the origins of their people. Myths play a vital role in every culture, giving us stories to explain our lives. Powerful tales, myths speak to every member of the culture. Momaday, for example, a modern man, may not exactly believe the myth that his people came into the world through a hollow log, but that myth offers him a vision that he cherishes as a poetic gift from the imagination of his people.

The Way to Rainy Mountain

A SINGLE KNOLL rises out of the plain in Oklahoma, north and west of the Wichita Range. For my people, the Kiowas, it is an old landmark, and they gave it the name Rainy Mountain. The hardest weather in the world is there. Winter brings blizzards, hot tornadic winds arise in the spring, and in summer the prairie is an anvil's edge. The grass turns brittle and brown, and it cracks beneath your feet. There are green belts along the rivers and creeks, linear groves

---

[1]In a **narrative essay**, the author writes in a personal way, often telling a story. Here, Momaday includes other types of writing as well, including history, myth, etc. But the main form of this essay is **narrative**.

of hickory and pecan, willow and witch hazel. At a distance in July or August the steaming foliage seems almost to writhe in fire. Great green and yellow grasshoppers are everywhere in the tall grass, popping up like corn to sting the flesh, and tortoises crawl about on the red earth, going nowhere in plenty of time. Loneliness is an aspect of the land. All things in the plain are isolate; there is no confusion of objects in the eye, but *one* hill or *one* tree or *one* man. To look upon that landscape in the early morning, with the sun at your back, is to lose the sense of proportion. Your imagination comes to life, and this, you think, is where Creation was begun.

I returned to Rainy Mountain in July. My grandmother had died in the spring, and I wanted to be at her grave. She had lived to be very old and at last infirm. Her only living daughter was with her when she died, and I was told that in death her face was that of a child.

I like to think of her as a child. When she was born, the Kiowas were living the last great moment of their history. For more than a hundred years they had controlled the open range from the Smoky Hill River to the Red, from the headwaters of the Canadian to the fork of the Arkansas and Cimarron. In alliance with the Comanches, they had ruled the whole of the southern Plains. War was their sacred business, and they were among the finest horsemen the world has ever known. But warfare for the Kiowas was preeminently a matter of disposition rather than of survival, and they never understood the grim, unrelenting advance of the U.S. Calvary. When at last, divided and ill-provisioned, they were driven onto the Staked Plains in the cold rains of autumn, they fell into panic. In Palo Duro Canyon they abandoned their crucial stores to pillage and had nothing then but their lives. In order to save themselves, they surrendered to the soldiers at Fort Sill and were imprisoned in the old stone corral that now stands as a military museum. My grandmother was spared the humiliation of those high gray walls by eight or ten years, but she must have known from birth the affliction of defeat, the dark brooding of old warriors.

Her name was Aho, and she belonged to the last culture to evolve in North America. Her forebears came down from the high country in western Montana nearly three centuries ago. They were a mountain people, a mysterious tribe of hunters whose language has never been positively classified in any major group. In the late seventeenth century they began a long migration to the south and east. It was a journey toward the dawn, and it led to a golden age. Along the way the Kiowas were befriended by the Crows, who gave them the culture and religion of the Plains. They acquired horses, and their ancient nomadic spirit was suddenly free of the ground. They acquired Tai-me, the sacred Sun Dance doll, from that moment the object and symbol of their worship, and so shared in the divinity of the sun. Not least, they acquired the sense of destiny, therefore courage and pride. When they entered upon the southern Plains they had been transformed. No longer were they slaves to the simple necessity of survival; they were a lordly and dangerous society of fighters and thieves, hunters and priests of the sun. According to their origin myth, they entered the world through a hollow log. From one point of view, their migration was the fruit of an old prophecy, for indeed they emerged from a sunless world.

* * *

In the last class, you worked on **NOUNS** and **VERBS**.

Notice a few of the **NOUNS** Momaday uses to name persons, places, things, or ideas in this paragraph: "people," "winds," and "grasshoppers."

Notice a few of the **VERBS** Momaday uses to name the actions in this paragraph: "rises," "gave," "turns."

Let's go just one more step today. Let's ask ourselves, what is an **IMAGE**?

The word **IMAGE** is familiar, but you don't really know what an **IMAGE** is.

what is an image?

An **IMAGE** is a picture of something. When you look at a painting, you are seeing an **IMAGE**. When you go to the movies, you see **IMAGES** on the screen. In language, **IMAGES** are those pictures you see in your mind when you read or hear certain words. If we say, "Your friend Billy went home," you might see Billy's house in your mind. If I say that your boyfriend or girlfriend called, you might see an image of your boyfriend or girlfriend in your mind. We use **IMAGES** in writing to describe the things we want our reader to see.

> **Describe =**
> From the Latin: *Describere*
> > De = the meaning is uncertain in this case
> > Scribe = [scribere] *to write*

IMAGES make your writing strong. They help the reader see what you want to say. How do we make **IMAGES** using language? Usually, we see that **NOUNS** make up the center of an **IMAGE**. However, verbs, adjectives, and adverbs can all play an important role in creating **IMAGES**.

Why do we want to think about **IMAGES**? An idea is abstract. An image is concrete. We can feel an **IMAGE**, we can see it, we can smell it, and we can hear it. If you say the word *love*, that's an abstract idea. If you say that Sally and Joe walk down the street hand in hand, that's a concrete image of love. You can't see love, but you certainly can picture Sally and Joe and feel their love.

In "The Way to Rainy Mountain," N. Scott Momaday uses the **NOUNS** *grasshopper* and *hill* to create **IMAGES**. If you close your eyes, and we say the noun **"grasshoppers"** you see grasshoppers.

That's an **IMAGE**. Nouns can make us see **IMAGES**. If you close your eyes, and we say the noun **"hill"** you see a hill. What you see in your mind is an **IMAGE** of a hill.

When you see the **IMAGE** of those grasshoppers, you imagine an open landscape where it is quiet enough to hear the grasshoppers chirp. When you see the **IMAGE** of this hill, together with hearing the sound of the grasshoppers, you get a picture of a natural environment which must have contributed to the Kiowas' culture by giving them a sense of quiet, peacefulness, openness, and a sense of gratitude and respect for the landscape they live in. As we can see, **IMAGES**, in a few words, can envelop us in a whole mood.

Now we understand how **NOUNS** work to make **IMAGES**.

For example, you might say:

> This morning, I had breakfast.

You use the **NOUNS** *morning* and *breakfast* to give us an **IMAGE.** We can picture you in the *morning* eating *breakfast.* We know something of how your day began. (As you read this, you might be seeing an **IMAGE** in your mind of yourself eating breakfast this morning.)

If you use more specific nouns, you might say:

> This morning, I had eggs, bacon, sausage, hash browns, fruit, cornbread, and coffee for breakfast.

You use the **NOUNS** *eggs, bacon, sausage, hash browns, fruit, cornbread,* and *coffee* to create a better **IMAGE.** We know you have a big appetite, and now we know a lot more about how your day began.

In another instance you might say:

> I saw a good movie last night.

You use the **NOUNS**, *I, movie,* and *night* to create an **IMAGE.** I know something about what you did last night.

But, if you tell us:

> Last night, downtown at the Rialto, my friend, Charlene, and I saw a good movie,

you have used the more specific **NOUNS** *night, downtown, Rialto, friend, Charlene,* and *movie* to give us a more specific **IMAGE** of your life.

You will use an abundance of **IMAGES** in all your essays. Looking back at N. Scott Momaday's essay, is it possible to say that his whole essay is images? Perhaps all essays are about creating **IMAGES**.

When you write, think in terms of **IMAGES**, think in terms of the images you use to describe what you write about.

How do you pull those **IMAGES** together into one cohesive, unified piece of work? You do that with your **THESIS.**

Chapter Review: Image

An **IMAGE** is a mental picture an author creates through the use of nouns, verbs, adjectives, and adverbs. These images make ideas concrete so the reader can grasp the ideas and most clearly understand the essay.

Exercises for Chapter 2

I. YOUR THOUGHTS

a. What do the **images** in Momaday's essay, "The Way to Rainy Mountain," make you think of or make you feel?

b. What do the **images** in Momaday's essay tell you about Momaday himself? Why do you think Momaday chose these particular **images**?

c. Why did N. Scott Momaday write this essay?
While there is no one right answer to this exercise, we've provided the entire essay at the back of the text to help you find your own answer to this question.

II. MOMADAY'S ART: PARTS OF SPEECH

a. Go back over Momaday's essay. List ten nouns that Momaday uses.

1. _____   6. _____

2. _____   7. _____

3. _____   8. _____

4. _____   9. _____

5. _____   10. _____

b. List ten verbs Momaday uses.

1. _____   6. _____

2. _____   7. _____

3. _____   8. _____

4. _____   9. _____

5. _____   10. _____

c. Momaday uses only four pronouns. They are:

1. _____

2. _____

3. _____

4. _____

d. List ten adjectives that Momaday uses.

1. _____ 6. _____

2. _____ 7. _____

3. _____ 8. _____

4. _____ 9. _____

5. _____ 10. _____

e. Momaday uses only three adverbs. They're a little tricky to spot, so if you get them, be proud of yourself.

1. _____

2. _____

3. _____

III. YOUR EXPERIENCE

a. Look around the classroom. List ten **nouns** that name things in the classroom.

1. _____ 6. _____

2. _____ 7. _____

3. _____ 8. _____

4. _____ 9. _____

5. _____ 10. _____

b. Momaday uses **nouns** to make **images** that describe his life and the life of his tribe, the Kiowas. List ten nouns that describe your life in and around your house, apartment, or dorm. Notice how those **nouns** alone tend to create **images.**

1. _____   6. _____

2. _____   7. _____

3. _____   8. _____

4. _____   9. _____

5. _____   10. _____

c. Pick one of the **nouns** you listed above. Write about that **noun**. Do you like the object it describes? Why? Do you not like it? Why? Does it have a special meaning in your life? Does that noun define you or your family in some way?

d. List a few of the verbs that name actions from your daily life (walk, talk, etc.).

1. _____   6. _____

2. _____   7. _____

3. _____   8. _____

4. _____   9. _____

5. _____   10. _____

e. List ten adjectives that describe some of your friends.

1. _____   6. _____

2. _____   7. _____

3. _____   8. _____

4. _____   9. _____

5. _____   10. _____

f. List five **adverbs** that *describe* actions (**verbs**) you might see people in a movie do. (Include the verb.)

Example: drive **fast**

1. _____   6. _____

2. _____   7. _____

3. _____   8. _____

4. _____   9. _____

5. _____   10. _____

IV. ACTIVE READING

Nouns name people, places, things, and ideas. N. Scott Momaday's people, the Kiowas, named their mountain "Rainy Mountain." We name things to make them part of our lives.

{Here is a real-life example.} When my father was a kid in the Bronx, New York, he used to tell his friends, "I'll meet you at *'the stables.'*" There had once been a horse stables at that place, 133rd Street and the Grand Concourse, but not for a hundred years. For those kids, the name, *the stables*, was a secret code, a secret naming of a special place. Even though my father lives in California now, he can still imagine that, if he went back to *the stables* in the Bronx, all his childhood friends would be there.

a. Write about a place that is important to you or an imaginary place that could be important to you. Notice the **nouns** you use to describe that place. Feel free to make up names, like "the stables."

b. Momaday writes, "Loneliness is an aspect of the landscape."

1. Do certain words in Momaday's piece evoke loneliness?

2. Do certain words in Momaday's essay evoke a feeling of home?

3. Describe a place that feels lonely to you.

4. Describe a place that feels comfortable to you.

c. Momaday writes about the relationship between nature and people. Is there a strong relationship between nature and the people where you live? Write about that relationship. If there isn't, write about why the place where you live is important to the people who live there.

CHAPTER03

the act of writing | what's the point | all about thesis

Your **THESIS** is a gift you give to your essay. Better, even, your **THESIS** is a gift you give to your reader. To make an essay work beautifully, and to help the reader understand you, the **THESIS** clearly sets forth the direction the essay will take. The thesis organizes your ideas for you as you write your essay; it organizes the ideas of the essay as a reader reads it. Your **THESIS** is the heart of the communication that unites you with your essay and unites your essay with your reader.

what is a thesis?

What is a **THESIS**? What can a **THESIS** do for you?

- Your **THESIS** states the *main idea* of your essay.
- Your **THESIS** tells your reader *why* you are writing this essay.

To understand what a **THESIS** does, we can learn from the way that scientists use **THESIS**:

The Thesis in Science

In scientific research, scientific theory, and scientific knowledge, the scientist always has a **THESIS**, and s/he has to prove it or disprove it. Some great moments from the history of science:

- **THESIS:** The earth is flat. (Christopher Columbus took care of that one.)
- **THESIS:** The sun and the planets all revolve around the earth. (Copernicus **disproved** that **THESIS** in the 16th Century.)
- **THESIS:** Penicillin can cure many bacterial infections. (Alexander Fleming **proved** that **THESIS** in 1928, curing, among other serious diseases, staphylococcus infections, strep throat, etc.)
- **THESIS:** The moon is made of green cheese. (Astronauts Neil Armstrong, Michael Collins, and Buzz Aldrin **disproved** that **THESIS** when they landed on the moon on July 21, 1969.)

What Makes a Good Thesis?

A good **THESIS**:

- States something that is not obvious and is not just a statement of facts;
- States an idea that requires discussion, evidence, and proof;
- Is narrowly focused;
- Makes an argument—an argument you *care* about. The more you care, the better you will write.

Not a good THESIS:	*A good THESIS:*
Today is Monday. (Obvious)	History supports the superstition that bad things happen on Mondays. (Not obvious; requires discussion, evidence, and proof.)
Abraham Lincoln was the 16th President of the United States. (Obvious)	We still rely, today, on the human values Abraham Lincoln defined for us when he delivered the Gettysburg Address on November 19, 1863. (Not obvious; requires discussion, evidence, and proof.)
Rain is wet. (Obvious)	Acid rain is a major destructive ecological problem. (Not obvious; requires discussion, evidence, and proof.)
Bears live in the woods. (Obvious)	As humans take over more wild land for development, bears come into towns in search of food. When they do, we should kill them (or: we should not kill them). (Not obvious; requires discussion, evidence, and proof.)
Beethoven was an important composer. (Too broad, too general.)	Beethoven's late quartets broke the mold of musical composition to establish new forms that would last into the 21st Century. (Specific and focused.)
Weather is important. (Too broad, too general.)	As we face global warming, we should look to past major climate changes, such as the Irish Potato Famine, the Depression-era drought in the U.S., the Biblical famine in Egypt, etc. to guide us in planning for the challenges global warming presents to us. (An argument.)
Public schools generally serve bad food in their lunchrooms. (A statement, not an argument.)	Schools that serve bad food in their lunchrooms harm their students and should turn to fresh, unprocessed, whole foods for better health and eating patterns. (An argument.)
Beautiful architecture is nice. (A statement, not an argument.)	The historical architecture of Chicago makes it an important, vital city to visit. (An argument.)

Let's now review the first paragraph of N. Scott Momaday's essay "The Way to Rainy Mountain" to both refresh our memory and determine his **THESIS**. We'll repeat the first paragraph of "The Way to Rainy Mountain." Read it over to remind yourself of what Momaday writes. Then, we'll find Momaday's **THESIS**.

An author (including you) might put the **THESIS** at the beginning of an essay or put it in later, after he or she has developed the work. Or, as in the case of N. Scott Momaday's essay, the **THESIS** may be implied. The author may not state it directly, but we can discover the **THESIS** from reading the work. Momaday doesn't state his thesis, but we can figure it out pretty easily.

The Way to Rainy Mountain

A SINGLE KNOLL rises out of the plain in Oklahoma, north and west of the Wichita Range. For my people, the Kiowas, it is an old landmark, and they gave it the name Rainy Mountain. The hardest weather in the world is there. Winter brings blizzards, hot tornadic winds arise in the spring, and in summer the prairie is an anvil's edge. The grass turns brittle and brown, and it cracks beneath your feet. There are green belts along the rivers and creeks, linear groves of hickory and pecan, willow and witch hazel. At a distance in July or August the steaming foliage seems almost to writhe in fire. Great green and yellow grasshoppers are everywhere in the tall grass, popping up like corn to sting the flesh, and tortoises crawl about on the red earth, going nowhere in plenty of time. Loneliness is an aspect of the land. All things in the plain are isolate; there is no confusion of objects in the eye, but *one* hill or *one* tree or *one* man. To look upon that landscape in the early morning, with the sun at your back, is to lose the sense of proportion. Your imagination comes to life, and this, you think, is where Creation was begun.

* * *

When you write an essay, we have suggested that you ask yourself our signature question: WHY AM I WRITING THIS ESSAY? The answer to that question will lead you to your **THESIS**. When we ask this same question of Momaday—**why is N. Scott Momaday writing his essay?**—we will discover his **THESIS**. In the second line, Momaday writes about "my people." In the rest of this paragraph, he describes his people with an intensely detailed description of the landscape they inhabit. He concludes that the landscape is so unique and so beautiful that you may think this "is where creation was begun."

From all this, we might decide that Momaday, wanting to tell us about his heritage, has this **THESIS** in mind:

> A severely beautiful and sacred-feeling landscape has shaped the life and culture of my people, the Kiowas.

As you learn to write well, it would serve you better to <u>state</u> your **THESIS** early on in your essay. For example, Momaday might have begun his essay:

> A severely beautiful and sacred-feeling landscape has shaped the life and culture of my people, the Kiowas.

Do you think Momaday continues, in his full essay, to develop this **THESIS**?

Looking back at the selection from Momaday in Chapter 2, page 21, if we were to write an essay *about* Momaday, would any of the following work well as our **THESIS**?

> In "The Way to Rainy Mountain," N. Scott Momaday demonstrates that the landscape shapes the culture of a people.

> *or*

> When N. Scott Momaday returns home to honor the death of his grandmother, he also revisits the culture of the golden age of the Kiowas.

> *or*

> In his journey home to honor the death of his grandmother, N. Scott Momaday preserves the dying culture of the Kiowas by writing about it.

Chapter Review: Thesis

A Good Thesis:

- States the main idea of the essay.

- Tells the reader why you are writing this essay.

- States an idea that requires discussion, evidence, and proof.

- Is narrowly focused.

- Makes an argument—makes an argument you *care* about. The more you care, the better you will write.

Exercises for Chapter 3:

A. THESIS

1. Which of the following seem to be a good **THESIS** or bad **THESIS**?"

    Red is my favorite color.   Good Thesis _____   Bad Thesis_____

    Tuition at public colleges should be free.   Good Thesis _____   Bad Thesis_____

    I'm really hungry right now.   Good Thesis _____   Bad Thesis_____

    We should (or should not) lower the drinking age to 18.   Good Thesis _____   Bad Thesis_____

    We should (or should not) legalize marijuana.   Good Thesis _____   Bad Thesis_____

    The United States of America is 234 years old.   Good Thesis _____   Bad Thesis_____

    California is the most populous State of the
    United States.   Good Thesis _____   Bad Thesis_____

    Any immigrant living, working, and paying taxes in the
    United States should (or should not) be allowed to
    become a citizen.   Good Thesis _____   Bad Thesis_____

    Every young American should have to do two years
    of military service   Good Thesis _____   Bad Thesis_____

    My dog's name is Dog.   Good Thesis _____   Bad Thesis_____

2. Read the following excerpts. What is the thesis of the each one? The author may or may not
    state it directly. Copy each author's **THESIS** in their own words, or write in your own words what
    you think the main idea—the **THESIS**—will be.

    from AN ORGY OF POWER

    I am reluctant to write about torture. It holds no special fascination for me—on the contrary,
    I find the subject repellent. But I did not choose the times I live in, nor do I choose what I am
    compelled to write. As a writer, I am committed to speaking from my own experience, which
    may seem to counsel silence. I have not been to Iraq, Afghanistan, or Guantánamo Bay. I am
    not a journalist or an authority on the history of torture. But the perimeters of experience do
    not end with what is immediate. In today's world, almost everything connects with everything
    else. The coffee that fuels my editing was raised in Kenya, my shirt was made in China.
    Reports arrive daily from around the world. The problem is sorting the relevant from the

irrelevant, the true from the false, and assigning each bit of information something like its proper weight. These things make learning gradual, writing slow, and these notes very late.

— GEORGE GESSERT

What is this author's **THESIS**?

_____

_____

_____

BASEBALL FOR LIFE

Jarrod Petree has spent his whole life throwing. The first things he threw, according to his mother, were assorted toys and a fair amount of food from the highchair. Before long, he moved on to throwing balls. Some babies, of course, are throwers. But from the very start, Jarrod had an especially determined arm. At least this is the view taken by his father, Tim, who played Division II baseball at the Florida Institute of Technology in the late '80s, graduating only a few years before his son was born: the kid basically arrived on earth wanting to throw.

— SARA CORBETT

What is this author's **THESIS**?

_____

_____

_____

LONG DAY'S JOURNEY INTO DINNER

Sometimes in life, there is a thing you long for so deeply that you are willing to wait for years – almost lying in ambush! – until you can get it. Suppose there's a woman you've always desired, but her heart belongs to another. Or maybe there's a job you've always fancied, or a wristwatch, or a car. You wait for it. Or perhaps there's a sovereign nation that you and your family have always wanted to invade, but the moment never seemed right. What do you do? You *wait*.

— ELIZABETH GILBERT

What is this author's **THESIS**?

_____

_____

_____

Assignment for Chapter 3:

Write an essay in which you either:

1. • Analyze the relationship of any group of people to the landscape they live in.

    How do they relate to that landscape? How does the landscape shape them? You could write about the community that you come from, or you could write about any other group of people: farmers in Central California, fishermen in Texas, Parisians in Paris, any group that strikes your imagination.

    or

    • Analyze the relationship of a group of people to their language.

    or

    • Analyze the relationship of a group of people to their history.

    or

    • Analyze the relationship of a group of people to at least one of their myths.

2. Using N. Scott Momaday's essay as a model, write about your home and your culture. How might you write about your culture to keep your cultural history and your cultural identity alive?

> *Remember:*
> Whether you choose option #1 or option #2, formulate a clear, strong **THESIS** for your essay.

PART02

the origins of language II: native american myths

Speech distinguishes man among the animals; language distinguishes nations from each other; one does not know where a [person] comes from until [they] have spoken.

Jean-Jacques Rosseau
1712–1778

The Aztecs ruled a large area of Central Mexico during the 14th, 15th, and 16th centuries. We identify most ethnic groups in the world not by where they live, nor by their religious beliefs, nor by their political structures, but by their **LANGUAGE.** In 1520, about 20,000,000 Aztecs, people who spoke Nahuatl, lived in Central Mexico.

Many Native American cultures tell a story about a great deluge that covered the earth. The Aztecs say that only a man, Coxcox, and a woman, Xochiquetzal, floating on a huge piece of bark, survived this great flood.

Coxcox and Xochiquetzal finally found themselves on dry land. Together, they had many children, but those children were unable to speak until, upon the arrival of a dove, the children were given language. Language came to them through a dove, a bird we associate with peace. But each child was given a different speech, so they could not understand each other.

CHAPTER 04

the art of language | what language can do | parts of speech (continued)

In Chapter 1, we studied the first five PARTS OF SPEECH: NOUNS, VERBS, PRONOUNS, ADJECTIVES, and ADVERBS. Now, let's look at the remaining four:

- Articles
- Conjunctions
- Interjections
- Prepositions

> Remember: it's all about **_nouns_** and **_verbs._** All these other PARTS OF SPEECH relate somehow to **_nouns_** and **_verbs_**.

Parts of Speech VI: Articles

What is an ARTICLE? What can an ARTICLE do for your sentence?

ARTICLES are a special kind of **adjective.** (ARTICLES are also sometimes now called **determiners.**) Like all **adjectives,** ARTICLES modify a noun. ARTICLES tell us:

- whether the **noun** names someone or something that is singular or plural
- whether the **noun** names someone or something *in general* or someone or something *specific.*

This definition might confuse you at first, but as you read on, we will make it all clear.

In English, we have only three ARTICLES. They are:

- **A**
- **An**
- **The**

A & An:

A and **An** have the <u>same function</u>, almost exactly.

- **A** and **An** both indicate that the **noun** is **singular**
- **A** and **An** both indicate that the **noun** names someone or some thing **in general**.

The only difference between **"A"** and **"An"** is this:

- We use **"A"** before a **consonant** because it is easier to pronounce.

If you don't know whether to use **"A"** or **"An,"** say the words out loud to yourself. Which of the following is easier to pronounce?

[**An** bird flew into my house] — difficult to pronounce

A bird flew into my house. — easy to pronounce

"A" **BEFORE THE** consonant "b" of "bird"

- We use **"An"** before a **vowel,** because it sounds right.

If you don't know whether to use "A" or "An," say the words out loud to yourself.

An elephant walked through the classroom, and we all just watched it go.

"An" **BEFORE THE** vowel "e" of "elephant"

Let's look at some additional examples of **"A"** and **"An,"** all before *singular* **nouns** that name someone or something *in general:*

"A" before a consonant

A guy who lives on my block won the lottery.
Robert went to **a d**esert somewhere in California.
Louise bought **a n**ew computer yesterday.
The people voted for **a d**emocracy.

	An actor spoke to our drama class this morning.
"An" before a vowel	She lives in **an a**rea of the city I don't know.
	You had **an i**ce cream from that new place.
	The country was ruled by **an a**utocracy.

BUT, what is the difference between **"A/An"** and **"The,"** and why do we need them? We said, on page 42, that **A** and **An** both indicate that the noun names someone or something in general. As for **THE**:

- We use **"THE"** before a noun that names a *specific* person/place/thing/idea, either *singular* or *plural:*

Let's look at some additional examples of **"The,"** some before *singular* nouns, some before *plural* nouns, but all before nouns that name something *specific.*

Examples of **"The"** before *specific* **nouns,** either singular or plural.

> **The** guy who lives next door to me won the lottery.
> Robert went to **the** desert called Mojave.
> Louise bought **the** computer she had been wanting for a long time.
> The people voted for **the** way of life they believed in.
> I have read all **the** books in the library.
> We fed **the** birds that came into our backyard.
> **The** students in my class all got the difference between **"A"** and **"And"** and **"The."**

What happens when you don't use the right **articles**? Let's say that you go home at night where you have dinner with your family and you want to tell them this fantastic story of what happened during the day; you wouldn't say:

Elephant walked into our classroom today. Nobody did anything about it. Everybody, the Professor, the students, just stared. Elephant walked to the back of the room then, like it was a ghost, it walked out through the back wall! It was amazing! It was incredible! When elephant left, the Professor just said, "OK, turn to page 95. Let's talk about President Truman and the atom bomb."

To communicate this story well, you need to tell us **which** elephant walked into the room: Was it some random elephant, any elephant, an elephant in general; or was it *the specific* elephant your Professor bought last week for his daughter to ride because his daughter loves to ride elephants?

You tell us more if you say:

> **AN** elephant walked into our classroom today.

> *or*

> **THE** elephant walked into our classroom today.

We use "**AN** elephant" *if* it is some *random* elephant, any elephant, or just *one among many* elephants in the world.

We use "**THE** elephant" if it is a *specific* elephant, **THE** elephant your Professor just bought for his daughter. Let's say it was **THE** elephant your professor just bought for his daughter {we have put all **ARTICLES** in bold red}

THE Elephant walked into our history classroom today. Nobody did anything about it. Everybody, **THE** Professor, **THE** students, just stared. **THE** Elephant walked to the back of **THE** room, then, like it was a ghost, it walked out through **THE** back wall! It was amazing! It was incredible! When **THE** elephant left, **THE** history Professor just said, "OK, turn to page 95. Let's talk about President Truman and **THE** atom bomb."

Here are some more examples of when to use **A** versus **THE**. You would say:

> I couldn't get any sleep. **A** baby was crying all night long,

You would say this if it were some *random* baby, any baby, or *one among many* babies—if, for example, it was <u>a</u> baby in your neighborhood, but you don't know which baby.

You would say:

> **A** computer started writing on its own, and it wrote a whole novel before anyone knew it,

if it were some *random* computer somewhere, any computer, or <u>one among all the many</u> computers in the world.

You say:

> **THE** baby was crying all night,

if it were a *specific* baby, a baby you know, for example, <u>the</u> baby your sister had last week.

You would say:

THE computer started writing on its own, and it wrote a whole novel before anyone knew it,

if it were a ***specific*** computer, for example, <u>the</u> computer you bought yesterday.

OK? Got it?

- **A/AN**
- **THE**

A/AN & THE

General & Specific
- **A** and **AN** both point to a noun that names someone or some thing **in general.**
- We use **"THE"** to point to a noun that is **specific.**

Consonants & Vowels
- We use **"A"** before a **consonant** sound because it is easier to pronounce.
- We use **"AN"** before a **vowel** sound because it is easier to pronounce.
- We use **"THE"** before *both* **consonants** and **vowels.**

Singular & Plural
- **A** and **AN** both point to a noun that is **singular.**
- We use **"THE"** before nouns that are either singular *or* plural.

After all of this, of course, we still don't know how the elephant managed to walk through the back wall of the classroom without destroying it, but we'll have to leave that for some other time.

A LITTLE MORE COMPLICATED

It gets a little more complicated. It always does!

ARTICLES describe **NOUNS.** But there are different kinds of **NOUNS** with different rules for the **ARTICLES** that describe those **NOUNS.** We've been talking about ***common*** nouns. Let's look at just one more kind of **NOUN:**

PROPER NOUNS
PROPER NOUNS name **specific** persons, places, things, or ideas that begin with a ***Capital Letter.*** We don't use any **ARTICLES** in front of **PROPER NOUNS.**

~~The~~ Chicago.
~~The~~ Steve and ~~the~~ Andrew went to ~~the~~ New York.

EXERCISES ON ARTICLES

Fill in the **articles** missing in the following sentences:

1. Rodrigo watched _____ movie I had told him about.

2. My father bought me _____ new watch for my graduation.

3. _____ new watch that my father bought me for my graduation looks very sharp.

4. When I saw _____ movie star walk down the street, I played it very cool.

5. I took _____ picture of Robert pitching in the game last night.

Parts of Speech VII: Conjunctions

What are **CONJUNCTIONS?** What can **CONJUNCTIONS** do?
Simple. **CONJUNCTIONS** either:

- *join things* together

  or

- they *separate* one thing from another.

The two main **CONJUNCTIONS** are:

- **And**—joins things together
- **But**—separates things one from another

There are more **CONJUNCTIONS,** and different kinds of **CONJUNCTIONS,** and we'll give you an index of them—the Index of Conjunctions—on page 243, but you will use mostly the **CONJUNCTIONS** "**and**" and "**but.**"

AND:

"**And**" joins things together:

- **nouns**

I had a hamburger **AND** a milkshake **AND** French fries.

- **pronouns**

He **AND** she both kept daily diaries.

- **verbs**

I walked five blocks **AND** took the bus from there.

- **adjectives**

My new brother-in-law is very tall **AND** very handsome **AND** very smart.

- **adverbs**

I ran hard **AND** fast down the track.

But:

"But" separates, or distinguishes, one thing from one another

- **nouns**

Billy, **BUT** not Sandy, worked at the hotel for the summer.

- **pronouns**

He, **BUT** not she, kept a daily diary.

- **verbs**

That winter it rained, **BUT** it never snowed.

- **adjectives**

My new brother-in-law is very tall **BUT** not very handsome.

- **adverbs**

I dressed quickly **BUT** nicely.

EXERCISES ON CONJUNCTIONS

Fill in the missing **conjunctions** in the following sentences:

1. I had math _____ physical science _____ anthropology today.
2. After three classes in a row, I'm hungry _____ tired.
3. I bought a new bicycle _____ not a new moped.
4. I sent a package to my brother in Afghanistan, _____ I didn't put any music in it.
5. I read two novels for my English class _____ one chapter in physical science, _____ I didn't get to the homework for history yet.

Parts of Speech VIII: Interjections

What are **INTERJECTIONS**? What can **INTERJECTIONS** do for you?

INTERJECTIONS are pretty simple. You add **INTERJECTIONS** to a sentence to add emphasis. We've given you some examples of **INTERJECTIONS** that will make this clear. We've put the **INTERJECTIONS** in *italics*.

Oh no, I forgot my house keys.

Uh oh, we just ate, but I don't have money for the check.

Ouch, I stubbed my toe!

Hey, that's hot. Don't touch it!

AN EXERCISE ON INTERJECTIONS

Find and circle all the **interjections** in the following paragraph:

Wow, I loved that air show we saw. Man, those planes flew incredibly close in formation. And, hey, they were so fast flying overhead you couldn't turn away for one second. Oh, I forgot to tell you, my buddy flew one of them.

Parts of Speech IX: Prepositions

What exactly are **PREPOSITIONS**? How do we use **PREPOSITIONS**? What can **PREPOSITIONS** do for us? We saved the most challenging **PART OF SPEECH** for last so give it all your attention. **PREPOSITIONS** can be tricky; they can be difficult to get right. If you are careful, you will do well with them.

- **PREPOSITIONS** describe the *relationship* between two **NOUNS.**
- **PREPOSITIONS** often {but not always} modify another word in the sentence.

Modify =

From the French: *modifier*

Modifier = to change

Two hints about how to use **PREPOSITIONS:**

- **PREPOSITIONS** *always* come before a noun.
- *Most*, but <u>not all</u>, **PREPOSITIONS** tell us:
- **<u>WHERE</u>** something is

or

- <u>**WHEN**</u> something happens.

A. <u>WHERE</u>

Take any two **NOUNS.** For example, take "bird" and "tree." You can say:

The bird is *in* the tree.
The bird is *near* the tree.
The bird is far *from* the tree.

The **PREPOSITIONS,** *in, near,* and *far from,* describe the *relationship* between the two nouns,

"bird" ⟷ "tree."

The **PREPOSITIONS** *in, near,* and *far from* also modify the **noun** bird. Those prepositions tell us something more about the bird; they tell us <u>where</u> the bird is.

> "To modify" means <u>to change</u> something. When we use the prepositions in, near, or far from to modify the **NOUN** "bird," we change our understanding of that word. We change what we know about the bird. Now we know where the bird is.

Let's take another example. In this one, if we give you the two nouns "lake" and "farm" and the **PREPOSITION** "behind," you might give me the sentence:

NOUN   PREPOSITION   NOUN
The lake is **behind** the farm.

You describe the relationship between the two nouns,

"lake" ⟷ "farm"

with the **PREPOSITION** *behind.*
You also *modify* the **noun** *"lake."* You tell us <u>where</u> the lake is.

Now let's take the two **nouns** "mouse" and "house." You could say:

The mouse ran through the house.
The mouse ran in the house.
The mouse ran under the house.

- The **PREPOSITIONS** *through, in,* and ***under*** describe the relationship between the nouns,

"mouse" ⟷ "house"

- The **PREPOSITIONS** *through, in,* and ***under*** <u>*modify*</u> the **noun** "mouse." They tell us more about the mouse. They tell us where the mouse is.

B. <u>WHEN</u>

Let's take the **nouns** "tree" and "bird." You can say:

Before the huge wind blew, the bird sang happily in the tree.
When the huge wind blew, the bird was quiet in the tree and just hung on.
During the huge wind, it was hard to see the bird in the tree.
After the huge wind blew, the bird was no longer in the tree.

- The **PREPOSITIONS** ***Before, When, During****,* and ***After*** describe the relationship between the **nouns**

"tree" ⟷ "bird."

- The **PREPOSITIONS** ***Before, When, During****,* and ***After*** <u>*modify*</u> the **NOUN** "wind." They tell us more about the wind. They tell us about **when** the wind blew.

C. THE <u>*MOST DIFFICULT*</u> PREPOSITION *OF* THEM ALL: OF

"Of," like all the **PREPOSITIONS**, describes the ***<u>relationship</u>*** between two **NOUNS**. But, *"of"* does not exactly tell us <u>**where**</u> something is, nor does it exactly tell us <u>**when**</u> something happens.

Why is *"<u>**of**</u>"* so difficult? Why is it so hard to tell you *how* and *when* to use *"<u>**of**</u>"*? Why do students make so many mistakes with *"<u>**of**</u>"*?

We have said that **language is alive**, that words in a sentence all interact with each other. Language is **alive** because it is always changing, always growing. The English language grows and changes faster than any other language in the world. It's challenging to keep up with all the rapid changes in the English language.

> **Hip** =
>
> In 1900, "hip" just meant a part of your body. By 1970, if you were "hip," you were aware of things like jazz, rock 'n roll, certain ways of dressing, and certain ways of thinking. What does "hip" mean today, if anything? Do we still use it? Language is ever changing. It's alive.

"Of" is an old word that has changed so much in the last thousand years that we would never recognize its original meaning. Originally, "*of*" meant "**away from**."[1] It's even difficult to define what "*of*" means today.

Look at a few examples of the use of "*of.*"

She came out *of* the house.

It is a quarter *of* ten.

He was one out *of* ten winners.

I told him to get out *of* my way.

It was sad. They had to shoot the horse to put him out *of* his misery.

I live ten miles north *of* the college.

I arrived at ten o'clock. She arrived within an hour *of* me.

An ogre lives in back *of* their house. They don't know what to do!

There were upwards *of* three hundred students in my high school class.

He was cured *of* his cold.

The Boston Red Sox were finally cleansed *of* "The Curse of the Babe."

They had to clear the street *of* all traffic.

---

[1] Strangely enough, if you were to substitute "*away from*" in each of the following sentences, it kind of works – even after a thousand years of the history of this word, "*of.*"

We emptied the rooms *of* all the waste baskets, so they could wash the floors.

It feels pretty good to be rid *of* that guy who was bugging me.

Yesterday, he was robbed *of* all his money.

This list could go on and on!

This list could go on and on, and yet it's still hard to tell the difference between the use of "*of*" in each of these examples. How then can you learn to use "*of*" properly? You will have to learn from reading a lot and from paying attention. You will also learn when your Professor corrects your misuse of "*of*" in your papers. Eventually, you'll get the feel *of* it, but for now, you have all nine **PARTS OF SPEECH**.

Before finishing this Chapter, let's look at one way we use one of the **PARTS OF SPEECH,** prepositions, to make what we call **PREPOSITIONAL PHRASES.**

Prepositional Phrase

What is a **PREPOSITIONAL PHRASE**? What can a **PREPOSITIONAL PHRASE** do for us?

We have seen how prepositions work to tell us, mostly, where something is or when something happens. When we <u>begin</u> a phrase *with* a **PREPOSITION,** we call that phrase a **PREPOSITIONAL PHRASE**[2].

PREPOSITIONAL PHRASE

<u>Before</u> the cat bit the dog, no one thought such a thing possible.
<u>When</u> the cat bit the dog, everyone talked about it all evening.
<u>After</u> the cat bit the dog, and after everyone talked about it all evening, everyone knew such a thing could happen.
<u>Of</u> all the crazy things that ever happened in my life, I think I'll never hear of a cat biting a dog.

PREPOSITIONAL PHRASE

The cat, with its sharp teeth, bit the dog.
The cat jumped onto the dog, and then gave him a playful nip.

PREPOSITIONAL PHRASE

The cat bit the dog on the ear.
The cat lies beside the dog.

---

[2]For the different types of prepositional phrases, see the Index of How Prepositions Work on page 247.

EXERCISES ON PREPOSITIONS

Fill in the missing **preposition:**

1. She took the candy _____ the baby.

2. I typed my notes _____ the computer.

3. I saw the performance _____ my girlfriend.

4. I planted a fig tree _____ my new garden.

5. We ate _____ the new restaurant on Delancy Street.

EXERCISES ON THE PREPOSITION OF

To get used to using this strange "*of,*" in each sentence below we have just left "*of*" out. All you have to do is fill it in. It's simple, it's obvious, but hopefully it will help you to hear and to feel when to use *"of."*

1. He got out _____ his car to talk to George.

2. She took two _____ the candies he offered her.

3. The table was made _____ Brazilian oak.

4. Out _____ all the exercises in this book, this is the strangest!

5. Out _____ all the PREPOSITIONS we have studied, "*of*" is the strangest!

Chapter Review: Parts of Speech

Articles:

We have only three **ARTICLES.** They are:

- **A**
- **An**
- **The**

Conjunctions:

The two main conjunctions are:

- **And**—joins things together
- **But**—separates things one from another

Interjections:

We use **interjections** in a sentence to add emphasis.

Prepositions:

Describe the *relationship* between two **nouns;**
modify a noun in the sentence.

HINTS ABOUT PREPOSITIONS:

- **PREPOSITIONS** *always* come before a noun.
- **PREPOSITIONS** often tell us:

- <u>**WHERE**</u> something is or
- <u>**WHEN**</u> something happens.
- The most difficult PREPOSITION of them all is: **of.**

Prepositional Phrases

When we <u>begin</u> a phrase *with* a **PREPOSITION,** we call that phrase a **PREPOSITIONAL PHRASE.**

Exercises for Chapter 4

I. ARTICLES

a. Go for a walk. Take a notebook with you. Write down ten **nouns** that name things you see. Include the appropriate **article** that goes with that noun.

Examples: **a** bicycle
           the library

1. _____   6. _____

2. _____   7. _____

3. _____   8. _____

4. _____   9. _____

5. _____   10. _____

b. In the following sentences, write **article** above <u>each</u> **article**. (Some of these sentences have more than one article.)

Example:

                article   *article*
           A man just bought the car I wanted.

1. The man in the grey fedora looks great.

2. The dress Sally bought fit her perfectly.

3. Roger asked Sally out to a movie.

4. The waitress brought us our tacos.

5. The big airplane landed noisily.

6. Rodrigo checked out the iPhone an aunt of his just gave him.

7. The balloons flew in the wind.

8. The band played at a wedding all night long.

9. Judy made millions in the stock market.

10. The earthquake sent the books flying from the shelves and rattled everybody's nerves.

c. Write ten sentences about your college campus using the **article "A."**

1. _____

2. _____

3. _____

4. _____

5. _____

6. _____

7. _____

8. _____

9. _____

10. _____

d. Write ten sentences about your friends using the **article "An."**

1. _____

2. _____

3. _____

4. _____

5. _____

6. _____

7. _____

8. _____

9. _____

10. _____

e. Write ten sentences about your house using the **article "The."**

1. _____

2. _____

3. _____

4. _____

5. _____

6. _____

7. _____

8. _____

9. _____

10. _____

II. Conjunctions

a. Fill in the missing **conjunction** in each of these sentences:

1. Alicia served us ham _____ eggs.

2. Jessica bought a gift for her brother _____ not for her sister.

3. Tyrone wanted a new watch _____ a new computer for his birthday.

4. Mark washed his car _____ his dad's car.

5. Miguel built his own airplane _____ not his own car.

6. Susanna wrote a novel _____ an article for the newspaper.

7. Francesco played both the cello _____ the violin.

8. Marguerite wore red shoes _____ a red hat.

9. Kevin owned a dog _____ not an elephant.

10. Janet liked classical _____ not jazz music.

b. Write ten sentences using the **conjunction** "and."

1. _____

2. _____

3. _____

4. _____

5. _____

6. _____

7. _____

8. _____

9. _____

10. _____

c. Write ten sentences using the **conjunction** "but."

1. _____

2. _____

3. _____

4. _____

5. _____

6. _____

7. _____

8. _____

9. _____

10. _____

d. Fill in the missing **conjunctions** below:

My friend, Melissa, _____ I went to the movies last night. Before going in, we

bought popcorn _____ soda. Melissa likes popcorn, _____ I don't. I like soda,

_____ Melissa doesn't. Melissa likes to sit close, _____ I like to sit further away, so we

sat in the middle. There were three trailers before the feature: one for the new Godzilla movie

_____ one for a new romantic comedy _____ one for an adventure film. They all

looked boring, _____ the Godzilla remake might be good.

Are Melissa _____ I boyfriend _____ girlfriend, or are we just friends? I'll leave

that up to you. Did I put my arm around Melissa's shoulder _____ kiss her during the

movie, or did we just watch the movie?

Being hungry after the movie, we went to a burger place. I had a hamburger _____

French fries _____ a milk shake, _____ Melissa just had a tuna melt. Did I get a

little sick from all the fat _____ the sugar? I did. Did I care? No, I didn't. It was all good.

I dropped Melissa off at her dorm _____ went home.

III. INTERJECTIONS

Fill in an **interjection** in each of these three sentences.

_____ Billy hit eight homeruns in the game yesterday!

_____Stay away from there!

_____That hurt!

III. PREPOSITIONS

a. Give us *two* **prepositions** (or prepositional phrases) that could fit into each of these sentences:

1. The bus stopped _____ the traffic light.

   _____   _____

2. He left the water hose _____ the garage.

   _____   _____

3. She walked _____ her car.

   _____   _____

4. I wrote _____ the book.

   _____   _____

5. We sat _____ the campfire.

   _____   _____

6. _____ I left for work, I called Tom.

   _____   _____

7. When I saw the accident, I ran _____ it.

   _____   _____

8. He hit the ball _____ the park.

   _____   _____

9. The astronauts flew _____ outer space.

   _____   _____

10. Hurricane Sally flew _____ our neighborhood.

   _____   _____

b. Fill in the following sentences with the appropriate **preposition**.

1. When I got out _____ my car, the traffic whizzed by.

2. The whizzing traffic scared me out _____ my wits.

3. There were hundreds _____ flies all around the picnic table.

4. I took a piece _____ cake and a piece _____ pie.

5. My mother ran _____ the burning house.

6. My father came out _____ the garage.

7. I almost ran out _____ ideas for grammar exercises, but luckily I found some more.

8. When I came back to my apartment _____ school, I found a mysterious letter awaiting me.

9. When the bus pulls out _____ the bus barn, they always have to stop traffic.

10. It was so cold that night I slept _____ three blankets.

c. Write ten sentences using **prepositions**. (You might want to look at the Index of Prepositions on page 245.)

1. _____

2. _____

3. _____

4. _____

5. _____

6. _____

7. _____

8. _____

9. _____

10. _____

CHAPTER 05

the act of reading | image is evidence

N. Scott Momaday uses language to describe the images, ideas, and feelings he had about his home, his tribe, and his family. In the following essay, "The Story of an Eyewitness: The San Francisco Earthquake," which first appeared in *Collier's* magazine, Jack London uses strong images to convey the aftermath of the 1906 San Francisco earthquake, estimated at 7.8 on the Richter scale.

The earthquake hit at 5:12 a.m. on April 18, 1906. *Collier's* Magazine called Jack London, who then lived 40 miles away, to go have a look at what had once been his hometown, San Francisco. London, as well as being a journalist, was a successful and popular American author who was also a pioneer in the rapidly growing world of commercial magazine fiction.

The Story of an Eyewitness: The San Francisco Earthquake

THE EARTHQUAKE SHOOK down in San Francisco hundreds of thousands of dollars worth of walls and chimneys. But the conflagration that followed burned up hundreds of millions of dollars' worth of property. There is no estimating within hundreds of millions the actual damage wrought. Not in history has a modern imperial city been so completely destroyed. San Francisco is gone. Nothing remains of it but memories and a fringe of dwelling-houses on its outskirts. Its industrial section is wiped out. Its business section is wiped out. Its social and residential section is wiped out. The factories and warehouses, the great stores and newspaper buildings, the hotels and the palaces of the nabobs, are all gone. Remains only the fringe of dwelling houses on the outskirts of what was once San Francisco.

Within an hour after the earthquake shock the smoke of San Francisco's burning was a lurid tower visible a hundred miles away. And for three days and nights this lurid tower swayed in the sky, reddening the sun, darkening the day, and filling the land with smoke.

On Wednesday morning at a quarter past five came the earthquake. A minute later the flames were leaping upward. In a dozen different quarters south of Market Street, in the working-class ghetto, and in the factories, fires started. There was no opposing the flames. There was no organization, no communication. All the cunning adjustments of a twentieth century city had been smashed by the earthquake. The streets were humped into ridges and depressions, and piled with the debris of fallen walls. The steel rails were twisted into perpendicular and horizontal angles. The telephone and telegraph systems were disrupted. And the great water-mains had burst. All the shrewd contrivances and safeguards of man had been thrown out of gear by thirty seconds' twitching of the earth-crust.

— 0 —

image is evidence

We often use **NOUNS** as the basis of **IMAGES,** but **VERBS, ADJECTIVES,** and **ADVERBS** can all play an important role in creating **IMAGES.** Images give you a picture that you see in your mind as you read. In writing your own essays, you can use **IMAGES** as **EVIDENCE** to prove your **THESIS.**

In Chapter 2, N. Scott Momaday writes clear **IMAGES** of his homeland. He gives us a concrete picture that we can see. For example, he writes of the "high gray walls" that surround the "old stone corral" where the U.S. Calvary imprisoned the Kiowas. Those "high gray walls" and that "old stone corral" are concrete **IMAGES** of objects we can actually see.

In "The Story of an Eyewitness: The San Francisco Earthquake," Jack London writes about how, after the earthquake, "the steel rails were twisted into perpendicular and horizontal angles." With this concrete writing about actual things, we see how concrete **IMAGES** tell the story of what happened and how the **IMAGES** in London's essay provide **EVIDENCE** that *prove* his **THESIS.** Before we look specifically at how these **IMAGES** in London's essay *prove* his thesis, let's first look at what we mean by **EVIDENCE.**

evidence

Evidence =
From the Latin: *Evident*
e = *out of*
vident = [videre] *to see*

What is **EVIDENCE**? **EVIDENCE** **proves** or **disproves** something. For example:

- If a lawyer, in court, says that Joe killed Sam, the lawyer has to prove that with **EVIDENCE.**

  The lawyer presents a gun found at the murder scene with Joe's DNA on it.

  That gun is the **EVIDENCE.**

- If we bought you a textbook for $20.00, and we want you to pay us back,

  We have the receipt from the bookstore as **EVIDENCE** that we paid $20.00 for the book.

- If we say that the Constitution of the United States guarantees free speech for all Americans,

  We can quote from the First Amendment to the Constitution, and that quote is our **EVIDENCE:** "Congress shall make no law…abridging the freedom of speech…."

Now let's look at how Jack London uses **IMAGES** as **EVIDENCE** to prove his **THESIS.** Let's say that Jack London's **THESIS** in "The Story of an Eyewitness: The San Francisco Earthquake" is:

Nature destroyed a great man-made city in the San Francisco earthquake of 1906.

How can Jack London prove this **THESIS?** He gives us **IMAGES** of the destruction as **evidence** that prove his **THESIS.**

The smoke of San Francisco's burning was a lurid tower visible a hundred miles away. And for three days and nights this lurid tower swayed in the sky, reddening the sun, darkening the day, and filling the land with smoke.

These images—the smoke, the reddening sun, and the darkening day—convey important pictures to us. They prove Jack London's **THESIS** that the natural destruction was enormous.

You now have a good idea of what an **IMAGE** is.

For example, let's say we wrote a brief essay, with the **THESIS:**

We have terrific students in our class.

We need to find **EVIDENCE** to prove that **THESIS.** We would like to use some **IMAGES** to use as **EVIDENCE** to support our **THESIS.**

We have terrific students in our class. We feel their desire to learn, and that inspires us to teach well. This morning we noticed, as we passed by the tables outside the small cafeteria on the South Quad, that one of our students sat by herself with a coffee, a textbook, and a notebook on the table in front of her. As she wrote in her notebook, she glanced back every few seconds at her textbook. She was apparently taking careful notes on the material in her textbook. This is not an uncommon sight for us. We often see our students studying around campus.

We have used this **IMAGE** of a student at her studies as **EVIDENCE** to prove our **THESIS**.

Chapter Review: Image Is Evidence

- Images give you a picture that you see in your minds as you read.
- In writing your own essays, you can use **IMAGES** as **EVIDENCE** to prove your **THESIS.**
- We often use **NOUNS** as the basis of **IMAGES,** but **VERBS, ADJECTIVES,** and **ADVERBS** can all play an important role in creating **images.**
- Evidence **proves** or **disproves** something.

Exercises for Chapter 5

I. YOUR THOUGHTS

a. What do the **images** in Jack London's essay, "The Story of an Eyewitness: The San Francisco Earthquake," make you think of or make you feel?

b. What do the **images** in London's essay tell you about London himself? Why did London choose these particular **images**?

c. Why did Jack London write this essay?

Remember that there is no one right answer to this exercise. London's entire essay "The Story of an Eyewitness: The San Francisco Earthquake" appears on p. 273. We recommend reading the whole essay to help you answer this question.

II. JACK LONDON'S ART: PARTS OF SPEECH

a. From Jack London's essay, list ten **articles** and the **noun** that goes with each of those **articles**.

Example: The telephone

1. _____   6. _____

2. _____   7. _____

3. _____   8. _____

4. _____   9. _____

5. _____   10. _____

b. List ten **conjunctions** that Jack London uses, along with the phrase that **conjunction** is a part of.

Example: factories **and** warehouses

1. _____

2. _____

3. _____

4. _____

5. _____

6. _____

7. _____

8. _____

9. _____

10. _____

c. Rewrite five of Jack London's sentences, adding **interjections.**

Example: Incredible! The earthquake shook down in San Francisco hundreds of thousands of
dollars worth of walls and chimneys.

1. _____

2. _____

3. _____

4. _____

5. _____

d. "The Story of an Eyewitness: The San Francisco Earthquake" contains twenty-nine **PREPOSITIONS!** We naturally use **PREPOSITIONS** often. List ten **PREPOSITIONS** that Jack London uses and the two nouns they connect.

Examples: hundreds of thousands

this lurid tower swayed in the sky

1. _____

2. _____

3. _____

4. _____

5. _____

6. _____

7. _____

8. _____

9. _____

10. _____

III. YOUR EXPERIENCE

a. List ten **IMAGES** that represent life on your campus as you experience it.

Example: We always have to wait in long lines at the registrar's office.

1. _____

2. _____

3. _____

4. _____

5. _____

6. _____

7. _____

8. _____

9. _____

10. _____

b. Have you ever witnessed a dramatic act of nature? Or, have you ever experienced nature as being still, quiet, and at peace? Write down five **IMAGES** that describe nature as either dramatic or peaceful.

1. _____

2. _____

3. _____

4. _____

5. _____

c. Looking at exercise "b," what verbs did you use?

1. _____

2. _____

3. _____

4. _____

5. _____

d. Prior to writing "The Story of an Eyewitness: The San Francisco Earthquake," Jack London had not lived in San Francisco for quite some time. Returning home often provides us with a fresh view of what we have left behind. Write one paragraph in which you describe a time when you left home, even briefly, and what you saw, felt, or discovered upon your return.

IV. ACTIVE READING

a. Write down four **IMAGES** from Jack London's essay that prove his **THESIS:**

_____

_____

_____

_____

b. Jack London uses strong, descriptive **VERBS** to describe the violent action of the 1906 San Francisco earthquake. Choose ten of the strongest **VERBS** and list them here.

1. _____   6. _____

2. _____   7. _____

3. _____   8. _____

4. _____   9. _____

5. _____   10. _____

c. In one paragraph, describe a city you have visited that has made either a positive or negative impression on you. Notice the **IMAGES** you use in your description.

d. Jack London shows his skill as a close observer and a good writer when he uses **IMAGES** of the two opposing forces of nature in his essay, fire and water. Copy those images down here from the essay: one of fire and one of water.

Fire: _____

Water: _____

CHAPTER06

the act of writing | develop it!

Having reviewed the **PARTS OF SPEECH** and explained what **THESIS, IMAGE** and **EVIDENCE** are, you are now ready to write your next essay. First, you will need to select a thesis and ask yourself our signature question—**"Why am I writing this essay?"** Having answered this question for yourself, you are now ready to write, but how will you **DEVELOP** your essay? That's the question, and here is the answer. Let's call these the **PARTS OF AN ESSAY.** You will follow these steps:

PARTS OF AN ESSAY: STEPS FOR DEVELOPING YOUR ESSAY

Step 1—<u>Present</u> your thesis

Step 2—<u>Present</u> examples as evidence that *prove* your thesis

Step 3—<u>Discuss</u> the evidence

Step 4—<u>Discuss</u> *how* the evidence proves your thesis

Step 5—Move on to <u>further develop</u> your evidence

    or

    <u>Present</u> new evidence

These are the steps for developing your essay. We'll now put them into practice, so you can see how they work together. Let's begin with the following thesis:

Step 1: Present Your Thesis

Jack London saw the 1906 San Francisco Earthquake as a force of nature more powerful than mankind and civilization.

You can't just make a statement like this and expect your reader to believe you. You have to prove it. How do you prove it? You prove it with **EXAMPLES** that you use as **EVIDENCE** that prove your thesis. Where do you get examples? You get examples from <u>inside</u> the essay or the books you're writing about, or you get them from the real world that you're writing about. You could take the following **EXAMPLE** from Jack London's essay: "The earthquake shook down in San Francisco hundreds of thousands of dollars worth of walls and chimneys," and use it as **EVIDENCE** to **PROVE** your thesis.

Step 2: Present Examples As Evidence That *Prove* Your Thesis

Jack London saw the 1906 San Francisco Earthquake as a force of nature more powerful than mankind and civilization. In his essay "The Story of an Eyewitness: The San Francisco Earthquake," Jack London writes, "The earthquake shook down in San Francisco hundreds of thousands of dollars worth of walls and chimneys."

You have found a good quote—an example (in red)—from Jack London's essay to prove your thesis. Now, you want to *discuss* that example in your own terms.

Step 3: Discuss the Evidence

Jack London saw the 1906 San Francisco Earthquake as a force of nature more powerful than mankind and civilization. In his essay "The Story of an Eyewitness: The San Francisco Earthquake," Jack London writes, "The earthquake shook down in San Francisco hundreds of thousands of dollars worth of walls and chimneys." Jack London thought of himself as an "Eyewitness," someone who saw this devastation.

Now, you're going to discuss *how* this example provides evidence of your thesis. Remember, the thesis is: *Jack London saw the 1906 San Francisco Earthquake as a force of nature more powerful than mankind and civilization.*

Step 4: Discuss How the Evidence Proves Your Thesis

Jack London saw the 1906 San Francisco Earthquake as a force of nature more powerful than mankind and civilization. In his essay "The Story of an Eyewitness: The San Francisco Earthquake," Jack London writes, "The earthquake shook down in San Francisco hundreds of thousands of dollars worth of walls and chimneys." Jack London thought of himself as an "Eyewitness," someone who saw this devastation. An earthquake comes not on mankind's schedule, but on its own schedule. It strikes not where mankind decides it should strike but wherever it happens to come. It can destroy all that mankind has built up: walls, chimneys, whatever happens to be caught in its circle.

Now, you can move on to offer another **EXAMPLE** as further **EVIDENCE** of your **THESIS.** Remember, again, that your **THESIS** is: *Jack London saw the 1906 San Francisco Earthquake as a force of nature more powerful than mankind and civilization.*

Step 5. Move on to Further Develop Your Evidence *or* Present New Evidence

Jack London saw the 1906 San Francisco Earthquake as a force of nature more powerful than mankind and civilization. In his essay "The Story of an Eyewitness: The San Francisco Earthquake," Jack London writes, "The earthquake shook down in San Francisco hundreds of thousands of dollars worth of walls and chimneys." Jack London thought of himself as an "Eyewitness," someone who saw this devastation. An earthquake comes not on mankind's schedule, but on its own schedule. It strikes not where mankind decides it should strike but wherever it happens to be. It can destroy all that mankind has built up: walls, chimneys, whatever happens to be caught in its circle.

In "The Story of an Eyewitness: The San Francisco Earthquake," London goes on to say that "Not in history has a modern imperial city been so completely destroyed. San Francisco is gone." London has seen his own city razed to the ground. By 1906, San Francisco was a powerful, important city that had been built up over the last hundred years. But nature was more powerful. It could destroy an entire city, a whole development mankind had worked over a long time to build.

Now, we know the steps that go into developing an essay. You don't want to just throw a lot of ideas down in your essay. You want to organize them, so they *develop* your **THESIS,** so that they *prove* your **THESIS,** so that your reader can see what you want to say. And that's what it's all about, isn't it?

You are using language to say what you have to say, to break the silence of your own life. You want the reader to understand what you want to say.

Let's use our method to write an essay where your **THESIS** is not about something you've read but about your life. The **EXAMPLES** you use as **EVIDENCE** to *prove* your **THESIS** will come from your life. Let's just call this essay, "I Want to Run for Public Office."

Step 1: Present Your Thesis

I want to run for public office because I want to help change our society as I saw my mother do.

Step 2: Present Examples As Evidence That *Prove* Your Thesis

I want to run for public office because I want to help change our society as I saw my mother do. I come from a family with a history of strong political involvement. The inhabitants of the small town I come from in Pennsylvania included Native Americans, African Americans, and other multi-cultural immigrants, my Irish family among them. Those communities were involved in both the Republican and Democratic parties, but my family was strongly Democratic. My mother was Commissioner of the School Board and then Mayor.

Step 3: Discuss the Evidence

I want to run for public office because I want to help change our society as I saw my mother do. I come from a family with a history of strong political involvement. The inhabitants of the small town I come from in Pennsylvania included Native Americans, African Americans, and other multi-cultural immigrants, my Irish family among them. Those communities were involved in both the Republican and Democratic parties, but my family was strongly Democratic. My mother was Commissioner of the School Board and then Mayor.

My mother began her political career when she ran for the School Board of our town. She wanted to improve the education we were getting as kids. By the time she became Commissioner of the School Board, she had begun changing our schools, bringing in art and music specialists, purchasing new technologies, inspiring worn-out teachers and administrators. During the Civil Rights era of the mid-'50s and '60s, my mother served as Mayor, dedicating herself to the fight for civil rights, inter-racial harmony, and universal equality.

Step 4: Discuss *How* the Evidence Proves Your Thesis

I want to run for public office because I want to help change our society as I saw my mother do. I come from a family with a history of strong political involvement. The inhabitants of the small town I come from in Pennsylvania included Native Americans, African Americans, and other multi-cultural immigrants, my Irish family among them. Those communities were involved in both the Republican and Democratic parties, but my family was strongly Democratic. My mother was Commissioner of the School Board and then Mayor.

My mother began her political career when she ran for the School Board of our town. She wanted to improve the education we were getting as kids. By the time she became Commissioner of the School Board, she had begun changing our schools, bringing in art and music specialists, purchasing new technologies, inspiring worn-out teachers and administrators. During the Civil Rights era of the mid-'50s and 60s my mother served as Mayor, dedicating herself to the fight for civil rights, inter-racial harmony, and universal equality.

All the time I was growing up, we had meetings, gatherings, and parties at our house with all the politically involved people in our town. Soon, we also had State officials coming over. Eventually, national political figures joined those events. At first, I listened in on all the conversations, which fascinated me. After a while, I felt sure enough of myself to join the conversations, expressing my own opinions. People listened to me. Not only did they listen to me, they thought my ideas were interesting. This made me feel so good that I wanted to keep up this activity after I left home. I joined the student Democratic Club when I came to college. Now, I want to keep going. Someday, I will run for public office myself. Who knows, I could be the Governor of Pennsylvania. I could be a Senator from Pennsylvania. Why be shy? I could be President of the United States!

Step 5: Move On To Further Develop Your Evidence Or Present New Evidence

I want to run for public office because I want to help change our society as I saw my mother do. I come from a family with a history of strong political involvement. The inhabitants of the small town I come from in Pennsylvania included Native Americans, African Americans, and other multi-cultural immigrants, my Irish family among them. Those communities were involved in both the Republican and Democratic parties, but my family was strongly Democratic. My mother was Commissioner of the School Board and then Mayor.

My mother began her political career when she ran for the School Board of our town. She wanted to improve the education we were getting as kids. By the time she became Commissioner of the School Board, she had begun changing our schools, bringing in art and music specialists, purchasing new technologies, inspiring worn-out teachers and administrators. During the Civil Rights era of the mid-'50s and 60s my mother served as Mayor, dedicating herself to the fight for civil rights, inter-racial harmony, and universal equality.

All the time I was growing up, we had meetings, gatherings, and parties at our house with all the politically involved people in our town. Soon, we also had State officials coming over. Eventually, national political figures joined those events. At first, I listened in on all the conversations, which fascinated me. After a while, I felt sure enough of myself to join the conversations, expressing my own opinions. People listened to me. Not only did they listen to me, they thought my ideas were interesting. This made me feel so good that I wanted to keep up this activity after I left home. I joined the student Democratic Club when I came to college. Now, I want to keep going. Someday, I will run for public office myself. Who knows, I could be the Governor of Pennsylvania. I could be a Senator from Pennsylvania. Why be shy? I could be President of the United States!

I'm not always happy with Democratic Party policies, and yet they represent my ideas about politics better than the Republicans. While I agree with some Republican positions, I sometimes have ideas of my own that neither party subscribes to. When I move up in the Democratic Party, and when I come to run for office myself, I hope to influence the Democratic Party with my ideas and to change it for the better.

Chapter Review: Essay Development

Step 1. <u>Present</u> Your Thesis

Step 2. <u>Present</u> Examples And Evidence To *Prove* Your Thesis

Step 3. <u>Discuss</u> The Evidence

Step 4. <u>Discuss</u> *How* The Evidence Proves Your Thesis

Step 5. Move on to <u>Further Develop</u> Your Evidence

        or

<u>Present</u> New Evidence

Exercises for Chapter 6:

DEVELOPMENT

A. Jack London's "The Story of an Eyewitness: The San Francisco Earthquake"

   a. How does Jack London develop his essay "The Story of an Eyewitness: The San Francisco Earthquake"? Answer the following questions. These questions follow the five steps for developing an essay we have given you.

      1. What is Jack London's **THESIS** in "The Story of an Eyewitness: The San Francisco Earthquake"?

      2. What is the first example Jack London uses as evidence to prove his **THESIS**?

      3. What does Jack London say about the first example he has used to prove his **THESIS**?

      4. How does the first example Jack London uses actually prove his **THESIS**?

      5. Does Jack London go on to further develop the first example he uses as evidence to prove his **THESIS,** *or* does he then go on to present another example as evidence to prove his **THESIS**?

      6. In Step 5 of the **STEPS FOR DEVELOPING YOUR ESSAY,** <u>either</u> you *further develop* your evidence, or you *present new evidence.*

         a. *If* Jack London *further develops* his evidence to prove his **THESIS,** what does he say about that evidence?

- or -

         b. *If* Jack London presents *another example* as evidence to prove his **THESIS,** what example does he present?

B. "I Want to Run for Public Office"

1. What is the **thesis** in "I Want to Run for Public Office?"

2. What example the does the author use as evidence to prove the **THESIS**?

3. What does the author say about the first example s/he used to prove the **THESIS**?

4. Does the first example the author use actually prove his/her **THESIS**?

5. In Step 5 of the **STEPS FOR DEVELOPING YOUR ESSAY,** either you *further develop* your evidence, **or** you *present new evidence*

   a. *If* the author further develops the evidence to prove his/her **THESIS,** what does s/he say about that example?

   b. *If* the author then *presents another example* as evidence to prove his/her **THESIS,** what example does s/he present?

C. Organizing an Essay

   a. We have jumbled up the following parts of an essay. Organize them according to the **STEPS FOR DEVELOPING YOUR ESSAY.** Write down the number of the **STEP** that describes each of these parts of a paragraph. Which one of these parts of an essay is the thesis (Step #1), which is the example (Step #2), which discusses the example (Step #3), and so on?

   Example:

   Step # ___2___
   (An example that proves the thesis)

   At the end of the Civil War, in 1865, Abraham Lincoln signed the Emancipation Proclamation, freeing the slaves.

   Step # ___1___
   (Thesis)

   Abraham Lincoln became a great American President.

Step # _____ My father, who works at a stressful job, spends an hour before dinner every day playing the piano. After playing the piano, he's relaxed enough to enjoy dinner.

Step # _____ Listening to music or playing an instrument will give you one of life's great relaxations.

Step # _____ Having watched my father for years, I took up piano lessons. Now I'll sit at the piano after school, playing until I feel relaxed, refreshed, and refocused to go on with the evening.

Step # _____ At family gatherings or at parties with friends, people will often ask my father to play the piano. I think he likes this aspect of his playing most of all, giving pleasure not only to himself but to others as well.

Step # _____ My father loves to play Mozart, but he also likes a lot of other composers. He loves to play the Blues, Jazz, Pop, or Rock. In short, he just loves music. I like best the way he plays Mozart, but if he plays a Pop song I know, sometimes I'll sing along with him.

b. Now, rewrite the elements of this essay into an ordinary paragraph. (To make it sound better, you can use "he" in place of "my father" where appropriate.)

Assignment for Chapter 6

In "The Story of an Eyewitness: The San Francisco Earthquake," Jack London writes about mankind's relationship to nature. Nature turns out to be more powerful than mankind and civilization. Write an essay about your own environment. What is the relationship between your environment and nature? Is it a harmonious relationship? Is your environment threatened by nature? Does mankind dominate nature in your environment?

Remember to create one clear **THESIS** for yourself, then follow that **THESIS** throughout your essay.

PART 03

the origins of language III: greek myth

The ancient Greeks believed that Zeus, their chief god, was the sole ruler of the universe. He lived, with the other gods, atop Mount Olympus. During the age of the rule of Zeus, all people spoke only one language. Everyone understood each other. They had no laws.

Rules, or laws, clarify acceptable behavior and misunderstandings of language. All of our laws are based on language. During the time of the rule of Zeus, everyone spoke the same language, so everyone understood the rules that governed social, civic, and commercial life. In that age, the Greeks had no need for laws. They all spoke with the same clarity of language. But this world of only one language would not last forever. Things changed.

The god Hermes, whose role it was to carry messages into the world, was responsible for language. According to Greek myth, it was Hermes who brought other languages into the world.

It is possible that, as the Greeks expanded their horizons by traveling around the Mediterranean and meeting other people who spoke other languages, they created the myth that it was Hermes, the messenger god, who brought other languages into being.

However the myth originated, once Hermes brought other languages into the world, people couldn't communicate effectively any more, giving rise to misunderstandings, discord, and separation into diverse nations.

This chaos so dismayed Zeus that he resigned his position as ruler of mankind, retiring to his position as ruler of all the gods. The first King, Phoroneus, rose to take Zeus's place as ruler of mankind.

With many languages among many nations, we need laws to govern ourselves. Law is our imperfect attempt to define with language what we allow and what we prohibit in society. We look to lawyers to express opposing interpretations of events and laws, while we leave it up to judges and juries to decide which language, which version of right and wrong, prevails.

We don't live in an ideal age of Zeus and universal understanding, but with our genius for language, we find ways to organize our lives to achieve as much understanding as we possibly can.

CHAPTER 07

the art of language | parts of a sentence

In Chapters 1 (page 3) and 4 (page 41), we learned all nine PARTS OF SPEECH:

- nouns
- verbs
- pronouns
- adjectives
- adverbs
- articles
- conjunctions
- interjections
- prepositions

These nine categories make up **one system** that we use to organize language, and we call that system PARTS OF SPEECH. In that system, PARTS OF SPEECH, we categorize every word as a **NOUN,** a **VERB,** an **ADJECTIVE,** etc.

Another system we use to organize language, we call PARTS OF A SENTENCE. What are the PARTS OF A SENTENCE? How do the PARTS OF A SENTENCE work? How do we use the PARTS OF A SENTENCE?

First, we'll look at the two necessary PARTS OF A SENTENCE:

- SIMPLE SUBJECT
- SIMPLE PREDICATE

Every sentence must have a:

- SIMPLE SUBJECT
- SIMPLE PREDICATE

What is a SIMPLE SUBJECT?

What is a SIMPLE PREDICATE?

We use the PARTS OF SPEECH as building blocks to make the PARTS OF A SENTENCE. For example:

- **NOUNS** are a **PART OF SPEECH.**

We use **NOUNS** (or **PRONOUNS**) to make the **PART OF A SENTENCE** that we call

SIMPLE SUBJECT

- **VERBS** are a **PART OF SPEECH.**

We use **VERBS** to make the **PART OF A SENTENCE** that we call:

SIMPLE PREDICATE

To make **any sentence** work, we need at least two **PARTS OF A SENTENCE:**

- We need a **SIMPLE SUBJECT** – always a **NOUN** (or **PRONOUN**)
- We need a **SIMPLE PREDICATE** – always a **VERB**

> *simple subject*

In <u>every</u> sentence, somebody (*or something*) <u>*does*</u> something.

The **SIMPLE SUBJECT** of a sentence *tells us* **WHO** or **WHAT** <u>**does something**</u> in that sentence.

Remember: we always use a **NOUN** (or **PRONOUN**) to make the **SIMPLE SUBJECT.**

Examples of **SIMPLE SUBJECT.**
Here the **NOUN** "Sam" becomes the **SIMPLE SUBJECT** of the sentence.

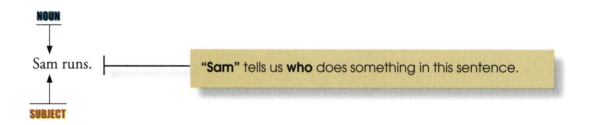

NOUN

Sam runs.

SUBJECT

"Sam" tells us **who** does something in this sentence.

The **NOUN** "Charles" becomes the **SIMPLE SUBJECT** of this sentence.

NOUN

Charles talks.

SUBJECT

"Charles" tells us **who** does something in this sentence.

Here, the **NOUN** "Roderigo" becomes the **SIMPLE SUBJECT** of this sentence.

"Roderigo" tells us **who** does something in this sentence.

Here, the **NOUN** "building" becomes the **SIMPLE SUBJECT** of this sentence.

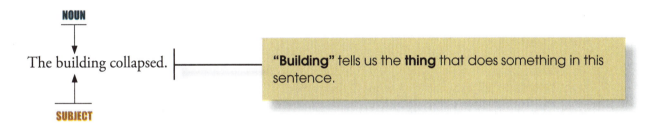

"Building" tells us the **thing** that does something in this sentence.

The **SIMPLE SUBJECT** of a sentence is *always* a **NOUN** (or **PRONOUN**). Fill in five **SUBJECTS** in the following sentences. Notice that each **SUBJECT** you choose is a **NOUN**.

EXERCISES ON SIMPLE SUBJECT

Example: _____ talks.   __*Billy*__ talks.

1. _____ sings.
2. _____ cooks.
3. _____ drives.
4. _____ writes.
5. _____ plays.

simple predicate

The **SIMPLE PREDICATE** tells us **WHAT** the **SUBJECT DOES.**

We always make a **SIMPLE PREDICATE** from a **VERB**

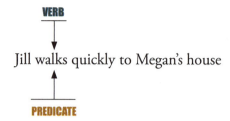

In the sentence above, the **VERB** "walks" becomes the **SIMPLE PREDICATE.** It tells us what the **subject** Jill does.

Remember, *two* systems we use to organize language and grammar:

- **PARTS OF SPEECH**
- **PARTS OF A SENTENCE.**

- **PARTS OF SPEECH** tell us what each word is on its own.
- **PARTS OF A SENTENCE** tell us how each word *works together* with all the other words in a sentence.

Examples of **SIMPLE PREDICATE**:

Here, the **VERB** "runs" becomes the **SIMPLE PREDICATE** of the sentence.

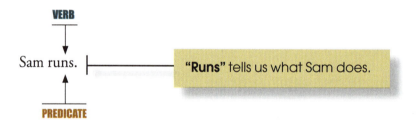

The **VERB** "talks" becomes the **SIMPLE PREDICATE** of this sentence.

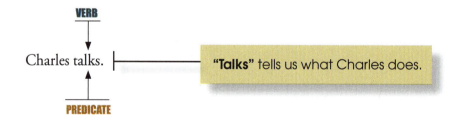

Here, the **VERB** "listens" becomes the **SIMPLE PREDICATE** of this sentence.

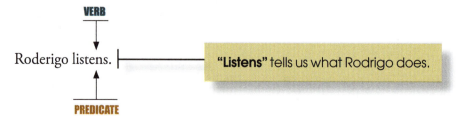

Here, the VERB "collapsed" becomes the SIMPLE PREDICATE of this sentence.

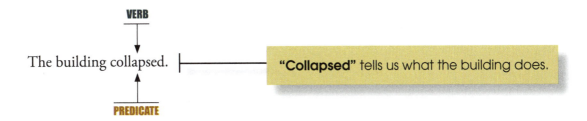

"**Collapsed**" tells us what the building does.

EXERCISES ON SIMPLE PREDICATE

In the following five sentences, fill in the SIMPLE PREDICATE that tells us **what** the SUBJECT of the sentence **DOES**:

1. Jim _____ his car.

SUBJECT   PREDICATE

2. Latasha _____ her bedroom.

SUBJECT   PREDICATE

3. Gloria _____ a book.

SUBJECT   PREDICATE

4. Pasquale _____ to the store.

SUBJECT   PREDICATE

5. Roger _____ in the ocean.

SUBJECT   PREDICATE

The SIMPLE PREDICATE is *always* a VERB.

a complete thought

Every **complete** sentence has *at least*

- a SUBJECT
- a PREDICATE

and

- expresses a COMPLETE THOUGHT.

This group of words:

you wrote a

has a SUBJECT ("you"), and it has a PREDICATE ("wrote"), **but** it does not express a COMPLETE THOUGHT. It is not a sentence.

In the following group of words, you have a COMPLETE THOUGHT, and you have a complete sentence:

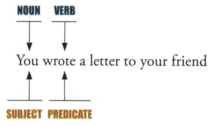

NOUN   VERB

You wrote a letter to your friend

SUBJECT PREDICATE

Now, you have a **complete sentence,** with:

- a SUBJECT ("You")
- a PREDICATE ("wrote")
- a COMPLETE THOUGHT [a letter to your friend.]

what is a sentence fragment?

If you don't have **both** a SUBJECT and a PREDICATE in your sentence, or if your sentence does not express a COMPLETE THOUGHT, you have a

SENTENCE FRAGMENT

(also called an INCOMPLETE SENTENCE)

You have not written a **complete** sentence but only a FRAGMENT of a sentence.

> **Fragment =**
> From the Latin: *Frangent-um*
> *Frangere* = to break
> A fragment is something broken off from the whole; it is only
> a part of something, not the whole of something.

Slept late on Sunday. = **sentence fragment** (no SUBJECT. WHO slept late on Sunday?)

Martin late on Sunday. = **sentence fragment** (no PREDICATE. WHAT did Martin DO?)

Because Martin arrived. = **sentence fragment** (not a COMPLETE THOUGHT.)

> If you write a **sentence fragment,** your Professor may write
> the proofreading mark *"frag"* above your mistake. You
> can correct that mistake by adding a SUBJECT, or by adding a
> PREDICATE, or by making the sentence a **complete thought.**

independent clause

What is an **independent clause?** Like every sentence, every **independent clause** has *at least* a SUBJECT and a PREDICATE.

- If **any** <u>group of words</u>
- has a SUBJECT and a PREDICATE,
          - **and** -
- that group of words **can stand alone as a complete thought**
  because it expresses a complete thought,

we call it an INDEPENDENT CLAUSE.

- It can stand alone, independent of any other words.
- We can easily turn any INDEPENDENT CLAUSE into a sentence merely by adding punctuation: a **period**, an **exclamation mark**, or a **question mark**. Let's take the two groups of words we used at this Chapter's beginning:

I come from Chicago   [**Subject:** "I;" **Predicate**: "come"]

My mother just went back to college   [**Subject:** "mother;" **Predicate**: "went"]

Each of these two groups of words has a SIMPLE SUBJECT:

- "I"
- "mother"

Each of these two groups of words has a SIMPLE PREDICATE:

- "come"
- "went"

Each one of these two groups of words can **stand alone** as a sentence. They are each an INDEPENDENT CLAUSE. To make these INDEPENDENT CLAUSES into sentences, we just add punctuation; in this case, we add periods.

I come from Chicago.

My mother just went back to college.

EXERCISES ON INDEPENDENT CLAUSES:

Indicate which of the following groups of words is an independent clause:

	independent clause	not an independent clause
1. I went	_____	_____
2. I came home	_____	_____
3. You stood up	_____	_____
4. The cup the table	_____	_____
5. I drink coffee	_____	_____

one sentence = one thought

The following sentence has *more than* **one** thought:

one thought   another thought

I come from Chicago my mother just went back to college.

How can we fix this problem? We can fix it by adding some punctuation, in this case, a period. Yet, these two thoughts are so different, they even belong in different paragraphs.

I come from Chicago.

My mother just went back to college.

Perfect! Now, we have *two* thoughts, and we have *two* sentences.

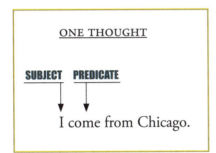

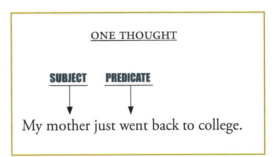

Chapter Review: Parts of a Sentence

We use two systems to organize language and grammar:

- Parts of Speech
- Parts of a Sentence

The two essential parts of a sentence are:

- simple subject:

  tells us who or what does something in that sentence;

- simple predicate:

  tells us what the subject does.

  We always make the simple subject from a noun.
  We always make a simple predicate from a verb.

<u>Every **complete**</u> sentence has

- a subject
- a predicate

and

- expresses a complete thought.

If you don't have ***both*** a SUBJECT and a PREDICATE in your sentence, or if your sentence does not express a COMPLETE THOUGHT, you have a

SENTENCE FRAGMENT (also called an incomplete sentence)

If **any** *group of words*
- has a SUBJECT and a PREDICATE

-and-

- that group of words can stand alone,

we call it an INDEPENDENT CLAUSE.

We can easily turn any INDEPENDENT CLAUSE into a sentence merely by adding punctuation: a period, an exclamation mark, or a question mark.

Each sentence expresses one and only one thought. One Sentence = One Thought.

Exercises for Chapter 7:

I. SUBJECT - PREDICATE

a. In the following sentences, fill in both the SIMPLE SUBJECT and the SIMPLE PREDICATE.

1. _____ _____ dogs.
   SUBJECT   PREDICATE

2. _____ _____ the piano.
   SUBJECT   PREDICATE

3. _____ _____ in her notebook.
   SUBJECT   PREDICATE

4. _____ _____ the bus.
   SUBJECT   PREDICATE

5. _____ _____ her boyfriend.
   SUBJECT   PREDICATE

6. _____ _____ the glass.
   SUBJECT   PREDICATE

7. _____ _____ a dress.
   SUBJECT   PREDICATE

8. _____ _____ TV.
   SUBJECT   PREDICATE

9. _____ _____ baseball.
   SUBJECT   PREDICATE

10. _____ _____ jewelry.
    SUBJECT   PREDICATE

b. Fill in the **PREDICATES** that tell us the things that the **SUBJECT** "I" does:

1. I _____.
   PREDICATE

2. I _____.
   PREDICATE

3. I _____.
   PREDICATE

4. I _____.
   PREDICATE

5. I _____.
   PREDICATE

6. I _____.
   PREDICATE

7. I _____.
   PREDICATE

8. I _____.
   PREDICATE

9. I _____.
   PREDICATE

10. I _____.
    PREDICATE

II. COMPLETE THOUGHT

a. Each of the following has at least one **SIMPLE SUBJECT** and one **SIMPLE PREDICATE.** Put in a **period** wherever necessary to make each sentence **ONE THOUGHT.** Fix the capitalization where necessary.

Examples: a. I went swimming yesterday
                     I went swimming yesterday.

b. I'll try to call you later it's very hot today
                     It's
    I'll try to call you later. it's very hot today.

1. I drove my mother to the doctor's office

2. My sister is a singer her husband is a doctor

3. I bought a new watch yesterday

4. My parents are very religious they go to church every Sunday

5. Parakeets are my favorite pets

6. Computers are great fun computers are also very expensive

7. I went shopping with my girlfriend I bought two sweaters

8. We went to New York for Christmas my grandparents live there

9. My brother and I love to play baseball we play baseball every Tuesday and Saturday

10. We went to a great movie last night we also went to a restaurant my sister picked out

b. Write ten complete sentences about your life in college. Make sure each sentence expresses only **ONE THOUGHT.**

1. _____

2. _____

3. _____

4. _____

5. _____

6. _____

7. _____

8. _____

9. _____

10. _____

c. The following are not sentences because they do not express a **COMPLETE THOUGHT.**
Complete each of the following **FRAGMENTS**:

1. Because the Dodgers didn't score in the 9ᵗʰ inning _____

2. If I eat the whole pizza _____

3. The customers in the restaurant _____

4. I saw where the birds _____

5. I wrote the essay before _____

6. When we listened to the song _____

7. After opening the garage door _____

8. Walking down the street _____

9. While drinking coffee _____

10. Inside the house _____

d. Write a sentence based on each of the following thoughts. Make sure each sentence expresses **ONE THOUGHT,** and that it has a **SUBJECT** and a **PREDICATE**.

Example: The thought: rollercoasters
                  The sentence: I hate rollercoasters.

1. The thought: baseball
   The sentence: _____

2. The thought: TV
   The sentence: _____

3. The thought: America

   The sentence: _____

4. The thought: sleep

   The sentence: _____

5. The thought: music

   The sentence: _____

6. The thought: war

   The sentence: _____

7. The thought: marriage

   The sentence: _____

8. The thought: ice cream

   The sentence: _____

9. The thought: love

   The sentence: _____

10. The thought: home

    The sentence: _____

IV. INDEPENDENT CLAUSES

a. If any of the following groups of words is an **independent clause**, add the appropriate punctuation to make it into a sentence. If any of the following groups of words is **not** an **independent clause**, cross it out.

   Example: I ran home   =   I ran home.

   Sally heartbreak = ~~Sally heartbreak~~

1. The women played basketball

2. The ice cream melted quickly

3. Did the ice cream melt quickly

4. The horrible accident

5. The school day was

6. The waiters cleared

7. My father is a waiter

8. Let's free pizza from my father

9. Did you do well on the math quiz

b. Complete each group of words below, so that it *becomes* an **independent clause**. Make sure that each group of words has all three:

    —a **simple subject,**
    —a **simple predicate,**
    —and it can **stand alone** as a complete thought.

1. My father _____

2. My dog, Alex, _____

3. The restaurant _____

4. The Professor came _____

5. She bought _____

6. The infant ran _____

7. The college announced _____

8. Aunt Sally did her _____

9. The team arrived _____

10. The boxer threw _____

c. Each of the sentences below is made up of two **independent clauses**. Underline *one of* the **independent clauses**, and *circle* the other **independent clause.**

1. Music filled the street, and my girlfriend and I danced.

2. The fireworks went off over the river, and my dad and I ran down to the river together.

3. The siren blared through our neighborhood, but our dog slept blissfully.

4. My favorite shop had a great sale, so I bought as much as I could afford.

5. I told Francine I would go shopping with her, or we could go to a movie.

6. My Grandfather went into the hospital yesterday, but he'll be all right.

7. I'm going to study abroad in Paris, or I'm going to intern in a law office in New York.

8. I wanted to work for the U.N., but now I want to work on my own.

9. We went to a great dance concert, yet we wanted to see a movie, too.

10. The lecturer talked about physics, yet he touched on religion.

CHAPTER 08

the act of reading | a community of writers

N. Scott Momaday, in "The Way to Rainy Mountain," and Jack London, in "The Story of an Eyewitness: The San Francisco Earthquake," each describe their home. In her book *The History of Love,* Diane Ackerman writes about how people in different cultures and in different times think about love, how they come together to express love in different ways.

Why do we write? Writing is a solitary act that joins us together in a community of writers and readers. Every time we write, we express something about who we are and where we're from.

The cave painters at Lascaux used painted images to break the silence of their lives and to speak about what mattered to them. N. Scott Momaday, in "The Way to Rainy Mountain," and Jack London, in "The Story of an Eyewitness: The San Francisco Earthquake," create images with words to speak about their homes and where they came from. Here, Diane Ackerman uses language to talk about all of us, to look at how we all live and love.

Modern Love

WHEN I THINK about the essence of being modern, the changes in attitude that led to the life we now know, three things come to mind: choice, privacy, and books. As a child of the seventies, I find it almost impossible to fathom a time when people couldn't make choices in their lives—whimsical choices, let alone solemn ones. Personal freedom has a long, slow history, based in part on the growing size of the world's population, which gave people a chance to be anonymous. If they couldn't be exempt from the moral law, they could at least toy with exemption in private. Despite arranged marriages, people stole the freedom to love whom they chose, without shame; then to choose whom to marry; and in time they even made the shocking leap to wishing to marry someone they loved. As wealth and leisure grew, houses began to have specific rooms for specific uses, including a bedroom where couples could be unobserved. Soon, young marrieds wanted a place of their own, separate from their in-laws. They wanted to be "alone together," a new idea based on a newly won sense of privacy.

The invention of printing aided and abetted lovers. Once people became more literate they could take a book with them to some quiet place and read to themselves and think. Reading changed society and readers could discover in romantic and erotic literature what was possible, or at least imaginable. They could dare controversial thoughts and feel bolstered by allies, without telling anyone. Books had to be kept somewhere, and with the library, came the idea of secluded hours, alone with one's innermost thoughts. Lovers could blend their hearts by sharing sympathetic authors; what they could not express in person they could at least point to in the pages of a book. A shared book could speak to lovers in confidence, increasing their sense of intimacy even if the loved one was absent or a forbidden companion. Books opened the door to an aviary filled with flights of the imagination, winged fantasies of love; they gave readers a sense of emotional community. Somewhere in another city or state another soul was reading the same words, perhaps dreaming the same dreams.

— 0 —

In Chapter 1, we asked what we would do without language? What would we do if we couldn't speak to each other? Now, let's ask ourselves what would we do without books? Five hundred years ago, scribes had to hand-write a copy of each book. A book was far too expensive for most people to buy. Imagine how long it must have taken to produce one handwritten copy of the Bible. Without books, most people were illiterate. Without reading, people had no idea they could think for themselves and achieve their own freedom. In the mid-fourteen hundreds, Johannes Gutenberg, of Mainz, Germany, invented moveable type and the printing press. Among his first printing projects, Gutenberg printed the Bible. With this invention, books became more common. Today, we all have them.

We have already pointed out and talked about the relationship between silence and writing. Language and literacy give us the power and knowledge to break our silence. This power allows us to think as individuals and to question how we choose to live. In writing about the history of love, Diane Ackerman traces the role that books have played in changing how we choose whom to love. Today, about five hundred years after Gutenberg, about 98%[1] of the population in developed countries is literate. Each one of us, as we read, joins in the language of our whole world. We join in a community of readers; we join in a DIALOGUE with everyone who has read what we have read. If you and I have both read Diane Ackerman's entire essay, we are thinking about the same things. We can have a great conversation, a dialogue about what love means to us in our lives.

Diane Ackerman writes about real things in our lives, and she also writes about how we live a life of human imagination. She writes, "Books opened the door to an aviary filled with flights of

---

[1]http://www.search.eb.com.libproxy.chapman.edu:2048/eb/article-281687

the imagination, winged fantasies of love; they gave readers a sense of emotional community." In our community of readers, we share similar ideas, but we also share similar emotions. And we share our imaginations.

the dictionary

Diane Ackerman emphasizes how important books are in our lives, and books are made up of **words.**

If your friend says to you:

I just saw the **zeppelin,**

and if you don't know what a *zeppelin* is, you're lost.

The dictionary is one of our great language tools.

English is the largest language in the world. It grows at a terrific rate, taking in new words from other languages, from new technology, and from slang. The Oxford English Dictionary is the most comprehensive of it's kind. When last printed, in 1989, it had 20 volumes, with approximately 600,000 definitions; it was 21,730 pages in length! Fortunately, we can now tap easily into dictionaries online.

When you come across a word that you don't know and skip over it without looking it up, you've read something, but you don't understand what you've just read. You've cheated yourself out of knowing what's going on. You always end up a little frustrated. You may not even notice it until you pay attention, but once you do notice that frustration, you want to relieve it. So let's begin using the dictionary to satisfy our curiosity and our desire to know what the words we read mean.

AN EXERCISE ON DICTIONARY USE

Look up five words from Diane Ackerman's piece that you don't know. List them and write a brief definition from a dictionary.

For example:

WORD	DEFINITION
whimsical	imaginative and impulsive

1. _____   _____
2. _____   _____
3. _____   _____
4. _____   _____
5. _____   _____

We've used the dictionary on our computer to get this definition. Often, since words can have different meanings, a dictionary will give you more than one definition. See if you can't pick the definition that you think best fits Diane Ackerman's use of that word.

In our example, above, if you don't know what "impulsive" means, you may want to look that up. You could spend the whole day at this, chasing down one definition after another!

Chapter Review: A Community of Writers

Books make it possible for us all to think about and talk about the same ideas. They can certainly help us to understand ourselves and to understand one another. Hopefully, they can even bring us all closer together.

Diane Ackerman sets an example in her own writing by laying out for us the history of love, so that we understand how we have come to enjoy the freedom to love that we have today.

Dictionaries are a key that give us the power to read accurately and to write with clarity, precision, and vitality.

Exercises for Chapter 8

I. YOUR THOUGHTS

a. Why does Diane Ackerman write this essay? Again, remember, there is no one right answer to this important question. Just tell us why you think she might have written this essay.

b. How are books important to modern love?

II. DIANE ACKERMAN'S ART: PARTS OF SPEECH; PARTS OF A SENTENCE

a. List ten nouns that Diane Ackerman uses in "Modern Love."

1. _____   6. _____

2. _____   7. _____

3. _____   8. _____

4. _____   9. _____

5. _____   10. _____

b. List ten verbs that Diane Ackerman uses in "Modern Love."

1. _____   6. _____

2. _____   7. _____

3. _____   8. _____

4. _____   9. _____

5. _____   10. _____

c. In the following sentences from "Modern Love," indicate the SIMPLE SUBJECT and the SIMPLE PREDICATE.

Example:

SUBJECT
↓
I find it almost impossible to fathom a time when people couldn't make choices in their lives.
↑
PREDICATE

1. Personal freedom has a long, slow history.

2. People stole the freedom to love whom they chose.

3. Houses began to have specific rooms for specific uses.

4. Young marrieds wanted a room of their own.

5. They wanted to be "alone together."

6. They could take a book with them to some quiet place.

7. They could dare controversial thoughts.

8. Lovers could blend their hearts.

9. Books opened the door.

10. They gave readers a sense of emotional community.

d. Diane Ackerman, skillful with language, writes clear sentences we can easily understand. She can make herself understood, something we all want to do. We want you to move from writing excellent, clear **sentences** to writing well-constructed **paragraphs** to building a well-written, well-developed **essay.** Take a look back at Ackerman's sentences. Pick out one sentence that reads particularly clearly to you. Copy that sentence here.

What is the SIMPLE SUBJECT of this sentence? What is the SIMPLE PREDICATE of this sentence?

Write down in your own words what you think Diane Ackerman says in this sentence.

III. Your Experience

a. Give an example from your own life when you exercised the freedom of choice.

b. Give an example from your own life of where you can experience privacy.

c. Give an example from your own life when a book has been important to you.

d. Books break the silence of our lives. If you were to write a book that would be published, describe what you would write about.

e. Think about the idea of a shared book. Have you ever shared a book with someone? Describe that book. Why was it important to you?

IV. Active Reading

a. Diane Ackerman lists three developments that led to modern life and modern love: choice, privacy, and books. Give one example she uses to demonstrate choice in modern life.

    b. Give one example she uses to demonstrate privacy in modern life.

    c. Give one example she uses to demonstrate the importance of books in modern life.

    d. Looking at the three things Diane Ackerman lists that have changed our lives: choice, privacy, and books, discuss how these things shape modern life as you know it.

    e. Ackerman writes that, "Books opened the door to an aviary filled with flights of the imagination." What does she mean?

    f. Look up ten words from Diane Ackerman's essay that you don't know. Then look them up in the dictionary and write out their definitions. (If you don't find ten words that you don't yet know, bravo! Look up a few words that you do know, so that you have ten.) Let's all start with the same word.

WORD   DEFINITION

1. _____zeppelin_____   _____

                          _____

2. _____   _____

                          _____

3. _____   _____

                          _____

4. _____   _____

                          _____

5. _____   _____

_____

6. _____   _____

_____

7. _____   _____

_____

8. _____   _____

_____

9. _____   _____

_____

10. _____   _____

_____

CHAPTER 09

the act of writing | develop it! | paragraph unity

When you write an essay, developing your **THESIS** with argument, evidence, proof, and discussion, you do it one paragraph after another, developing your **THESIS** from one paragraph to the next. Right? In order to communicate your ideas, in order to make your argument clear, each paragraph must have **PARAGRAPH UNITY**. So what do we mean by **PARAGRAPH UNITY**?

PARAGRAPH UNITY means that, in <u>each paragraph,</u> you write about **one** and *only* **one** and *not more than* **one** idea. You will organize each paragraph around one **MAIN IDEA**. For example, Diane Ackerman would not have written:

> The invention of printing aided and abetted lovers. All the people who had been friends said good-bye to each other.

You would not write:

> I am a Freshman in college. Only 6% of Americans now smoke cigarettes.

You have begun with **one** idea, so you must continue with that idea:

> I am a Freshman in college. I graduated high school the year before last, but I couldn't begin college because I had to work for a year to save enough money for tuition and books.

You could go on writing more in this paragraph, as long as you stick to your **one** idea:

> I am a Freshman in college. I graduated high school the year before last, but I couldn't begin college because I had to work for a year to save enough money for tuition and books. Working in a gas station as a mechanic, I saved up enough for my first year. I'm hoping now to get a scholarship to help me go on.

One idea: "I am a Freshman in college." Everything else is about that **one** idea.

I've decided to go to law school. My uncle became a lawyer, and he loves it. Every day he spends the whole day fighting for peoples' rights.

> Next paragraph, also **one** idea: "I've decided to go to law school."

The second paragraph begins with the *next* idea, **developing** the author's THESIS.

> one paragraph = one idea
> each paragraph *develops from* the last paragraph

Let's imagine that we're in a class where the Professor gives us this assignment:

Write an essay analyzing the importance of books in Diane Ackerman's "Modern Love."

We're going to write this essay for you, reviewing all of the STEPS FOR DEVELOPING AN ESSAY. Notice that each paragraph focuses on one idea, so that each paragraph has PARAGRAPH UNITY, and each paragraph develops the THESIS. In the essay that follows, we will indicate, in the boxes beside each paragraph, the *one idea* that gives PARAGRAPH UNITY to that paragraph.

> *steps for developing an essay*

Let's say we write an essay with the following thesis:

Step 1. (Present Your Thesis)

In the modern world, we are free to choose whom we love, and books have helped us to find that freedom. But it wasn't always that way.

> **Main Idea:**
> Books have helped us find the freedom to choose our love.

Step 2. (Present Examples As Evidence That Prove Your Thesis)

You can't just state your thesis and expect your reader to believe it. You have to prove it. *How* do you prove it? You use EXAMPLES as EVIDENCE that prove your thesis. Where do you get examples that you can use for evidence? You get those examples from <u>inside</u> the essay or the books you're reading, or you get them from the real world. We're going to take **EXAMPLES** from world literature, and from Diane Ackerman's essay and use these examples as **EVIDENCE** to **PROVE** our thesis.

In her essay "Modern Love," Diane Ackerman writes, "When I think about the essence of being modern, the changes in attitude that led to the life we now know, three things come to mind: choice, privacy, and books." In the modern world, we are free to choose whom we love, and books have helped us to find that freedom. But it wasn't always that way. **Shakespeare's famous characters, Romeo and Juliet, who lived in the old world, did not have this choice.**

> **Main Idea:**
> Choice, privacy, and books have given us the freedom to choose our love, a freedom Romeo and Juliet did not have.

Step 3. (Discuss the Example/Evidence)

In her essay "Modern Love," Diane Ackerman writes, "When I think about the essence of being modern, the changes in attitude that led to the life we now know, three things come to mind: choice, privacy, and books." In the modern world, we are free to choose whom we love, and books have helped us to find that freedom. But it wasn't always that way. Shakespeare's famous characters, Romeo and Juliet, who lived in the old world, did not have this choice.

Could "choice, privacy, and books" have saved Romeo and Juliet? When Romeo and Juliet tried to live as modern lovers, they chose each other. But their families, in the ways of the old world, prohibited their love. In the end, Romeo and Juliet both die for their love.

> **Main Idea:**
> While Romeo and Juliet chose each other, their families prohibited their love.

How is it that, in the modern world, books give us choice, including the choice to choose our love? Books give us many freedoms, many choices. **For example, if you read about people who have freedom of religion, you see that you are free to practice your own religion. If you read about people who have the freedom to choose their love, you see that you, too, are free to choose your own love.**

> **Main Idea:**
> Books give us many freedoms.

Now, we'll discuss *how* this example provides **EVIDENCE** for our **THESIS**. Remember, our **THESIS** is: *In the modern world, we are free to choose whom we love, and books have helped us to find that freedom. But it wasn't always that way.*

Step 4. (Discuss How the Evidence Proves Your Thesis)

In her essay "Modern Love," Diane Ackerman writes, "When I think about the essence of being modern, the changes in attitude that led to the life we now know, three things come to mind: choice, privacy, and books." In the modern world, we are free to choose whom we love, and books have helped us to find that freedom. But it wasn't always that way. Romeo and Juliet, for example, who lived in the old world, did not have that choice.

Could "choice, privacy, and books" have saved Romeo and Juliet? When Romeo and Juliet tried to live as modern lovers, they chose each other. But their families, in the ways of the old world, prohibited their love. By the end of the story, Romeo and Juliet both end up dying for their love.

Books can give us many freedoms, many choices. If you read about people who have freedom of religion, for example, you see that you are free to practice your own religion. If you read about people who have the freedom to choose their love, you see that you, too, are free to choose your own love.

If Romeo and Juliet's parents had had easy access to books and read about the freedom to choose love, maybe they would have just let Romeo and Juliet choose each other. If that happened, poor Romeo and poor Juliet would not have died for their love. Of course, if that happened, we wouldn't have Shakespeare's wonderful play.

> **Main Idea:**
> Perhaps access to books would have saved Romeo and Juliet, but, not having that access, they died for their love.

Now, We'll move on to offer another **EXAMPLE** as further **EVIDENCE** of our thesis. Remember, that the **THESIS** is: *In the modern world, we are free to choose whom we love, and books have helped us to find that freedom. But it wasn't always that way.*

Step 5. (Further Develop Your Evidence or Present New Evidence)

In Step 5, we'll begin with another idea. **NOTICE** that our new idea *grows out of* what we have already written. Our new idea *still supports* our thesis, but it develops that support in a new direction. We'll put that new idea in red.

In her essay "Modern Love," Diane Ackerman writes, "When I think about the essence of being modern, the changes in attitude that led to the life we now know, three things come to mind: choice, privacy, and books." In the modern world, we are free to choose whom we love, and books have helped us to find that freedom. But it wasn't always that way. Romeo and Juliet, for example, who lived in the old world, did not have that choice.

Could "choice, privacy, and books" have saved Romeo and Juliet? When Romeo and Juliet tried to live as modern lovers, they chose each other. But their families, in the ways of the old world, prohibited their love. By the end of the story, Romeo and Juliet both end up dying for their love.

Books can give us many freedoms, many choices. If you read about people who have freedom of religion, for example, you see that you are free to practice your own religion. If you read about people who have the freedom to choose their love, you see that you, too, are free to choose your own love.

If Romeo and Juliet's parents had had easy access to books, and read about the freedom to choose love, maybe they would have just let Romeo and Juliet choose each other. Of course, if that happened, we wouldn't have Shakespeare's play. But, of course, if that happened, poor Romeo and poor Juliet would not have died for their love.

If a book is good, it can give us a powerful experience. If you and I read the same book, we can relate to each other's feelings.

> **Main Idea:**
> Good books can allow us, as readers, to relate to each other's feelings.

Step 2. (Present Evidence for the New Idea)

In her essay "Modern Love," Diane Ackerman writes, "When I think about the essence of being modern, the changes in attitude that led to the life we now know, three things come to mind: choice, privacy, and books." In the modern world, we are free to choose whom we love, and books have helped us to find that freedom. But it wasn't always that way. Romeo and Juliet, for example, who lived in the old world, did not have that choice.

Could "choice, privacy, and books" have saved Romeo and Juliet? When Romeo and Juliet tried to live as modern lovers, they chose each other. But their families, in the ways of the old world, prohibited their love. By the end of the story, Romeo and Juliet both end up dying for their love.

Books can give us many freedoms, many choices. If you read about people who have freedom of religion, for example, you see that you are free to practice your own religion. If you read about people who have the freedom to choose their love, you see that you, too, are free to choose your own love.

If Romeo and Juliet's parents had had easy access to books, and read about the freedom to choose love, maybe they would have just let Romeo and Juliet choose each other. Of course, if that happened, we wouldn't have Shakespeare's play. But, of course, if that happened, poor Romeo and poor Juliet would not have died for their love.

If a book is good, it can give us a powerful experience. If you and I read the same book, we can relate to each other's feelings. **Diane Ackerman writes, "A shared book could speak to lovers in confidence, increasing their sense of intimacy even if the loved one was absent or forbidden."**

> **Main Idea (more developed):** Good books can allow us, as readers, to relate to each other's feelings.

Step 3. (Discuss Evidence for New Idea)

In her essay "Modern Love," Diane Ackerman writes, "When I think about the essence of being modern, the changes in attitude that led to the life we now know, three things come to mind: choice, privacy, and books." In the modern world, we are free to choose whom we love, and books have helped us to find that freedom. But it wasn't always that way. Romeo and Juliet, for example, who lived in the old world, did not have that choice.

Could "choice, privacy, and books" have saved Romeo and Juliet? When Romeo and Juliet tried to live as modern lovers, they chose each other. But their families, in the ways of the old world, prohibited their love. By the end of the story, Romeo and Juliet both end up dying for their love.

 Books can give us many freedoms, many choices. If you read about people who have freedom of religion, for example, you see that you are free to practice your own religion. If you read about people who have the freedom to choose their love, you see that you, too, are free to choose your own love.

If Romeo and Juliet's parents had had easy access to books, and read about the freedom to choose love, maybe they would have just let Romeo and Juliet choose each other. Of course, if that happened, we wouldn't have Shakespeare's play. But, of course, if that happened, poor Romeo and poor Juliet would not have died for their love.

If a book is good, it can give us a powerful experience. If you and I read the same book, we can relate to each other's feelings. Diane Ackerman writes, "A shared book could speak to lovers in confidence, increasing their sense of intimacy even

> **Main Idea (more developed):** Good books can allow us, as readers, to relate to each other's feelings.

if the loved one was absent or forbidden." **Books can cross the most difficult distances that might separate us from one another.**

Step 4. (Discuss How Your Evidence Supports Your Thesis)

In her essay "Modern Love," Diane Ackerman writes, "When I think about the essence of being modern, the changes in attitude that led to the life we now know, three things come to mind: choice, privacy, and books." In the modern world, we are free to choose whom we love, and books have helped us to find that freedom. But it wasn't always that way. Romeo and Juliet, for example, who lived in the old world, did not have that choice.

Could "choice, privacy, and books" have saved Romeo and Juliet? When Romeo and Juliet tried to live as modern lovers, they chose each other. But their families, in the ways of the old world, prohibited their love. By the end of the story, Romeo and Juliet both end up dying for their love.

Books can give us many freedoms, many choices. If you read about people who have freedom of religion, for example, you see that you are free to practice your own religion. If you read about people who have the freedom to choose their love, you see that you, too, are free to choose your own love.

If Romeo and Juliet's parents had had easy access to books, and read about the freedom to choose love, maybe they would have just let Romeo and Juliet choose each other. Of course, if that happened, we wouldn't have Shakespeare's play. But, of course, if that happened, poor Romeo and poor Juliet would not have died for their love.

If a book is good, it can give us a powerful experience. If you and I read the same book, we can relate to each other's feelings. Diane Ackerman writes, "A shared book could speak to lovers in confidence, increasing their sense of intimacy even if the loved one was absent or forbidden." Books can cross the most difficult distances that might separate us from one another.

If you and your lover are separated, or if your families forbid your love, and you decide that you will each read the same book, you have shared something, you have become intimate, and you can feel closer to each other. **If you feel close enough to each other through your reading, you may end up together, even if your parents continue to forbid it.** Hopefully, your parents will come around to your point of view, and you will end up much better off than Romeo and Juliet did.

Main Idea:
The shared intimacy of books could make your love work.

Perhaps our parents or grandparents were not free to choose whom to marry and their families chose for them. This happened to two of our grandparents. They met in Romania, but their families didn't like each other and forbade the marriage. Luckily, our grandparents could flee to America, which they did, where they married and raised a family.

> **Main Idea:** The free choice of our parents and grandparents.

If your parents don't believe in this free choice, you can certainly give them books to read that talk about the modern freedom to love. That may bring them around. On the other hand, maybe your parents already believe in your freedom of choice. In that case, you and your chosen can sit out on the porch together, each reading your own copy of *Romeo and Juliet*.

> **Main Idea:** Dealing with your parents in regard to the freedom to choose your love.

We have written this essay using this pattern:

STEP 1 — Thesis
STEP 2 — Evidence
STEP 3 — Discuss evidence
STEP 4 — Discuss *how* evidence proves thesis
STEP 5 — Present a new idea in support of your thesis
STEP 2 — Present evidence for new idea
STEP 3 — Discuss evidence
STEP 4 — Discuss *how* evidence proves new idea

Chapter Review: Paragraph Unity

Paragraph unity means that, in <u>each paragraph,</u> you write about **one** and *only* **one** and *not more than* **one** idea.

Each paragraph develops from the last paragraph and develops the thesis.

Review of steps for developing an essay:

Step 1 — Thesis

Step 2 — Evidence

Step 3 — Discuss evidence

Step 4 — Discuss *how* evidence proves thesis

Step 5 — Present a new idea in support of your thesis

Step 2 — Present evidence for new idea

Step 3 — Discuss evidence

Step 4 — Discuss *how* evidence proves new idea

Exercises for Chapter 9:

PARAGRAPH UNITY

a. We have mixed up the sentences in the following paragraph. Some of them belong to one paragraph that makes up one unified idea; some of them belong to a separate paragraph that makes up another unified idea.

Rewrite the following paragraph into <u>two</u> paragraphs, each having clear **PARAGRAPH UNITY**. It might help to use a highlighting pen to highlight all of the sentences that belong to one paragraph.

When I went to college, I was determined to become a doctor. Just before World War II, my great-grandparents moved to Shanghai, China, where my great-grandfather had a good business opportunity. Shanghai, during the war, was an "Open City," meaning that you could come and go without a passport. Anyone could get into Shanghai. I took some science classes, including biology, chemistry, physiology, and I did well in all of them. I liked them a lot. I was learning fascinating things. Because Shanghai was an "Open City," refugees from war-torn Europe who could escape came to Shanghai for a safe place to live during the war. Then I had to take a human anatomy class, which involved working with actual human cadavers. Not only could I not do the work, I couldn't even walk into the lab! I stopped right there, at the door. No one could budge me. My great-grandmother became head of a Committee that helped these European refugees settle in Shanghai. Many of them stayed on after the war, and their families still live in Shanghai, well integrated into the Chinese way of life. So, now you know why I am a chef and not a doctor. I love this restaurant I opened 22 years ago and have built up into the best restaurant for a hundred miles around!

First paragraph:

_____

_____

_____

_____

_____

_____

_____

_____

_____

Second paragraph:

_____

_____

_____

_____

_____

_____

_____

_____

b. In the sample essay below, write out the main idea of each paragraph in the space provided.

Here are the basic background facts to the American Civil War: in 1860 – 1861, eleven states in the American south formed a new country, which they named the Confederate States of America. That left 25 States and Territories in the United States of America. During the period of the Civil War, we call the government and the army of the Confederate States of America the "Confederacy;" we call the government and the army of the United States of America the "Union."

The **one** main idea of this paragraph is:

_____

_____

_____

_____

_____

_____

_____

_____

All of the States of the Confederacy had slaves, while all the States and Territories of the Union had either abolished slavery or had promised to abolish slavery. Fearing that the United States would abolish slavery in the eleven States of the Confederacy, the Confederacy declared independence from the United States of America in 1861, but the government of the United States refused to accept that declaration of independence, insisting that all the States of the Confederacy remain in the United States.

The **one** main idea of this paragraph is:

_____

_____

_____

_____

_____

_____

_____

_____

Determined to gain independence and to preserve slavery, the Confederacy attacked the Union at Fort Sumter, South Carolina on April 12, 1861. The Union, under President Abraham Lincoln, raised an army from each State in the Union and fought back.

The **one** main idea of this paragraph is:

_____

_____

_____

_____

In September 1861, President Lincoln issued a document called the Emancipation Declaration. It is one of the most important documents in American history, honored and

The **one** main idea of this paragraph is:

_____

_____

_____

revered as a milestone in our progress toward freedom for all. It declared that the goal of the Civil War was to keep the United States of America together and to abolish slavery in all States of the United States of America, including all those States of the Confederacy.

_____
_____
_____
_____
_____

At first, the Confederacy won important victories. Over time, however, the Union took the upper hand. The Union won the Battle of Gettysburg, which occurred in and around the town of Gettysburg, Pennsylvania, from July 1 – July 3, 1863. In one of the most horrific battles in history up until that time, about 50,000 soldiers were killed.

The **one** main idea of this paragraph is:

_____
_____
_____
_____
_____

On November 18, 1863, President Lincoln traveled to Gettysburg for the dedication ceremony for the Soldiers' National Cemetery, a cemetery where the bodies of the soldiers who fell at the Battle of Gettysburg were buried. There, President Lincoln delivered one of the most famous speeches in American history, called The Gettysburg Address. Lincoln opened by reiterating our founding principle that "all men are created equal" and closed with the hope that "government of the people, by the people, for the people, shall not perish from the earth."

The **one** main idea of this paragraph is:

_____
_____
_____
_____
_____
_____
_____
_____
_____

Having begun on April 12, 1861, the Civil War ended on April 9, 1865, when the Confederacy General Robert E. Lee surrendered his army to the Union General Ulysses S. Grant at the McLean House in the village of Appomattox Court House, Virginia. Over 600,000 soldiers died in service to the Confederacy and the Union.

The **one** main idea of this paragraph is:

_____
_____
_____
_____
_____
_____

Assignment for Chapter 9

Diane Ackerman writes: **"When I think about the essence of being modern, the changes in attitude that led to the life we now know, three things come to mind: choice, privacy, and books."**

Choose EITHER

- **choice**

– or –

- **privacy**

– or –

- **books**

Create a thesis for yourself. For example: "Diane Ackerman says that having choice has changed modern life."

REMEMBER:

- Create a **THESIS** of your own. Then, *prove* your thesis. Stick to proving your thesis. ONLY write about what proves your thesis.

- Develop your essay along the lines we outlined in Chapter 8 and have reviewed in this Chapter.

- Organize your paragraphs so that they have paragraph unity.

PART 04
the origins of language IV: african myth

Millions of people in Africa speak one of the Bantu languages. The word "Bantu" means "people." One of the Bantu tribes, the Wa-Sania, in East Africa has a myth that in the beginning all people knew and spoke one language. During a severe famine, a madness ran through the population. In their madness, people wandered off in all directions, all of them muttering strange words. Eventually, those mutterings formed into different languages. It's interesting to note that in their madness, people spoke jibberish. This means that language is a part of our ordinary sanity. It's also interesting to note that this Wa-Sania, Bantu, myth presumes, like many other myths, that in the beginning we all spoke the same language. World-wide, myths repeat the tale that we all had a common language. Having separated and splintered off, we now can't understand each other easily.

CHAPTER 10
the art of language | the ever-changing verb

It's all about *nouns* and *verbs*. All the other **PARTS OF SPEECH**:

pronouns	adverbs	conjunctions	prepositions
adjectives	articles	interjections	

all relate to <u>nouns</u> and <u>verbs</u>.

For example:
- **adjectives** describe **nouns**;
- **adverbs** describe **verbs**;
- **articles** define **nouns**, etc.

It makes sense, then, for us to focus now on one of these central **PARTS OF SPEECH**: **VERBS**. **Nouns** are relatively easy to use, whereas **VERBS** require study. You change the *form* of **VERBS** in the sentence to make yourself understood. It's all about being heard, being understood, and effectively saying what you have to say.

You wouldn't say:

I reading the newspaper.

We wouldn't know what you mean. You have to use the right **VERB** in the ***right form.*** Instead, you would say:

I read the newspaper.

Notice that we've corrected the **incorrect VERB** form "**reading**" to the correct verb form "**read.**" The **VERB** always changes as it <u>responds</u> to two things:

- the **subject** of the sentence;
- **time.** The VERB tells us *when* something happens:

  in the present, in the past, or in the future.

the ever-changing verb

You already know how to use VERBS. You do it correctly all the time. For example, fill in the missing VERBS below. You'll see that the VERBS change and that you already know how to make those changes.

EXERCISES ON VERBS

1. I like _____ the newspaper.
2. Yesterday, I _____ the newspaper.
3. Tomorrow morning, I _____ the newspaper.
4. Almost every day, I _____ the newspaper.
5. When I _____ the newspaper this morning, I saw an article about a student studying grammar.

You see from the verbs you filled in above that the verb always changes, always *responds to* two things:

- the **subject** of the sentence;
- **time:** The VERB tells us *when* something happens:

  in the present, in the past, or in the future.

the base

IF the **verb** is ever-changing, **IT ALSO** has a home base, a basic form, a place it starts from. We call this THE BASE. Here are THE BASE forms of several verbs:

drive	walk
read	sing
speak	text
feel	

EXERCISES ON THE BASE

Write the base form for each of the five verbs below:

verb in another form	base form of the verb
1. I had written a good essay.	_____
2. I went to the club last night.	_____
3. I wanted a car for graduation!	_____
4. I played the trombone in high school.	_____
5. I will play the saxaphone in college.	_____

to conjugate

What does **"TO CONJUGATE"** mean? What can it do for us? When you **CONJUGATE** a **verb**, you take that **verb** from its base form, and you **change it** into the form you want. Remember: the **verb** changes from the base *in response* to two things:

- the **subject** of the sentence
- **time:** The **VERB** tells us *when* something happens:
  in the present, in the past, or in the future.

When you **CONJUGATE** a verb, you do both of these things. You make the **verb** *agree* with the **subject** it goes with, and you put the **verb** in the right form regarding time: the past, the present, or the future.

Here's how we **CONJUGATE** the **verb** "read" in the present tense.

READ   **PRESENT TENSE**

<u>Singular</u>   <u>Plural</u>

I read   We read

You read   You (plural) read

He She/It read**s**   They read

In English, the conjugation of verbs is often pretty simple. The verb doesn't change much. As you can see from above, we have six "persons" in English.

I	=	first person singular	**We**	=	first person plural
You	=	second person singular	**You**	=	second person plural
He/She/It	=	third person singular	**They**	=	third person plural

EXERCISES ON CONJUGATION

Now, you do it. Fill in the **verb** form of "speak" that goes with the pronoun below:

SPEAK   PRESENT TENSE

<u>Singular</u>   <u>Plural</u>

1. I _____   4. We _____

2. You _____   5. You (plural) _____

3. He/She/It _____   6. They _____

See? You already know how to do it. You've just conjugated the **verb** "speak" in the PRESENT TENSE. You know how to CONJUGATE **verbs.**

verb agreement

When talking or writing, you wouldn't say:

~~I speaks~~.

You would say:

He speaks.

-or-

I *speak.*

You make the **verb** ("speak") AGREE with the **subject** ("I" or "He").

If your Professor writes on your paper that you have a VERB AGREEMENT problem (va), you've used a **verb** that doesn't AGREE with the **subject.**

EXERCISES ON VERB AGREEMENT

Fix the examples below so the **verb** AGREES with the **subject**:

1. We ~~reads~~ the newspaper.

    We _____ the newspaper.

2. They ~~walks~~ to class from the bus stop every morning.

    They _____ to class from the bus stop every morning.

3. I ~~wanted~~ to have lasagna for dinner tonight.

    I _____ to have lasagna for dinner tonight.

4. We ~~return~~ to bring back the equipment tomorrow.

    We _____ to bring back the equipment tomorrow.

5. My mother ~~will buy~~ me a new pair of shoes yesterday.

    My mother _____ me a new pair of shoes yesterday.

---

verb tense

You know how to make the **verb** *agree* with the **subject.** The **verb** also tells us ***when*** something happens. An example:

I **walk** around campus looking for my dog.

Yesterday, I **walk*ed*** around the campus so much my feet hurt.

"Walk" is in the **PRESENT TENSE**   {It *happens* now, in the present}

"Walk*ed*" is in the **PAST TENSE**   {It *happened* in the past}

Often, we add **"ed"** to the end of the verb to make the past tense.

Here's a **CONJUGATION** of the **verb** "walk" in the **past tense**[1]:

Singular	Plural
I walk**ed**	We walk**ed**
You walk**ed**	You (plural) walk**ed**
He/She/It walk**ed**	They walk**ed**

AND, here's a **CONJUGATION** in the **future tense.**

Here, we use the **helping verb "will"**[2] to form the future tense.

WALK	FUTURE TENSE
Singular	Plural
I **will** walk	We **will** walk
You **will** walk	You (plural) **will** walk
He/She/It **will** walk	They **will** walk

EXERCISES ON VERB TENSE AND CONJUGATION

Fill in the **verb** below in the correct **TENSE.** Do you know the old saying, "Don't cry over spilled milk?" Using the correct tense for "cry," fill in the examples below.

1. My baby brother spills his milk, and he _____.

2. Yesterday, when my baby brother spilled his milk, he _____.

3. I bet that tomorrow, when my baby brother spills his milk, he _____.

Let's try one in the **<u>first person</u>:** "I." Let's use the **verb** "text."

4. I _____ my friend, Louise. {present tense}

5. Yesterday, when Louise hadn't called me, I _____ her. {past tense}

6. Tomorrow, as usual, I expect I _____ Louise a few times. {future tense}

---

[1]**Spanish** speakers often don't hear this **"ED"** past tense sound because of the way Spanish works, and because we often do not pronounce the **"ED"** clearly. If Spanish is your first language, or you grew up with Spanish, your particular attention to this **"ED"** could help you.
[2]See the **Index of Helping Verbs** on page 255 for all the **helping verbs** in English.

Got it? The **verb,** the ever-changing **verb,** does two things. You've done them both. The verb:

- *agrees* with the **subject**—we call this: **verb agreement**
- *tells* us <u>when</u> something happens—we call this: **verb tense**

the verb "be"

The verb **"be"** is a special case. You will need to know how to use it. We call the **verb "be"** a *passive* verb. **"Be"** is the *only* passive verb in English. You won't have to learn any other passive verbs.

Active verbs describe *action*; the **passive verb** <u>does not</u> describe any **action**; it indicates **being,** indicates that something exists, that it *is.*

Let's look at the **CONJUGATION** of "**be**" in the present, past, and future tenses.

BE	PRESENT TENSE
<u>Singular</u>	<u>Plural</u>
I *am*	We *are*
You *are*	You (plural) *are*
He/She/It *is*	They *are*

BE	PAST TENSE
<u>Singular</u>	<u>Plural</u>
I *was*	We *were*
You *were*	You (plural) *were*
He/She/It *was*	They *were*

BE	FUTURE TENSE
<u>Singular</u>	<u>Plural</u>
I *will be*	We *will be*
You *will be*	You (plural) *will be*
He/She/It *will be*	They *will be*

Again, the verb **"be"** is the <u>only</u> *passive verb* in English. **Every other verb** is an *<u>active</u> verb*. What's the difference between the *passive verb* (BE) and *active verbs* (<u>all</u> other verbs)?

> •• ACTIVE VERBS show **action,** they show the *subject* acting.

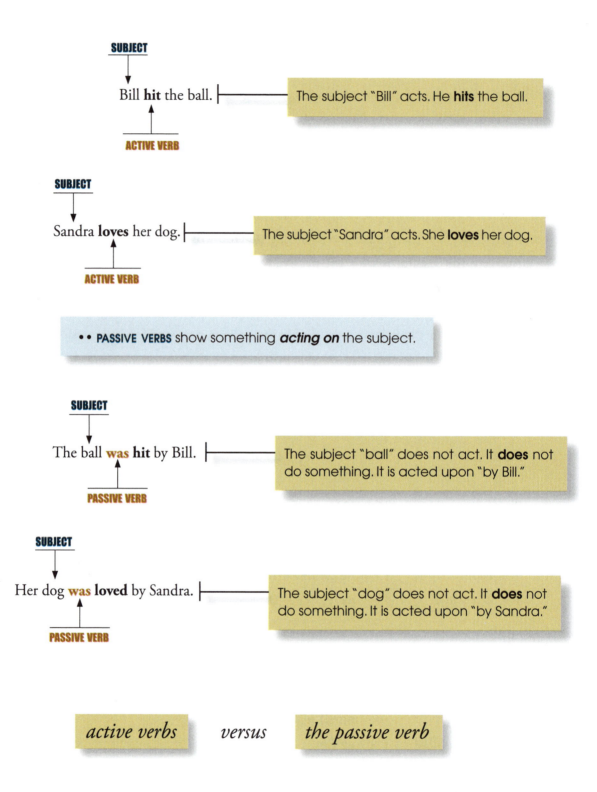

SUBJECT

Bill **hit** the ball.

ACTIVE VERB

The subject "Bill" acts. He **hits** the ball.

SUBJECT

Sandra **loves** her dog.

ACTIVE VERB

The subject "Sandra" acts. She **loves** her dog.

•• **PASSIVE VERBS** show something *acting on* the subject.

SUBJECT

The ball **was hit** by Bill.

PASSIVE VERB

The subject "ball" does not act. It **does** not do something. It is acted upon "by Bill."

SUBJECT

Her dog **was loved** by Sandra.

PASSIVE VERB

The subject "dog" does not act. It **does** not do something. It is acted upon "by Sandra."

active verbs   *versus*   *the passive verb*

This section on **passive verbs** will give you a tool to help you avoid a lot of errors in your writing. One simple trick can save you a lot of work.

The simple trick:

In general, <u>not always,</u> but usually, ***use* ACTIVE VERBS.**

Which is the better sentence?

Billy **hit** the ball. ├—— **ACTIVE VERB**

The ball **was hit** by Billy. ├——**PASSIVE VERB**

> When you use **ACTIVE VERBS,** you correct a lot of other problems, and you correct a lot of <u>awkwardness</u> in your sentence.

When my girlfriend *asked* me if I would *go* to the movies with her or with someone else, I told her I was too busy to go with anyone. ├—— **MOSTLY ACTIVE VERBS**

When I *was asked* by my girlfriend, *was* she the one I would go to the movies with, she had *to be* told by me that I *was* too busy to go with anyone. ├—— **ALL PASSIVE VERBS**

> **A Quick Trick:**
> When you want to change a passive verb into an active verb, you will often find the active verb already in the sentence but in the wrong form.

Watch this:

When I **was asked** by my girlfriend . . .

When my girlfriend **asked** . . .

- Change the **passive verb** *"was asked"* into the **active verb** *"asked."*
- Ask yourself: What does the **subject** of the sentence do? What does "my girlfriend" do? She **asks** me...

<u>Sometimes</u>, you want a **passive verb:**

The sky is blue.

But, most often, you want an **active verb:**

My dad *cut* down the tree that *blocked* our window.   ⎯⎯ **ACTIVE VERBS**
The tree that *had been* blocking our window *was cut* down by my dad. ⎯⎯ **PASSIVE VERBS**

BE *as a helping verb*

In the section "Active Verbs vs. The Passive Verb, on page 136, when we **CONJUGATGED** the verb "walk" in the **future tense** (I *will* walk, you *will* walk, etc.), we used the **helping verb "will"** to form the **future tense.**

Sometimes, we use **BE** as a **helping verb** to form other tenses. For example:

I ***am*** walking to class.	helping verb: ***am***;	verb: walking
I ***was*** drinking too much coffee.	helping verb: ***was***;	verb: drinking
I will ***be*** coming late to the party.	helping verb: ***be***;	verb: coming

EXERCISES ON ACTIVE AND PASSIVE VERBS

Indicate the **active verbs** and the **passive verbs** below:

1. I typed Sandy's paper for her. _____ (active or passive?)

2. Many of Sandy's errors were corrected by me. _____ (active or passive?)

3. Sandy's paper on solar eclipses was fascinating. _____ (active or passive?)

4. Sandy said she would take me out for dinner. _____ (active or passive?)

5. Sandy agreed with all the corrections I made. _____ (active or passive?)

Chapter Review: The Ever-Changing Verb

It's all about *nouns* and *verbs*. All the other PARTS OF SPEECH: **pronouns, adverbs, conjunctions, prepositions, adjectives, articles and interjections all** relate to *nouns* and *verbs*.

The VERB always changes as it *responds* to two things:
- the **subject** of the sentence
- **time:** The VERB tells us *when* something happens: in the present, in the past, or in the future.

When you CONJUGATE a verb, you do both of these things:
- You make the **verb** *agree* with the **subject** it goes with;
- you put the **verb** in the right form regarding time: the past, the present, or the future.

The **verb** also tells us *__when__* something happens.

"**Be**" is the *only* passive verb in English.

the **passive verb—be—**<u>does not</u> describe any **action**; it indicates **being.**

ACTIVE VERBS show **action,** they show the *subject* acting

PASSIVE VERBS show something *acting on* the subject.

In general, <u>not always,</u> but usually, *use* ACTIVE VERBS.

We also use BE as a helping verb.

Exercises for Chapter 10:

I. VERB CONJUGATION

   a. Fix the following errors in verb conjugation, writing the correct verbs next to the sentence.

   1. Yesterday, I go to the concert with Billy.   _____

   2. I will want to eat that cupcake, but I'll leave it for you. _____

   3. When I ask my mother about it, she said she
       know the answer but can't tell me.   _____

   4. Tomorrow, I took my dog for a walk.   _____

   5. I understood what she says.   _____

   6. I will come over yesterday to talk about it.   _____

   7. I don't knew anything about it.   _____

   8. When we walk across the city we
       saw a lot of great things.   _____

   9. We get a new pitcher. I think we can win games now. _____

   10. They finished that new building on campus.
       It was ugly.   _____

   b. Write a short paragraph with all the **verbs** in the **present tense.**

c. Write a short paragraph with all the **verbs** in the **past tense.**

d. Write a short paragraph with all the **verbs** in the **future tense.**

II. VERB AGREEMENT

a. Fix the following errors in **verb agreement**. Write the correct **verb** next to each sentence.

1. I writes an essay.   _____

2. He write an essay.   _____

3. The old guy lecture the young man on life.   _____

4. She go to class every day on time.   _____

5. Roger hide behind the bushes.   _____

6. My father come home late every night now.   _____

7. You has time to change your mind.   _____

8. My friend, Billy, call me every night.   _____

9. I does all the exercises in this book.   _____

10. I has fifty different ideas about what I want to do. _____

b. Write a short paragraph in the first person singular, "I," making sure all your **verbs** agree with that noun "I."

c. Write a short paragraph in the second person singular "you," making sure all your **verbs** agree with that noun "you."

d. Write a short paragraph in the third person singular "he," or "she," or "it," making sure all your **verbs** agree with that noun "he," "she," or "it."

e. Write a short paragraph in the first person plural "we," making sure all your **verbs** agree with that noun "we."

III. ACTIVE VERBS

Change the following sentences with **passive verbs** into sentences with **active verbs.**

Example: This book **was written** by Rebecca Goodman and Martin Nakell.
   <u>Rebecca Goodman and Martin Nakell wrote this book.</u>

1. The saxaphone in that piece **was played** by John Coltrane.

    _____.

2. The homerun **was hit** by me.

    _____.

3. The new building on campus **is being** visited by the Governor tomorrow.

    _____.

4. You **are being** kissed by your grandmother.

    _____.

5. The elephant **is being** chased out of the classroom by me.

    _____.

6. They **are asked** by the Professor to put away their cell phones.

    _____.

7. The thief **is being** arrested by the police.

    _____.

8. The biggest hot dog in the world **was eaten** by the biggest man at the fair.

    _____.

9. The fastest car at the race track **was driven** by my cousin, Shirley.

   _____ .

10. The last to arrive at the party **was** my fast cousin, Shirley.

   _____ .

   b. <u>Underline</u> the passive verbs in this paragraph and <u>circle</u> the active verbs.

When I was a kid growing up in Detroit, Michigan, my Dad often took us to Detroit Tiger games at Tiger Stadium. Tiger Stadium was in the heart of Detroit. Regular neighborhoods surrounded the stadium. People in the neighborhood were always renting out space in their driveways and on their lawns for Tiger fans to park. We always parked on the same guy's lawn, always for $1.00. He was a great guy, who sat out on his lawn during the games, listening to the radio. We got to know him so well, and he liked me so much, that my Dad once let me stay with him to listen to the game. My Dad and my sister went on to Tiger Stadium. I had a great time. The parking guy gave me lemonade and cookies, and all afternoon his neighbors came over, and we whooped and hollered for the Tigers. The Tigers were the winners of that game. We always had a story in my family that, if I stayed with the parking guy, the Tigers would win, but if I went to the stadium, the Tigers would lose. It wasn't true, but my sister always tried to make me stay with the parking guy, so she could have my Dad all to herself!

CHAPTER 11

the act of reading | dialogue with the text

What is **DIALOGUE**? What is a **TEXT**?

In every act of reading, you engage in a **DIALOGUE** with the **TEXT.**

• In **DIALOGUE** we talk *with* someone or something. When you talk with your friend, you have a **DIALOGUE.** When you talk with your parents, you have a **DIALOGUE.** When you talk with your dog, you have a **DIALOGUE**!

dialogue =

from the Greek: *dialogos*

dia = two

logos = word

• How do we define a **TEXT**?

Most of us think of a **TEXT** as a book. A **TEXT** can also be anything else we see or hear. We talk about a *movie* as a **TEXT.** We can talk about a song as a **TEXT.** We can also talk about a **TEXT** as *anything* we choose to look at or think about.

• If we go to the Grand Canyon, and we talk about what we see, we can think of the Grand Canyon as a **TEXT** we analyze.

• If you look at a picture, a photograph, an advertisement, you can think about those as **TEXTS** that you analyze.

• Even if we think about an idea, like love, we can look at love as a **TEXT** we analyze, as Diane Ackerman does in "Modern Love."

When you read, you talk with a book, you have a dialogue with that book?

yes!

the *text* talks to you
you talk to the *text*

the *text* talks *with* you
you talk *with* the *text*

from *Alice's Adventures in Wonderland*[1]

Alice was beginning to get very tired of sitting by her sister on the bank, and of having nothing to do: once or twice she had peeped into the book her sister was reading, but it had no pictures or conversations in it, "and what is the use of a book," thought Alice "without pictures or conversation?"

So she was considering in her own mind (as well as she could, for the hot day made her feel very sleepy and stupid), whether the pleasure of making a daisy-chain would be worth the trouble of getting up and picking the daisies, when suddenly a White Rabbit with pink eyes ran close by her.

There was nothing so VERY remarkable in that; nor did Alice think it so VERY much out of the way to hear the Rabbit say to itself, "Oh dear! Oh dear! I shall be late!" (when she thought it over afterwards, it occurred to her that she ought to have wondered at this, but at the time it all seemed quite natural); but when the Rabbit actually TOOK A WATCH OUT OF ITS WAISTCOAT-POCKET, and looked at it, and then hurried on, Alice started to her feet, for it flashed across her mind that she had never before seen a rabbit with either a waistcoat-pocket, or a watch to take out of it, and burning with curiosity, she ran across the field after it, and fortunately was just in time to see it pop down a large rabbit-hole under the hedge.

Lewis Carroll
Alice in Wonderland

---

[1]In **fiction**, or **imaginative writing**, the author is free to abandon reality and write using only his or her imagination. A **fiction** will usually tell a story.

When you read *Alice in Wonderland*, you just about hear the **TEXT,** the book, talk to you, telling you all about Alice and her lazy afternoon with her sister just before she falls down that famous rabbit hole that begins her great adventures. And what do you say back to the text, to the book? Read this opening paragraph from *Alice in Wonderland* again, then have a dialogue with this text. What are all the thoughts you have while reading this text? Write them down, whatever they are. There are no wrong answers. We'll give you an example, writing down some of the ideas we have while reading this text.

> *I can picture Alice sitting by a riverbank, stretched out on the grass under a tree, while her sister sits beside her. It looks very inviting. I wouldn't get bored. I'd just take a nap. But Alice got bored. Even her sister's book bored her because it didn't have any pictures or conversation in it. If I were bored, I'd just lie back in the sunshine and take a nice long nap. But Alice isn't just bored. She looks around for something to do. Something will happen to Alice, and I want to read on. Who knows? Maybe if I took a nap I would dream the whole book of Alice in Wonderland!*

See? When we read, we listen to the book, and we talk with the book. We hear what the text says to us, and we think about that. That's our dialogue with the text. Most often, that dialogue doesn't take place out loud, it takes place silently, in our thoughts. When we see a movie, we have a dialogue with that film. We think about it. When see something beautiful, the ocean, a great mountain, we take it in, and we think about it, and we have a dialogue with it. When we read a good book, we think about it. That's our dialogue with the text. The text is alive! When you read, you read a living language that speaks to you.

In your dialogue with this excerpt from *Alice in Wonderland,* think especially about what images strike you. What images do you remember from the text? Perhaps some images seem particularly amusing or funny. Have your own dream-images ever been anything like the images in *Alice?* You might also think about other books you have read that *Alice* reminds you of. Have you ever read anything like *Alice in Wonderland* ?

analysis

What is **ANALYSIS?**
What can **ANALYSIS** do for us?

Once we have a dialogue with a text, we are ready to **ANALYZE** that text. That **ANALYSIS** will help us to form a **THESIS,** which will lead us to write a well-formed essay.

from dialogue ⟶ to analysis

THINKING about the text *is* **ANALYSIS**

- **ANALYSIS** is all about thinking. And, of course, how do we think? We think in words, we think in language, and we think in images.
- When we **ANALYZE** something, we take it apart, we look at it, we think about it.

When you *think about* what to wear today, you **ANALYZE** your wardrobe.
 What clothes fit the season?
 What colors would you like to wear today?
 What pants or skirt might go with what shirt or top?
 What shoes would look the best?

When you *think about* whom you like and whom you don't like, you **ANALYZE** your friends.
 One friend might be smart but not be a nice person.
 Another friend might be fun but not be so smart.
 Another friend might like the things you like. You have a lot in common.
 Another friend might be okay, but their family is terrific.
 Another friend might be a little dangerous in their impulses. It might be good to be careful.
 Another friend might be a bad gossip, spreading bad impressions.

When you *think about* that girl/guy you met last night, you **ANALYZE** your love life.
 You might like someone, but they're not available.
 You might like someone, but you don't know if they like you.
 You might like someone who has given you signs they like you.
 You might like someone, but your best friend doesn't have a good feeling about it.

When you *think about* your life, you **ANALYZE** your life.
 What should you pick as a major?
 What kind of career do you want?
 Should you get married? Have kids?
 How can you realize your goals?
 How can you best understand your parents or your family?
 How can you heal the argument you had with your brother?

When you think about why your car won't start, you **ANALYZE** your car.

Your car won't start. To **ANALYZE** the problem, we take the car apart. We take out the alternator. We look at it. It's ok. We take out the starter motor. We look at it. It's ok. We take out the ignition system. Ah. It got cracked. In this case, we won't write an essay. We'll fix the car. We'll replace the ignition system.

Chapter Review: Dialogue with the Text

In **DIALOGUE** we talk *with* someone or something.

A **TEXT** can be anything we see or hear. It can also be anything we choose to look at or think about.

ANALYSIS is all about thinking. We think in words, we think in language, and we think in images. When we **ANALYZE** something, we take it apart, we look at it, we think about it.

Exercises for Chapter 11:

I. Your Thoughts

a. This selection from *Alice in Wonderland* is the first piece of **imaginative** literature we have read so far. It's clearly not realistic—unless you have seen a rabbit somewhere at some time pulling a watch out of its pocket. The essays we have read so far, by N. Scott Momaday, Jack London, and Diane Ackerman, we call *expository writing*. We call *Alice in Wonderland* imaginative writing, or **fiction**. Do you prefer one or the other, expository writing or fiction? Or do you like both equally? Write a paragraph in which you express your feelings about these two kinds of writing.

b. Imagine that, like Alice, you sit by a riverbank. Imagine that a white rabbit stops right in front of you, takes a watch out of its waistcoat pocket and looks at the time. Imagine that the rabbit turns to you and says, "Oh, no. I'm late."

    1. How might you interpret this **image** of the white rabbit and his pocket watch? What might you say that it means?

    2. Write out a dialogue you might have with this strange white rabbit.

II. Lewis Carroll's Art

a. Each of the following from the *Alice in Wonderland* selection could be a separate sentence. Write down the SIMPLE SUBJECT and SIMPLE PREDICATE of each sentence.

1. Alice was getting very tired of sitting by her sister on the bank. _____ _____
   SUBJECT   PREDICATE

2. Once of twice she had peeped into the book her sister
   was reading. _____ _____
   SUBJECT   PREDICATE

3. It had no pictures or conversation in it. _____ _____
   SUBJECT   PREDICATE

4. Suddenly a White Rabbit with pink eyes ran close by her. _____ _____
   SUBJECT   PREDICATE

5. She ought to have wondered at this _____ _____
   SUBJECT   PREDICATE

6. I shall be late! _____ _____
   SUBJECT   PREDICATE

7. The Rabbit actually took a watch out of its waistcoat pocket. _____ _____
   SUBJECT   PREDICATE

8. Alice started to her feet. _____ _____
   SUBJECT   PREDICATE

9. It flashed across her mind that she had never before seen a rabbit
   with either a waistcoat pocket or a watch to take out of it. _____ _____
   SUBJECT   PREDICATE

10. She ran across the field. _____ _____
    SUBJECT   PREDICATE

b. Adjectives

   In the brief excerpt from *Alice in Wonderland,* Lewis Carroll uses only a few adjectives. List five of them.

   1. _____.

   2. _____.

   3. _____.

   4. _____.

   5. _____.

c. Passive Verbs / Active Verbs

   Lewis Carroll uses verbs with great skill. At the beginning of the story, he uses more **PASSIVE THAN ACTIVE VERBS.** When the White Rabbit shows up, **ACTIVE VERBS** take over: "…a White Rabbit with pink eyes **ran** close by her."

   List three **PASSIVE VERBS** from the story *before* the White Rabbit shows up.

   1. _____

   2. _____

   3. _____

d. List five **ACTIVE VERBS** from the story *after* the Rabbit shows up.

   1. _____

   2. _____

   3. _____

   4. _____

   5. _____

e. Why do you think Lewis Carroll uses **passive verbs** before the white rabbit shows up, while he uses mostly **active verbs** after the white rabbit shows up?

III. Your Experience

a. Look around the room. Pick out some person(s) and/or some object(s) in the room. Using your imagination, come up with a few sentences about the people and/or objects. Create an unrealistic situation, as Lewis Carroll did in *Alice's Adventures in Wonderland*.

Example: When I walked into the cafeteria, the first chair I passed by said, "Sit down." I looked at that chair suspiciously. "It's ok," the chair said to me, "sit down." When I sat down on the chair, the chair on the other side of the table said, "No, don't sit there. Sit here." Then another chair chimed in. "No, no. Sit here. Sit here." It was so crazy I went up the block to a little restaurant where the chairs all kept to themselves, and I had a very nice, quiet lunch.

b. Lewis Carroll is a great storyteller who creates imaginative fiction. Think of something fantastic that happened to you—it could be fantasy, but it doesn't have to be—and describe that event as though you were writing fiction. You could write about a dream you had.

c. Think about a text: a book you've recently read or a movie or TV show that you've recently seen. You could even choose an interesting text message or recall the first time you saw the Grand Canyon. Engage in a dialogue with that text.

d. Read the following brief fiction:

Sally & the Falling Sky

My friend, Sally, came rushing through the unlocked front door into my house. Her breath came quick and hard.

"What's up, Sally?" I asked her.

"The sky is falling, that's what's up. Isn't that enough?"

"Sally! The sky is *not* falling. Are you living in an old fairy tale? What's it called, *Chicken Little?* Are you Chicken Little all of a sudden?"

"Look," Sally said, holding out her hand. In it, she held a blue object, irregularly shaped, transparent, and not quite like anything I'd ever seen.

"Where did you get that?"

"On Delaney Street. I was on my way to get some ice cream and boom, this fell right in front of me. It's a piece of the sky! Have you ever seen the likes of it?"

Very hesitant to take it from the hand she held out to me, but very excited to see what it was, I let Sally pass it over into my hand. It was incredibly soft. It was not just warm but radiant. It seemed to float up from my hand at the same time as it seemed to rest easily, steadily in my palm. It moved around a little bit, giving me an odd sensation of peace and calm. Could it be the sky was falling? Could it be I held a piece of the sky in my hand? If I did, what should I do?

***

Write out a brief **dialogue** with this fictional text, *Sally & The Falling Sky.* How do you respond to this text? Do you think it's ridiculous? Do you think it's funny? Do you think it's charming? What does this text make you think of? What do the **images** make you think of? What do you think of this text?

e. Read through your own **dialogue with the text**, *Sally & The Falling Sky*. Take some idea from your dialogue with this text and formulate a THESIS for an essay based on that idea. (For example, you might write an essay with this THESIS: *When we look up at a clear sky, we often feel peaceful, and when the narrator of Sally & The Falling Sky held a piece of the sky in her hand, she felt peaceful. Blue is a peaceful color.*)

IV. ACTIVE READING

a. Lewis Carroll tells his story in what we call a third person POINT OF VIEW, but we see it all mostly through Alice's eyes. Make a list of things that Alice sees or thinks.

1. _____

2. _____

3. _____

4. _____

5. _____

b. Look up five words from *Alice in Wonderland* that you don't know. Write the definitions below.

WORD   DEFINITION

1. _____   _____

2. _____   _____

3. _____   _____

4. _____   _____

5. _____   _____

c. List five things in *Alice* that had a strong effect on you. These may be images, particularly good sentences, something funny, some description, some idea. In short, tell us what you think makes for good writing.

_____

_____

_____

_____

_____

d. How does the setting in *Alice in Wonderland* differ from the setting in:

• Momaday's "The Way to Rainy Mountain"

- or –

• Jack London's "The Story of an Eyewitness: The San Francisco Earthquake."

CHAPTER 12

the act of writing | dialogue to analysis to essay

from dialogue ⟶ to analysis ⟶ to essay

We always think, all day long, about what we see, what we read, what we do, and who we are. We naturally have a **DIALOGUE WITH THE TEXTS** of our lives. Sometimes, we want to **organize** our thoughts, our feelings, and our dialogues into a **formal essay**.

NOW, where do we get our **IDEAS** for an **ESSAY**?

We know how to develop an essay because we studied the **PARTS OF AN ESSAY** in Chapter 6, page 75. We get the ideas for our essays from within the text we are reading, from our **DIALOGUE WITH THE TEXT.**

As we said in Chapter 11, one way to have a **DIALOGUE WITH THE TEXT** is to respond to the text with our own writing. We call this **FREEWRITING.** In **FREEWRITING**, you are free to write anything. We have only one rule for **FREEWRITING**: you **cannot stop** writing. If you get stuck, without anything to write, write anything, write:

I can't think of anything to say. I'm so frustrated. I'm bored. Can I go now? My name is Cheryl. My name is Cheryl. My name is Cheryl. Wait a minute! I just thought of something to write about.

When you have finished with your freewriting, you may find that it contains good ideas for an essay. From those ideas, you can formulate a thesis for your essay. How do you go from:

freewriting ⟶ thesis

In Chapter 11, we did a **FREEWRITE** about *Alice's Adventures in Wonderland.* Now, we'll look at that **FREEWRITING** to discover a **THESIS** for our essay. After we've written the **FREEWRITING**, we'll make a list of things we wrote about:

I can picture Alice sitting by a riverbank, stretched out on the grass under a tree, while her sister sits beside her. It looks very inviting. I wouldn't get bored. I'd just take a nap. But Alice got bored. Even her sister's book bored her because it didn't have any pictures or conversation in it. If I were bored, I'd lie back in the sunshine and take a nice long nap. But Alice isn't just bored. Alice is restless. Restlessness can lead you to do something creative. Alice looks around for something to do. I think Alice will do something interesting. I think something will happen to Alice. I want to read on. Who knows what Alice might do? Maybe if I take a nap I will dream the whole book of Alice's Adventures in Wonderland! I will use my imagination to create a story.

> **The Ideas We've Written About**
> The way Alice is lying around, bored, looks inviting to me.
>
> I'd be lazy.
>
> I'd take a nap.
>
> Alice isn't just bored, she's restless. What will she do to cure her restlessness?
>
> If I were Alice, I'd fall asleep, and to cure my restlessness, I'd dream the whole story of Alice's Adventures in Wonderland.
>
> We use our imagination—the power of our minds to invent ideas, actions, images, and stories—to come up with fascinating dreams, writings, and art of all kinds.

Our **FREEWRITING,** our **DIALOGUE WITH THE TEXT,** our **ANALYSIS** of *Alice's Adventures in Wonderland,* gives us an idea:

> In the end, Alice was not as bored as we thought.

From that idea, we develop a **THESIS:**

> When you are bored, you are passive. When you are restless, you become active, and you *do* something. You become creative. Alice is not so much bored as she is restless, looking for something to do. Her restlessness leads her to use her imagination to do something creative.

With that **THESIS,** we can write the beginnings of an **ESSAY:**

Restless Alice

Boredom makes us passive. But, restlessness makes us active, and we *do* something; we become creative.

In *Alice's Adventures in Wonderland,* Alice, sitting on the river bank, "peeped into the book her sister was reading," but it didn't interest her because "it had no pictures or conversations in it." Alice certainly does not like that kind of book! "And what is the use of a book," thought Alice "without pictures or conversation?" Alice was "very, very tired of sitting by her sister on the bank with nothing to do." But, Alice is not just tired, she is impatient with having "nothing to do." Alice is not so much bored as she is restless. Alice's restlessness leads her to do something creative. Perhaps, at that moment of her restlessness, Alice wrote the story of *Alice's Adventures in Wonderland*. Perhaps she imagined the whole thing.

Alice's Adventures in Wonderland tells us that Alice saw a "White Rabbit with pink eyes" run "close by her." But, perhaps Alice, in her restlessness, <u>imagines</u> the White Rabbit with pink eyes. Perhaps Alice imagines the White Rabbit speaking, saying, "Oh dear! Oh dear! I shall be late!" Alice might imagine that the White Rabbit took a watch from his waistcoat pocket, "looked at it, and then hurried on" down a rabbit hole. Alice could imagine that she "started to her feet" to follow the White Rabbit down his rabbit hole into all of the adventures of *Alice's Adventures in Wonderland*.

Of course, we don't know if Alice sitting on the river bank imagined the whole book of *Alice's Adventures in Wonderland*. But if she did, she certainly used her creative imagination to lift herself out of her boredom and her restlessness. If she did, she might have enjoyed herself very much all afternoon.

We do know that Lewis Carroll used *his* imagination to give us Alice and her adventures. Perhaps Lewis Carroll lifted himself out of his own restlessness by writing *Alice's Adventures in Wonderland*.

* * *

We have gone from **DIALOGUE WITH THE TEXT** to **ANALYSIS** to **THESIS** to **ESSAY.**

Here's another **FREEWRITING,** a **DIALOGUE WITH THE TEXT** of *Alice in Wonderland*.

I just realized how the idea of <u>time</u> plays an important part in Alice's Adventures in Wonderland. The story begins with Alice almost outside of time. She dreamily sits, bored, on the banks of the river. Suddenly, the White Rabbit brings time into the picture. The White Rabbit says, "Oh dear! Oh dear! I shall be late." He took a watch out of his pocket, "looked at it, and then hurried on." When time comes into the story, things start to happen. The action begins!

Time is one of the most important aspects of our lives. We all experience time every day, from morning to evening. We know that we have to be somewhere, for example, at 1:30. We look at our lives in terms of time: we are infants; we are teenagers; we are adults. We look at time in history. We say, "in the Nineteenth Century," "in the 70s," "in the future." And we even know time in terms of the whole universe. Many scientists now believe that the universe is about 15–20 billion years old.

People have always contemplated **time**, written about it, and made paintings and drawings about it. In 1931, the Spanish surrealist painter Salvador Dalí painted a painting he titled *The Persistence of Memory*. That painting portrays a landscape with some fascinating images of **time.** In Chapter 8, page 105, we talked about the paintings in the Cave at Lascaux as a kind of early "language." All painting, in its desire to break the silence of our lives, speaks to us with a visual "language." Here, Dalí lets his imagination go, much as Lewis Carroll does in *Alice's Adventures in Wonderland*. We'll use this painting in the Exercises for this Chapter.

Surrealism =

From the French:
sur = super
réalisme = realism

Surrealism was one of the exciting art and literature movements that began in the early 1920s in Paris and spread around the world. It influenced the visual arts, literature, film, and music as well as political thought and practice, philosophy and social theory.

To convey a reality above our ordinary reality, including our dream life, surrealism uses imaginary, unusual images and language and puts images and ideas together in ways that we don't see in daily life. Surrealist artists and writers still practice that art style today.

Salvador Dali's *The Persistence of Memory*

Chapter Review: Dialogue with the Text

We naturally have a DIALOGUE WITH THE TEXT, and those TEXTS include the books we read and the art we see.

We get our ideas for an essay from *within* the text, from our DIALOGUE WITH THE TEXT.

In FREEWRITING, we generate ideas, and we see what we're thinking about, and we have a DIALOGUE WITH THE TEXT.

Exercises for Chapter 12:

I. DIALOGUE WITH THE TEXT

a. Write a DIALOGUE WITH THE TEXT of Dalí's painting. Describe the painting. What do you see? What does it make you think of? Write down whatever you think of. Write for about 10 minutes. No one will look at this if you decide to keep it to yourself.

We have only one rule for FREEWRITING: you **cannot stop** writing. If you get stuck, without anything to write, write anything, write: *I can't think of anything to say. I'm so frustrated. I'm bored. Can I go now? My name is Cheryl. My name is Cheryl. Wait a minute! I just thought of something to write about.*

b. When you finish freewriting, make a short list of the things you wrote about. For example:
what is time?
melting watches
how old I am
the alarm clock in the morning

c. Look over your DIALOGUE WITH THE TEXT of Salvador Dalí's painting and the list of subjects you wrote about. Find some idea in your FREEWRITING, your DIALOGUE WITH THE TEXT, or the list you wrote that you could make into a THESIS for an essay on **time**. Write an essay on **time** in *Alice's Adventures in Wonderland* or an essay on **time** in the painting by Salvador Dalí? Write your THESIS here.

_____.

II. THESIS AND EVIDENCE

a. What is the THESIS of our short essay, "RESTLESS ALICE"?

_____

b. Give two examples of **EVIDENCE** we use to support our **THESIS** in "Restless Alice." Indicate *how* each example of evidence supports our thesis.

1. _____.

_____.

_____.

_____.

2. _____.

_____.

_____.

_____.

c. Read three articles from today's newspaper. While any article will do, you may want to select a front-page article or an opinion piece from the op-ed section. Write down the thesis of each of those three articles.

1. _____

2. _____

3. _____

Assignment for Chapter 12:

Alice's Adventures in Wonderland and *The Persistence of Memory* are both works of the imagination. In her essay on page 311, Ursula LeGuin writes: "To make something is to invent it, to discover it, to uncover it." Every day, we use our imagination to invent, discover, and uncover our world and our lives. Write an essay in which you discuss what role the creative imagination plays in our lives.

A couple of example possibilities for this essay:

- I live in a 2 bedroom apartment with 6 members of my family. I imagine that we live in a huge mansion.

- Walking around my city, I realize that we have no parks at all. I imagine a great park in a specific space.

- Looking up at the sky, I imagine that we could explore the outer reaches of our galaxy, and I imagine myself as a scientist leading that project, and I imagine what we discover out there.

- Last night, I dreamt about a ship sailing across the sky. I write a story about that ship.

If you like, you can write an essay using the THESIS you developed from your **dialogue with the text** *The Persistence of Memory* or write a **dialogue with the text** of *Alice's Adventures in Wonderland* and develop a THESIS from that **dialogue.** Some ideas you might address in your freewriting include:

- secret passages

- rules and breaking them

- time and memory

- maturity and immaturity

PART 05

the origins of language V: australian myth

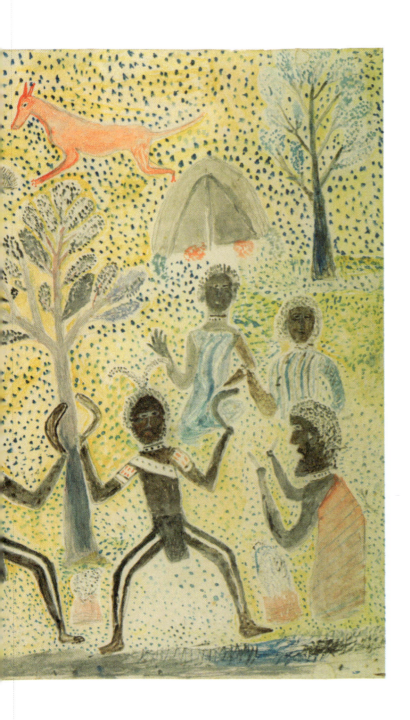

The Gunwinggu people of Australia have a particularly wonderful and somewhat unique myth of the origin of language. They distinguish between waking time and what they call dreamtime. In dreamtime, things happen that we don't see during waking time. If we think about our own dreams, of course, we find this to be certainly true. Dreamtime is a very potent experience out of which come important messages on which people base the values of their whole culture.

A Gunwinggu goddess, in dreamtime, gave each of her children their own language to play with. In the myths of many cultures, there was only one language to begin with, and something caused that language to splinter into many languages. This Gunwinggu origin of language myth tells of many different languages from the beginning, but those languages are all for the sake of play. We still use our language for play when we make puns, allusions, alliterations, rhymes, imaginative fictions, etc.

CHAPTER 13

the art of language | punctuation

When you walk into class, you see this on the board:

A woman without her man is nothing.

The Professor asks two students to come to the board to punctuate this sentence. The first student punctuates the sentence so it reads:

A woman, without her man, is nothing.

The Professor erases those punctuation marks and asks the second student to punctuate the sentence. The second student does it like this:

A woman: without her, man is nothing.

What is **PUNCTUATION?** How do we use **PUNCTUATION** in a sentence?
We can see from what's on the board: **PUNCTUATION** makes a difference!

When it rains cats and dogs run inside. — confusing

When it rains, cats and dogs run inside. — clear, with one meaning

When it rains cats and dogs, run inside. — clear, with a different meaning

PUNCTUATION helps us to understand the sentence. Language is alive. As the sentence moves along, we want to use every tool—grammar, punctuation, etc.—to make sure our readers understand us.

Our English language has many, **many** rules for PUNCTUATION. We'll give you the rules, along with some examples, for the *most common* PUNCTUATION. We'll give you some more detailed rules in an **Index** on page 257. But here's a good general rule that often works well with PUNCTUATION.

A GENERAL RULE THAT *OFTEN* WORKS WELL WITH PUNCTUATION:

Read your work aloud to yourself or to a friend. When you hear it aloud, you might hear where the PUNCTUATION goes and which PUNCTUATION MARK to use.

Sometimes, PUNCTUATION marks indicate the **breath** in a sentence. They tell you where you pause for a breath and for how long you pause. In our chart below, we'll let you know how long of a **breath stop/breath pause** each mark indicates.

Of course, you always want your work to **sound** right and to **read well** when you hear it. That's a good general test for your work. It helps to read aloud, to hear what your work sounds like.

The Most Common Punctuation Marks (and the Most Common Comma Rules)

Period

- a. **Full stop** at the end of a sentence

Example:

I stopped at the Corner Café this morning to get a coffee and pastry for breakfast.

For **Exercises**, fill in the missing punctuation

Exercise:

When we went to the zoo, we discovered a lion had escaped its dwelling

b. In abbreviations

Example:

Mr. Billingsly had coffee with Ms. Sharp. The Rev. Montgomery, Prof. Fernandez, and Sgt. Lee sat in the far corner talking about something in the morning paper, the N. Y. Times.

Exercise:

Mr Billingsly, the Zoo Manager, asked if we would join him, Sgt Battle, and Col Worth in searching for the lion.

Exclamation mark

! **Full stop** at the end of a sentence, used to add emphasis

Example:

I quit drinking coffee, and I quit eating sweets, but, unable to help myself, I stopped at the Corner Café this morning to get a coffee and pastry for breakfast! It was delicious!

Exercise:

We spent at least 6 hours scouring the zoo and the surrounding neighborhood looking for the escaped lion

Question mark

? **Full stop** at the end of a sentence to indicate the sentence is a question

Example:

Did you stop at the Corner Café this morning for breakfast? Didn't I see you there having coffee and a pastry?

Exercise:

As we searched the neighborhood, we asked everyone we saw the same question: Have you seen a lion   Of course, everyone looked at us in amazement.

Comma

,   **General Rule: Short Pause** in the sentence to separate parts of the sentence and to make the meaning clear. Whenever the meaning is unclear, you can add a comma if it will help.

Example:
At the Corner Café this morning, when I was eating a pastry, and my notebook fell on the floor, the man sitting next to me fainted!

Exercise:
When it got dark, and we had not yet found the lion and the flashlights were all back at the zoo, we ran back for flashlights to keep searching.

Specific Comma Rules:

a. *Before* a **coordinating conjunction** (see Chapter 4) joining **independent clauses** (see Chapter 7)

Example:
I looked for you at the Corner Café this morning, but you weren't there.

Exercise:
When we went out again, with flashlights, we split up into two teams and we took two different directions.

b. *After* a prepositional phrase (see Chapter 4, page 52)

Example:
At the Corner Café, they had a lot of new pastries on display. On my way out, I ran into Joey, Suzanne, and Paul.

Exercise:
After another hour Sgt. Battle and I grew tired, and we were ready to give it up.

c. Between all items in a series

Example:
On my way out of the Corner Café this morning, I ran into Joey, Suzanne, Rachel, Richard, Lujean, and Paul.

Exercise:
Although it was the lion who escaped the zoo, the zoo has a lot of other big animals, including tigers elephants jaguars zebras bears leopards camels and kangaroos.

d. Between adjectives **not** joined by "and."

Example:

The pastry I had this morning at the Corner Café was a warm, fresh, delicious, reasonably priced Italian kind.

Exercise:

The escaped lion could be perfectly tame, but if it became hungry disoriented tired or confused, it could turn violent. Sgt. Battle and I agreed that we had to keep looking on all the big long dark occupied or empty streets alleyways backyards and open lots in the neighborhood.

Semi-colon

; **Longer pause** than a comma; used between two **independent clauses** you want to join together.

Example:

I had the best breakfast this morning at the corner café; I go there often, mostly for breakfast.

Exercise:

We turned the corner from Round Street to Turner Street, and I sensed something nearby it felt like a lion. Do I have ancestors way back in the jungles of India or on the savannas of Africa or in the mountains of America from whom I inherited an intuitive sense for lions?

Colon

: A full **pause.** Use it to introduce a list of items:

Example:

I have used the Corner Café for meetings for different purposes: social, business, dating, studying, and creative collaborations on screenplays, poems, and stories.

Exercise:

I saw the lion peacefully asleep on someone's lawn. I knelt down to pet it. Suddenly, animals came from everywhere to play with the lion dogs, cats, birds, chipmunks, and squirrels. They all rolled around on the lawn with the lion until the zoo truck showed up, along with a lot of other vehicles police cars, an ambulance, a fire truck, an animal control van, and the rescue truck from the zoo. I'd had my fun. I went home. My family had been looking for me. They didn't believe my story at all, but it's true.

Chapter Review: Punctuation

PUNCTUATION helps us to understand the sentence.

Types of Punctuation Marks

Period (.)

Exclamation point (!)

Question Mark (?)

Comma (,)

Semi-colon (;)

Colon (:)

A Tip to follow when using PUNCTUATION:

Read your work aloud to yourself or to a friend. When you hear it aloud, you might hear where the PUNCTUATION mark goes and which PUNCTUATION mark to use.

Some PUNCTUATION marks indicate the **breath** in a sentence, where you pause for a breath, and for how long you pause.

Of course, you always want your work to **sound** right, to **read well** when you hear it. That's a good general test for your work. It helps to read aloud in order to hear what your work sounds like.

Exercises for Chapter 13

I. PERIODS

Insert **periods** and fix the capitalization where necessary:

1. A solar eclipse happens when the Moon passes between the Earth and the Sun, partially covering our view of the Sun each year we can have from two to five solar eclipses

2. For the last eclipse of the Sun, I went to a nearby mountaintop for a better view

3. In a solar eclipse, the Sun seems to disappear suddenly the sky quickly darkens ancient people feared an eclipse of the Sun they thought it signaled that their deities were angry

4. Don't look at an eclipse of the Sun with the naked eye you could go blind

5. In a total eclipse, the Moon completely obscures the Sun from our point of view this can happen up to twice a year

6. Prof Miller, Director of the Observatory, invited us to view the last eclipse from his facilities

7. Mr and Mrs Gonzales took Mrs Gonzales's 3rd Grade class to the Observatory

8. Although I was born during an eclipse of the Sun, everyone said it was neither a good sign nor a bad sign or a sign of any kind for my life

9. My little brother was born during an eclipse of the Moon many people thought our family was special I didn't think so at all I just thought it was funny

10. If an eclipse of the Sun, or an eclipse of the Moon, occurred while I was doing these exercises that would be too strange

II. EXCLAMATION MARK

Insert **periods** or **exclamation marks** where appropriate, fixing capitalization where necessary:

1. I saw the last eclipse from a nearby mountaintop it was fantastic

2. My brother knew someone who looked at the eclipse last night without any protection for his eyes he's blinded for life

3. I want to see an eclipse of the Sun I've never seen one before.

4. Although they say we can have no more than five solar eclipses per year, last year there were six

5. When we saw the solar eclipse, my baby brother wanted to climb up on my shoulders, so he could be closer to it

6. We drove all the way to Arizona for a clear view of the eclipse

7. Yes, we made that long trip in my old beat-up jalopy we had no trouble

8. Do you know what my baby sister did during the eclipse? She cried

9. Do you know what my little brother did during the eclipse? He laughed

10. Do you know what I did during the eclipse? I watched it

III. QUESTION MARKS

Insert **question marks** where appropriate:

1. Have you ever seen an eclipse

2. Would you like to see an eclipse

3. Would you drive all the way to Arizona for a clear view of a solar eclipse

4. Will any of these exercises ever be about something other than eclipses

5. Can a solar eclipse blind you

6. How many solar eclipses have you seen

7. When the sky darkens from a solar eclipse, should you go to sleep

8. Do you think a solar eclipse is a good luck sign

9. When your baby brother cried during the eclipse, did you rock him back and forth in your arms and whisper to him: it's alright, it's alright

10. Can you believe there are even more exercises coming, all based on eclipses

IV. COMMAS

Insert **commas** where appropriate:

1. I saw a solar eclipse and the man standing next to me screamed!

2. I fell asleep in the darkness of the solar eclipse and the man standing next to me awakened me.

3. After the solar eclipse we went to celebrate by having a milkshake.

4. So far I have seen a solar eclipse a lunar eclipse and the northern lights.

5. While my friend was watching the solar eclipse I was doing exercises on commas.

6. I went to see the solar eclipse from a nearby mountaintop with Jerry Lucinda and Jimmy.

7. On the day of the last solar eclipse I couldn't go out to see it and my brother had to tell me all about it.

8. I did all the exercises on solar eclipses and then I got a hamburger with my friend Charlie.

9. The hamburger I got just happened to be called "The Eclipseburger," so I got the "Moonshine Fries" to go with it.

10. In my short life I have seen an eclipse of the Sun an eclipse of the Moon and a night of the Northern Lights.

V. Semi-colons

Insert **semi-colons** where appropriate:

1. Because I was sick and had to stay inside, I couldn't go out to see the last solar eclipse my brother had to tell me about it.

2. My brother saw the last solar eclipse, but I couldn't I was terribly jealous of him.

3. To see a solar eclipse, you need some eye protection without it you could go blind.

4. The Sun is 92.58 million miles from the Earth it takes light from the Sun about 8 minutes to reach the Earth.

5. If you put your thumb up a few inches from your eye, you block the view of the Sun is your thumb bigger than the Sun?

6. It takes about 8 minutes for light from the Sun to reach the Earth why is that light still so warm?

7. I went out to watch the eclipse I came home to write about it in my diary.

8. I meant to write in my diary about the eclipse instead I found myself writing about my boyfriend.

9. I wrote seven pages in my diary about my boyfriend I then remembered that I wanted to write about the eclipse that we'd seen.

10. An eclipse of the Sun blocks the sun, and an eclipse of the Moon blocks the Moon when someone stands between you and the TV that you're watching you call it an eclipse of the TV.

V. COLONS

Insert **colons** where appropriate:

1. The greatest natural phenomenon I have witnessed include a solar eclipse, the Northern Lights, and Niagara Falls.

2. Four of us went out to witness the eclipse Jimmy, Jill, James, and Augusto.

3. This year, so far, there have been three solar eclipses one best visible in New Mexico, one best visible in Montana, and one best visible in New Hampshire.

4. We have eight planets in our solar system Mercury, Venus, Earth, Mars, Jupiter, Saturn, Uranus, and Neptune.

5. We have five dwarf planets in our solar system Ceres, Pluto, Haumea, Makemake, and Eris.

6. When I looked up at the night sky, I saw a million stars. They were in thousands of constellations the Big Dipper, the Little Dipper, Orion, Aries, Taurus, Gemini, Virgo, Lepus….

7. If you're at the beach at dusk, and you look across the water, you will see the following the land, the water, the horizon, and the setting Sun.

8. This afternoon, I looked up to see the eclipse of the Sun, but everyone my friend, Susan, the radio, the TV, and the newspaper said it would occur tomorrow, not today.

9. If you take an astronomy class, you will learn about these things, among others eclipses, stars, the Moon, the planets, the Sun, sunspots, etc.

10. The authors of this book had to look up a few things to write these exercises the distance from the Sun to the earth, the number of eclipses per year, etc.

VI. AN ESSAY IN NEED OF PUNCTUATION

a. In the following short essay, insert **punctuation marks** wherever needed:

From 1939 – 1945 World War II engulfed almost every country in the world Two main coalitions of countries dominated the fighting the Axis Powers Germany Italy and Japan on one side the Allied Powers France Great Britain the United States and the Soviet Union on the other side The Fascist party which then controlled both Germany and Italy had contempt for democracy and did not believe in elections They believed in extreme military control and rule by an elite class of people and they thought that the individual did not have rights but that the interests of the State superseded the interests of any citizen In short the Fascists believed in exactly the opposite kind of freedom we hold dear in America Since World War II the very word "fascism" has become equated with almost pure evil

In 1943 many in the Italian government fearing that Italy was losing the war and disillusioned with Fascism threw out the Italian Fascist government formed a new more democratic government and began negotiations with the Allies to end the war But the Germans who had no patience with losing Italy as a Fascist partner invaded Italy

By now many Italians had become disillusioned with Fascism and tired of the hardships of war To fight against the invading Germans they formed unofficial groups of citizen-fighters called Partisans who fought in the cities and the countryside from the farms and the mountains against the Germans They made the German army pay a high price for its invasion of Italy while the Germans captured and executed about 70,000 Partisans The Partisans took on the romantic aura of a small group of Italian citizens who fought for freedom against the giant invading German army Even today the history of the Partisans is held very dear by the Italian people You will find monuments to the Partisans even in small villages as you travel across Italy

Eventually of course the Allies won World War II Italy and Germany both turned to democratic rule Both flourish today as free nations

b. In the following short essay, insert **punctuation marks** wherever needed:

The history of art goes all the way back in human history The cave paintings at Lascaux which appear in the Origins of Language I following Chapter One come from about 15,000 years ago Whether in writing or painting or music or dance or any other art form we as humans have always been inspired by our imaginations

As art develops in different ages artists develop different techniques to represent the life around them in ways that express their feelings for that life Visual artists painters and sculptors have long been in love with the shapes and the colors of the objects we live with This love gave rise to an art form we call Still Life In Still Life paintings artists portray the common objects of their world in an artificial setting Typically painters will choose natural objects to portray such as flowers food plants rocks seashells etc or man-made objects such as musical instruments books tableware etc While a Still Life painting may include representations of people or landscapes it maintains its focus on the objects Although Still Life paintings usually use techniques to represent objects and people realistically in a sense we might call Salvado Dalí's *The Persistence of Memory* a Still Life painting

The period of time we call the Renaissance took place in Italy from about 1420–1600 It was an incredible time in Italy Culture flourished as it never had before Business and commerce rose to support the middle class Government developed new more efficient forms of organizing that served the Italian population well Art in particular exploded The Medici family in Florence and other wealthy Renaissance families became famous for supporting artists for giving them studios to work in for hiring younger artists to work in those studios for providing materials to work with and for commissioning paintings So many artists worked brilliantly in Italy during the Italian Renaissance that today we devote whole museums to them We study their styles to learn from them We lovingly restore their paintings and frescoes with the same kinds of paint they used We read books that Renaissance authors have written about their own time and the artists who worked in the Renaissance If you would like to see the greatness of Renaissance art perhaps the best place in the world to do so is at the Uffizi museum in Florence Italy In fact the Italian Renaissance began in Florence and Florence remained its center

Many Italian painters worked in Still Life called in Italian Natura Morta Enamored of the shapes the colors and the life in natural objects they painted literally hundreds of paintings of fruit in bowls delicately mixing paints to imitate the shades of color they saw in different light in the morning in the afternoon or in the evening They paid attention not only to the shapes and colors they saw but to the shadows cast by the natural light coming in through open windows for they had not yet developed window glass

CHAPTER 14

the act of reading | quote | paraphrase | summary

You have engaged in a **DIALOGUE WITH THE TEXT.** You have **ANALYZED** texts. You have written **ESSAYS** about texts. Now, when you want to **convey** part or all of the information from a text to someone else, you have a few options for how to do that.

> *quote* *paraphrase* *summary*

You will want to use each of these options for a different purpose.

Let's take the beginning of an article that the *New Yorker* magazine published on September 5, 2005. Then we'll look at how the author, John Seabrook, uses **quote, paraphrase, and summary** to prove his **THESIS.**

Renaissance Pears

The Fiorentina[1] is a squat and hippy pear, its dark-green skin blemished with black freckles. It is to supermarket fruit as real people are to supermodels. Until recently, the pear was thought to have disappeared from central Italy, where it once flourished. But Isabella Dalla Ragione, a forty-seven-year-old agronomist[2] in Perugia[3], continued to look for it.

Dalla Ragione[4] has straight brown hair and crooked teeth; she can look twenty years younger than her age or ten years older, depending on the angle of her head. She is a fast driver and an even faster talker, with a gift for making archeologia arborea,[5] as she calls her vocation—the pursuit and recovery of

---

[1] The Fiorentina is a type of pear that has almost become extinct.
[2] An agronomist studies soils and plants.
[3] A major city in central Italy, the capital of the province of Umbria.
[4] This is the family name of the woman, Isabella Dalla Ragione.
[5] Archeologia arborea is the study of the archeology, or the history, of trees

old varieties of fruit—sound thrilling. She finds clues in many places: Renaissance paintings[6], obscure books, and the records that were kept by former estate owners in Umbria and Tuscany[7], where the climate is peculiarly advantageous for many kinds of fruit. Last year, while studying the catalogue of a large estate that once belonged to the Bufalini family[8], on the northern tip of Umbria, she came across a reference to the Fiorentina. The Bufalini maintained villas[9] with extensive gardens and orchards, from the fifteenth century on up to the nineteen-eighties, when the final landlord left the property to the state.

Pear trees can live for more than two hundred and fifty years—among fruit trees, only olives live longer—and so Isabella thought a Fiorentina[10] might remain on the former Bufalini lands. She knew what the pear looked like, thanks to a memoir left by an itinerant[11] early-twentieth-century musician, Archimede Montanelli, whose travels had taken him all over Umbria. She also happened to have an uncle, Alvaro, who hunted in that part of Umbria and was acquainted with some of the farmers who lived there. Eventually, one of them told Alvaro that a Fiorentina remained on his farm.

Earlier this summer, I accompanied Isabella on a trip to visit the old pear tree. We drove into a mountainous region above the town of Pietralunga, a land of thick woods with small farms in the valleys. Stone houses where the landowners had once lived, many of them now abandoned, sit on the tops of hills. The old orchards are gone, but the landscape is dotted with a few rugged arboreal[12] survivors: almonds, olives, and pears.

The Fiorentina was growing in the Valdescura, the Valley of Darkness. When we arrived, relatives of several families, spanning four generations, were sitting under the big shade trees outside the farmhouse. The matriarch[13] was an eighty-four-year-old woman named Sergia. She wore a ragged shift and filthy slippers, and carried a long walking stick. Hearing my accent, she recalled the Americans who had escaped from a nearby Fascist[14] prison and turned up one night in 1943; she had given them shelter and something to eat.

There was a cherry tree beside the house, and Isabella walked with Sergia to gather some cherries. Or, rather, Isabella gathered them; Sergia ate them, the pits tumbling down her whiskery chin as more cherries went into her mouth.

Then the farmer, a nephew of Sergia's, led us through a potato field to the Fiorentina, which was growing next to a rutted[15] old road. Its black bark had deep crevices, and the trunk and lower branches were covered with scabrous[16] white lichen[17]. Isabella fought through the high weeds around

---

[6]The Renaissance is a period of time that took place in Italy from about 1420–1600.

[7]Tuscany is another Province of Italy, just to the west of Umbria.

[8]The Bufalini were a wealthy Renaissance Italian family, like the Medici family, that owned huge estates.

[9]A villa is a huge home on an Italian estate.

[10]The Fiorentin is the tree that bears the Fiorentina pear.

[11]An itinerant musician is someone who travels around to perform his or her art in different places.

[12]Arboreal is the adjective meaning trees.

[13]A matriarch is the oldest living female in a family, usually the grandmother or great-grandmother.

[14]The Fascists were the Party that governed Italy in the early 20th Century and took Italy into World War II.

[15]A rutted road is a bumpy, uneven, potholed road.

[16]Scabrous means something with a rough surface.

[17]Lichen are organisms that grows over rocks and trees.

the tree and patted its trunk. "Sometimes when I find one of these old trees I feel like weeping," she said. "If only they could talk—what a story they could tell." Then she frowned, and said, "But I think, Maybe it is better they cannot talk. They would probably curse us."

For thousands of years, peasants in Umbria and Tuscany cultivated fruit trees. Most tended small pomari, or family orchards, with no more than ten trees. A fruit tree provided food, shade in summer, fuel in winter, furniture, and children's shoes, which were made from the wood of fig trees. Fruit was also a staple of the cooking of the region, in dishes like salt cod with roasted pears, and pork with plums; whole cherries in agrodolce—pickled in vinegar and sugar—were served as a chutney[18] with roasted meat. The farmers planted as many varieties as possible because the different trees would bear fruit at different times over the growing season. The mountainous topography[19] of Umbria, and its lack of roads, insured that varieties common to one valley were unknown in the next. When a woman married, she often carried seeds from her family's farm with her in order to prepare her mother's recipes, which were based on the particular varieties of fruit in her home valley.

This feudal[20] way of life endured, more or less unbroken, for two thousand years, until it abruptly ended in the two decades following the Second World War.[21] Nine million Italians, about a sixth of the population at that time, left their rural homes and went to the cities. They acquired Fiats,[22] Vespas,[23] televisions, and fashionable clothes—all the trappings of modern Italian identity. The old fruit trees were among the things they left behind.

The varieties eaten in Umbria and Tuscany were replaced, first, by generic[24] fruit grown in the Emilia-Romagna[25] region, where much of Italy's agricultural industry is concentrated, and, more recently, by fruit from other countries—peaches and cherries from Spain, pears from Argentina, and apples from China. In most markets in Italy you can find only three kinds of apple (Golden Delicious, Stark Delicious, Rome Beauty), and lately the Fuji apple, from China, has begun to replace those. It's not hard to imagine a day when there will be only one kind of apple for sale in the whole industrial world.

The Dalla Ragiones' orchard is an open-air museum of Old World fruit. It was begun by Isabella's father, Livio, forty years ago, on his land in northwestern Umbria, and is now maintained by Isabella. The trees grow on a hilltop in San Lorenzo di Lerchi, a hamlet[26] about seventy miles southeast of Florence[27] and thirty miles northwest of Perugia; Livio lives in a stone farmhouse that overlooks the orchard. There are about four hundred trees in the collection: pears, apples, plums, cherries, peaches,

---

[18]Chutney is a relish served with food.
[19]Topography means a way of describing a landscape.
[20]A feudal system was a country way of life, where landowners dominated the peasants living on their land.
[21]World War II took place from 1939–1945.
[22]A Fiat is a European brand of car.
[23]A Vespa is a popular brand of motor scooter.
[24]Generic refers to something general, in this case, something not from a local family farm, but from a large corporate farm.
[25]Emilia-Romagna is another Province of Italy, south of Umbria and Tuscany.
[26]A hamlet is a small village.
[27]Florence is the capital city of the Province of Tuscany.

quinces,[28] and medlars.[29] Most were common in Umbria as recently as sixty years ago; now they have all but disappeared. Some of the Dalla Ragiones' specimens are believed to be the last examples of that variety.

* * *

Seabrook has written about saving varieties of fruit trees threatened by extinction. In doing that, he also writes about history, art, food, culture, and how the people he encounters form their identities by interacting with the landscape they live in. Notice how Seabrook handles all these different subjects, how he organizes his essay to include all this interesting material, while, at the same time, he never loses touch with his **THESIS.**

You can read the rest of this essay in the back of the book, or in the September 5, 2005 issue of the *New Yorker,* to find out what happened to Isabella Dalla Ragione and her adventures in saving the ancient fruit trees of Italy.

quote

We use a **QUOTE** to support and prove our thesis. To **QUOTE,** we copy the exact words from a text, be it a written text or an oral text (someone speaking). John Seabrook **QUOTES** Isabella Dalla Ragione in his essay. (We have put all the **QUOTES** in **bold.**)

> **"Sometimes when I find one of these old trees I feel like weeping,"** she said. **"If only they could talk—what a story they could tell."** Then she frowned, and said, **"But I think, maybe it is better they cannot talk. They would probably curse us."**

paraphrase

We may not always want to use the exact language of a text by **quoting** it. When we **paraphrase** language from a text, we restate that language in our own terms. A **paraphrase** is often about the same length, nearly the same number of words, as the original, but rewritten in our own words.

You may want to use **paraphrase** to vary the style of your essay. You might want to use **paraphrase** if a **quote** is too long for your essay. You might want to use **paraphrase** to give your reader the flavor of your own language or to make your reader feel that you are talking directly to him or her.

---

[28]A quince is a pear-shaped fruit.
[29]A medlar is an apple-shaped fruit.

She's a fast driver and an even faster talker, with a gift for making archeologia arborea, as she calls her vocation—the pursuit and recovery of old varieties of fruit—sound thrilling.

summary

When you **SUMMARIZE,** you give the main points of the material from the text. A **SUMMARY** should be much shorter than the original.

You might want to use a **SUMMARY:**
- if you give a **SUMMARY** of the text you're analyzing, your reader will better understand what you're talking about;
- to give your reader a lot of information with a few words;
- if you have a lot of information to convey to your reader, but you don't have a lot of space to do that in;
- if the original contains important information, but it does not read well or is boring;
- if you have a lot of information to convey from the original, but you want your reader to hear your voice speaking in the essay.

Here, John Seabrook **SUMMARIZES** Isabella Dalla Ragione's research.

She finds clues in many places: Renaissance paintings, obscure books, and the records that were kept by former estate owners in Umbria and Tuscany, where the climate is peculiarly advantageous for many kinds of fruit.

Seabrook doesn't want to go into all the detail of Isabella's work. He wants to give the sense of what she does and how she does it. He uses **SUMMARY** to do that.

Seabrook uses all these methods—**quote, paraphrase, and summary**—to convey information to us, information that, as **EVIDENCE**, supports his **THESIS**.

Chapter Review: Quote, Paraphrase, Summary

We use quote, paraphrase, and summary to give our reader information from the material are writing about.

- A quote repeats the original source language.
- A paraphrase restates the original source language in your own words.
- A summary conveys the main ideas of the original source.

Exercises for Chapter 14

I. YOUR THOUGHTS

a. John Seabrook covers a lot of topics in his essay. What ideas do you find most interesting?

b. Do these ideas have any relevance to your life?

c. Does Seabrook bring forth new ideas for you, things you may have never thought of?

II. JOHN SEABROOK'S ART: PUNCTUATION

a. John Seabrook uses seven different kinds of punctuation in his essay. Name each one of those seven different punctuation marks, then write out one sentence in which Seabrook uses that punctuation mark.

1. Name of Punctuation mark: _____
Sentence in which Seabrook uses that punctuation mark:

_____

_____

2. Name of Punctuation mark: _____
Sentence in which Seabrook uses that punctuation mark:

_____

_____

3. Name of Punctuation mark: _____

   Sentence in which Seabrook uses that punctuation mark:

   _____

   _____

4. Name of Punctuation mark: _____

   Sentence in which Seabrook uses that punctuation mark:

   _____

   _____

5. Name of Punctuation mark: _____

   Sentence in which Seabrook uses that punctuation mark:

   _____

   _____

6. Name of Punctuation mark: _____

   Sentence in which Seabrook uses that punctuation mark:

   _____

   _____

7. Name of Punctuation mark: _____

   Sentence in which Seabrook uses that punctuation mark:

   _____

   _____

III. YOUR EXPERIENCE

a. John Seabrook sought out Isabella Dalla Ragione because he liked the work that she does. Describe someone you know who does interesting work and describe the work that they do.

b. Seabrook's article talks about fruit trees on the verge of extinction. In your own environment, or somewhere you have heard about, do you know of any fruit, vegetable, tree species, or animal on the verge of extinction? What would we lose if we lost that natural thing?

c. Isabella Dalla Ragione, in her passion to save fruit trees on the verge of extinction, goes on a treasure hunt to save those species she can find. Following your own passions, if you went on a treasure hunt, what would you look for? How would you look for it? What might you want to preserve?

d. Seabrook relates the contrast between the "Old World" and modern life. Do you have any experience of that in your own or your family's life? Has your family experienced the contrast between rural life and urban life, perhaps? Or have some other changes taken place in the way you or your family live?

IV.   ACTIVE READING

a. What is John Seabrook's THESIS? _____

_____

_____

b. Write out five examples of EVIDENCE that Seabrook uses to support his THESIS.

1. _____

_____

_____

2. _____

_____

_____

3. _____

_____

_____

4. _____

_____

_____

5. _____

_____

_____

c. List five topics that Seabrook mentions in his article.

1. _____

2. _____

3. _____

4. _____

5. _____

CHAPTER 15

the art of writing | dialogue with the reader

Using Quote / Paraphrase / Summary to Present Evidence

When you read, you have a **DIALOGUE WITH THE TEXT.** When you write, you have a **DIALOGUE WITH THE READER,** *your* reader, the person who reads what you write. We like to think that when you write a text, a book, an essay, a letter, anything at all, it lies silent until someone picks it up to read or reread it. Then it comes alive again.

When you write an essay, when you speak to your reader, when you speak *with* your reader, you want to support your **THESIS** with **EVIDENCE.** You want to bring as much information to your reader as you can because you are in **DIALOGUE** with him or her. By using **QUOTE, PARAPHRASE,** and **SUMMARY,** as John Seabrook does in "Renaissance Pears," you can prove your **THESIS,** and you can bring information to your reader. You will make your essay more dynamic and richer in tone.

QUOTE, **PARAPHRASE,** and **SUMMARY** all present concrete evidence that proves your thesis. You don't use just any **QUOTE, PARAPHRASE, OR SUMMARY** to use in your essay. You choose **QUOTES, PARAPHRASES, AND SUMMARIES** that prove your **THESIS.**

In Chapter 14, page 181, we saw how John Seabrook used **QUOTE, PARAPHRASE,** and **SUMMARY** to prove his thesis. Now, let's look at how you might use **QUOTE, PARAPHRASE,** and **SUMMARY.** Imagine you write an essay in which you use **QUOTE, PARAPHRASE,** and **SUMMARY,** all taken from John Seabrook's "Renaissance Pears." Let's imagine that the essay you write has this **THESIS:**

After World War II, life in Europe and America changed from rural to urban, from small and personal communities in which people cared for each other to large, impersonal communities where the individual could get lost. Our culture even changed from an awareness of taking care of the environment that was close around us to one that exploits our environment for all the profit we can get.

To develop your essay and to prove your thesis, you could use **QUOTE, PARAPHRASE,** and **SUMMARY** in the following ways (we've put **QUOTE, PARAPHRASE,** and **SUMMARY** in bold type):

quote

We use a **DIRECT QUOTE** from a text when we take the *exact language* from that text and use it in our own writing. You always put the **DIRECT QUOTE** in quotation marks.

The journalist, John Seabrook, found an example of Old World Italy, and of how people took care of each other, when he met Sergia, an 84-year old Italian woman who wore a ragged shift, filthy slippers, and carried a long walking stick. Hearing Seabrook's American accent, Sergia **"recalled the Americans who had escaped from a nearby Fascist prison and turned up one night in 1943; she had given them shelter and something to eat"** (104).[1]

You have chosen this **direct quote** from "Renaissance Pears" because it proves your thesis. By quoting this woman, you show us how, in the old rural farms and villages, people took care of strangers.

We put quotation marks around a **direct quote** to indicate we have accurately reported what the author wrote.

A **direct quote** gives us the *exact language* of a text, so we know you have reported accurately to us what the text said. A **direct quote** also gives us a flavor of the original language, so we know what it sounds like.

paraphrase

When you want to convey information from a text but don't want to use a **direct quote,** you can use **PARAPHRASE.** When you **PARAPHRASE,** you convey an idea from a text, but you write it in your own language. So, when do you paraphrase? Perhaps you don't remember the **direct quote** or don't have the original text in front of you. Perhaps you have already used several **direct quotes** in your essay, and you want to add some variety of style. Perhaps you want to restate, in your own words, what someone else has written or said. Now, we will paraphrase the quote from "Renaissance Pears."

The journalist, John Seabrook, described an old Italian woman he met, Sergia, with her ragged shift, her dirty slippers, and her long walking stick. She told Seabrook about how she took in and cared for American soldiers who, during World War II, had escaped from a nearby Fascist prison (104).

---

[1] When you use *any* information from another source, **quote, paraphrase, summary,** or just a statement of fact, you must give credit to that source through **citation.** The *MLA Handbook,* or some other style reference book, will show you how to do **citations.**

We have given the same information as Seabrook, but we have used our own words. We have **PARAPHRASED** Seabrook's article in order to convey this information but to vary the style of quoting and to speak more directly to the reader in our own language.

In fact, we use **PARAPHRASE** all the time. When we tell someone about an event that happened in a book we read, we generally **paraphrase** that. When we talk about some scene in a film we saw, we **PARAPHRASE** that scene. Even if we just tell someone about an argument an article in the newspaper made, we **PARAPHRASE** that argument.

summary

A **SUMMARY** should be much shorter than the original text. A **SUMMARY** gives just the *main points* of the original text.

In your essay on the change of culture in Europe and America after World War II, you could write about many aspects of modern European and American life, about urban crowding, about industrialization, about traffic congestion, about religion, politics, etc. You might even write about the Dalla Ragione's orchard as one among many interesting things in modern Europe that relates to "Old World" Italy. You don't need all the rich details from "Renaissance Pears" for your essay, you just want the main ideas. Your **summary** gives you that.

Isabella Dalla Ragione and her father, Livio, search for species of trees in danger of extinction and save those species by planting a cutting in their orchard on a hilltop in the Italian province of Umbria.

Isabella learns about the existence of ancient trees from Renaissance paintings, from obscure books, and from old records kept by feudal landowners. Then she will ask around if anyone has seen a particular obscure fruit tree, such as the Fiorentina pear tree. People will tell her they have seen a tree on an old farm, in an old nunnery, or elsewhere. Isabella will travel to find the tree, to save it.

Modern agriculture in the industrialized world has reduced the variety of fruits available to us in our supermarkets. The Dalla Ragiones hope to save the tastes and flavors of the Old World in their orchard of ancient fruit trees.

When might you want to use a **SUMMARY**?

- **To provide a context for your reader.** In writing an analytical essay, you want to make sure your reader understands what you're analyzing. When you give a **SUMMARY** of that text, your reader will know what you're talking about when he or she reads your analysis. In this case, your **SUMMARY** gives a context for your reader to understand your essay.

- **To understand a text.** A SUMMARY helps you understand a text. If you want to know a text well, do a SUMMARY. It will engage you with the text. When you are done, you will know the text thoroughly, and you will understand it better.

- **To understand the thesis.** You must know the main point of a text to SUMMARIZE it. You must ask yourself, "Why did the author write this text?" When you answer that, you will know the THESIS of the text.

- **For a presentation.** A Professor may ask you to give a SUMMARY of something you have read. He/she may also ask you to give a SUMMARY of a paper you have written for the class.

- **In business.** Your boss may ask you to give her or him a SUMMARY of a business report. We call this an EXECUTIVE SUMMARY. If you have written a book you want to submit for publication, you might write a SUMMARY for the publisher. There are many business uses for a SUMMARY.

- **In your personal life.** In everyday life, you may SUMMARIZE for your friends a movie you saw, a vacation trip, an article you read, your life at college. In fact, almost every day we use SUMMARY.

Having learned about QUOTE, PARAPHRASE, and SUMMARY, you can now now use all three of them effectively in your writing. You will also become aware of how you use them in your daily life. Suppose you call your brother, who is at another college, to tell him about this interesting article you just read, "Renaissance Pears." You read to your brother from the article: **"Pear trees can live for more than two hundred and fifty years—among fruit trees, only olives live longer."** You ask him if the olive tree in your backyard at home might be that old. You have just used a QUOTE in your daily conversation with your brother.

Chapter Review: Using Quote/Paraphrase/Summary As Evidence

Use **quote, paraphrase,** and **summary** to present EVIDENCE that proves your THESIS.

A **direct quote** gives us the *exact language* of a text.

Put a **direct quote** in quotation marks.

A **paraphrase** gives us an idea from the text in your own language.

A **summary** gives just the main ideas from the text. Use a summary:

- to provide a context for your reader;
- to help you to understand a text yourself;
- to find and understand the thesis;
- for a presentation;
- in business;
- in your personal life.

Exercises for Chapter 15

I. DIALOGUE WITH THE READER

a. In writing "Renaissance Pears," John Seabrook engages us in a dialogue. What do you think he wants to tell us?

(This question is similar to our signature question: "Why Am I Writing This Essay?" It asks, "Why Does John Seabrook Write This Essay?" But it changes the focus a little bit, so we could rephrase our signature question: "What Does John Seabrook Hope to Tell Us?" You could also ask yourself that question of every essay you write: "What Do I Hope To Tell My Reader?")

b. Go back to your first essay, where you addressed someone in your family, or a good friend, who thought you should not go to college. What did you hope to tell them? How do you think they might have responded to you?

c. Going back to our selection from *Alice's Adventures in Wonderland* in Chapter 11, page 148, what do you think Lewis Carroll wants to tell us? With this example, in particular, you may think of a broad range of answers. Any one of them will do.

II. THESIS; QUOTE; PARAPHRASE; SUMMARY

Read the essay below, which we have written. The exercises that follow all relate to this essay.

Culture & Agriculture

What is culture? What is your culture, your cultural identity? For each one of us, our culture consists of all the ways we do everything we do, from the way we make the food we eat, to the art we make, to the kinds of houses we live in, the kinds of family structures we have, the kinds of work we do and how we do it, the entertainments we pursue and enjoy, and the sports we play. Even the kind of economic system we live in makes up part of our culture. We live in America, where we enjoy the benefits of a multi-cultural society. We live in and among not only our own cultural milieu but among the diversity of many cultures. Where does culture come from? How did all the many cultures in the world, so similar in origin, become so varied in the ways they live?

At the earliest times of human history, we had what we call "culture." The cave paintings at Lascaux represent a cultural artifact of the people who lived in that area about 15,000 years ago. But the word "culture" originally meant, "The science and art of cultivating the soil; including the allied pursuits of gathering in the crops and rearing live stock," or, farming (*Oxford English Dictionary*). Agriculture began "roughly 10,000 years ago" (*Wikipedia*). Before that, humans lived in small tribes, subsisting by hunting and gathering. We had to keep moving from season to season to follow the migration patterns of the animals we hunted and the growing seasons of the wild plants we took from the earth.

Once we figured out how to plant crops, which we call farming, and to raise animals for food, which we call husbandry, everything changed. We could settle down. We could organize our family life. We could live by regular schedules. We knew where we would be from day to day. We had the leisure time and the stable life it takes to organize all of our activities. Agriculture, the art of farming and husbandry, gave birth about 10,000 years ago to our way of life today.

Cultures developed differently around the world, but all cultures share the same elements in common. If we look at the culture of food, we see clearly that, while all cultures have developed food, each culture has developed its own style of preparing food with the ingredients most readily available to it. If you come from an island, you will likely eat a lot of fish. If you come from the mountains, you will likely eat goat or lamb, smaller animals that you can raise in rocky areas.

But beyond what is near at hand, each culture, over thousands of years, has finely tuned its cuisine. We have the leisure to make our food not only nutritious, but also varied and interesting and delicious. If you come from a Middle Eastern culture, your native food will include hummus, pita bread, a lot of lamb dishes, and shish-kebab. If you come from an Hispanic culture, your food will include rice and beans, tortillas, and more red meat from cows. If you come from an Indian background, your native food will include curries, naan bread, spice mixes, and basmati rice.

As we just read in John Seabrook's "Renaissance Pears," central Italian cuisine includes a healthy amount of fruit (102). "Fruit was also a staple of the cooking of the region, in dishes like salt cod with roasted pears, and pork with plums; whole cherries in agrodolce—pickled in vinegar and sugar—were served as chutney with roasted meat" (Seabrook 104).

Just think of how your family values the kind of food you eat, of how you identify with that food, of how you love to offer that kind of food for your friends and families at holidays and celebrations.

In modern life, as the world has become more connected through technology, we all share a universal culture. In the area of food, we now create fusions of foods from different cultures. One lunch truck, in Los Angeles, the Calbi BBQ truck, serves "Korean-style barbecued…corn tortillas" (*Los Angeles Times*). Another truck that carries mostly Japanese food —the Koji Roja truck—also serves "a $2 taco" (*Los Angeles Times).* Tortillas are not originally Korean, while tacos are certainly not typically Japanese! Our cultures are merging together.

Works Cited

-----. Agriculture. *Oxford English Dictionary*. June 2009. August 3, 2009. <dictionary.oed.com. libproxy.chapman.edu:2048/cgi/entry/50055634?quer y_type=word&queryword=culture&fir st=1&max_to_show=10&sort_type=al pha&result_place=1&search_id=9Xdl-xCAnqG-7476&hilite=50055634>.

-----. History of Agriculture. *Wikipedia*. August 2, 2009. August 3, 2009. <en.wikipedia.org/wiki/History_of_agriculture>.

-----. "The Food Trucks Just Keep Rolling." *Los Angeles Times*. July 22, 2009. August 4, 2009. <latimes.com/features/food/la-fo-foodtrucks 22 2009j ul 22,0,7542552.story>.

Seabrook, John. "Renaissance Pears." *The New Yorker.* September 5, 2005.102.

a. What is the thesis of our essay "Culture and Agriculture"?

_____

_____

b. Identify **two** of the five **direct quotes** we have used in our essay "Culture and Agriculture." Copy those **quotes** here.

_____

_____

_____

_____

c. Write a **paraphrase** of the first paragraph from our essay "Culture and Agriculture."

_____

_____

_____

d. Write a **summary** of our entire essay "Culture and Agriculture."

_____

_____

_____

_____

_____

_____

Assignment for Chapter 15

Write a paper where you discuss one of the following:

- Environmental and ecological dangers, especially to food.
- How agriculture in your own region has changed in modern times.
- How we can use art to describe the life around us—either in some historical period or in the present.
- In "Renaissance Pears," John Seabrook writes about different kinds of objects that become central to cultural identity—in this case, the ancient Fiorentina pear tree and Renaissance paintings. Referring to Seabrook's essay and/or your own culture, do you think it is important to preserve the things that make up our cultural identity?
- Some other topic which comes out of your reading of "Renaissance Pears," making sure to get your topic approved by your Professor. Your Professor can help you choose a good **THESIS.**

PART06
the origins of language VI: asian myth

The authors of the essays in our book, *The Assignment,* have all broken silence to speak about things important to them. From the Andaman islands of India, comes a rich myth of the origin of language which relates to our theme of silence and language.

For the Andamanese islanders, the myth of the origin of language begins in silence.

According to this myth, the first man and the first woman on earth lived together in silence. Then a great flood deluged the earth. The Andamanese deity, Pūluga, gave language to the first man and the first woman at their first union following the flood. The people of the Andaman islands still speak that language today, which they call Bojig-yâb. As with all people, the Andamanese refer to their language as the "mother tongue."

Even before the death of the first man or the first woman, their offspring became so numerous that their house could no longer accommodate them. When Pūluga decreed that the only solution was that all the offspring of the first man and the first woman had to leave the household and disperse, the first man and the first woman provided all their children with the necessary things of life: weapons to defend themselves, implements with which to build and sustain their homes, and the all-important fire.

As the children dispersed in pairs throughout the world, Pūluga gave each pair of them their own language, a dialect of the original Bojig-yâb. For the Andamanese, this explains why there are so many languages in the world, and why we can't all understand each other.

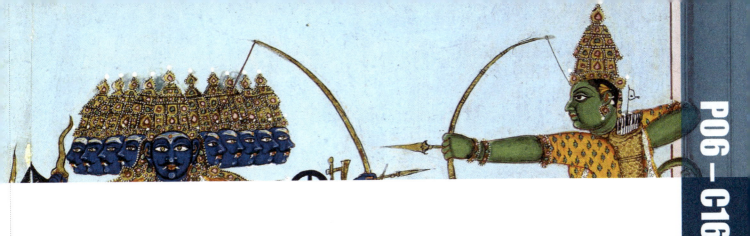

CHAPTER16

the art of language | making the sentence work right

For this last **"ART OF LANGUAGE"** chapter, we first need to do some review.

You already know about **INDEPENDENT CLAUSES** from Chapter 7, page 93. It's important that we review that now.

- An **INDEPENDENT CLAUSE** is any group of words that has a **SUBJECT** and a **PREDICATE** and can stand alone as a sentence.
- The basic building block of a sentence, an **INDEPENDENT CLAUSE,** expresses **ONE THOUGHT** and does so with at least a **SUBJECT + A PREDICATE.**

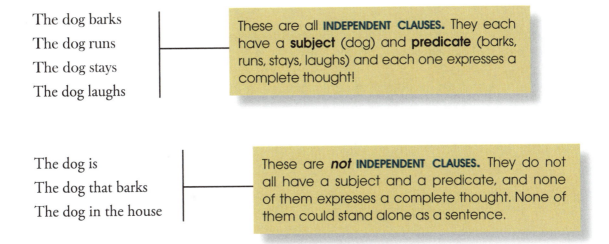

The dog barks
The dog runs
The dog stays
The dog laughs

> These are all **INDEPENDENT CLAUSES.** They each have a **subject** (dog) and **predicate** (barks, runs, stays, laughs) and each one expresses a complete thought!

The dog is
The dog that barks
The dog in the house

> These are *not* **INDEPENDENT CLAUSES.** They do not all have a subject and a predicate, and none of them expresses a complete thought. None of them could stand alone as a sentence.

The group of words below makes up one **INDEPENDENT CLAUSE:**

I come from Chicago = **INDEPENDENT CLAUSE**

This following paragraph is grammatically correct:

I come from Chicago. I love my hometown. Chicago is a great city. Chicago has great sports teams. Chicago has great restaurants. Chicago has fun clubs. Chicago has important art museums. There are parks in Chicago. You can walk along lake Michigan.

But, it doesn't *sound good*. We want our writing to sound good to the ear of our reader. But this paragraph gets clunky, awkward, and boring. We need to vary the **rhythm** of the language by joining independent clauses together.

joining independent clauses

To join two or more INDEPENDENT CLAUSES together, we need help from:

- **the punctuation marks: commas, periods,** and **semi-colons,**
-- and from --
- **coordinating conjunctions.**

COORDINATING CONJUNCTION

In Chapter 4, page 46, we saw that a **conjunction** joins words together. But there are different kinds of **conjunctions.**

A **COORDINATING CONJUNCTION** joins two **independent clauses** together. It <u>coordinates</u> the two **independent clauses.**

The two most common **coordinating conjunctions** are: and; but.

See Index III on page 243 for a list of all the conjunctions in English.

two common errors: run-on sentences

If you join two **independent clauses** together incorrectly, you have made an error that we call a RUN-ON SENTENCE. You could say that when you write a RUN-ON SENTENCE, you write a sentence that just *runs on* without the right punctuation. That can cause confusion. We have two types of RUN-ON SENTENCES:

- fused sentences, and
- comma splices.

If you can learn how to avoid these two common errors that arise from incorrectly joining **independent clauses**, you'll save yourself a lot of trouble.

fused sentences

If you put two or more **independent clauses** together *without* the *comma* and *without* the *coordinating conjunction*, you have a FUSED SENTENCE. If you write:

I come from Chicago   I love my hometown

FIRST INDENDENT CLAUSE   SECOND INDEPENDENT CLAUSE

you have *fused* the two **independent clauses** together, but you have not used the grammatical tools you need to join two **independent clauses**. If you add a *comma* and a *coordinating conjunction:*

COMMA

I come from Chicago, and I love my hometown.

COORDINATING CONJUNCTION

you have a complete sentence.

We can't write:

The dog barks the dog runs home the dog stays home the dog lies on the rug the dog laughs.

It doesn't work. We have joined together **five different** INDEPENDENT CLAUSES, but it doesn't make sense. Let's look at three ways to fix this FUSED SENTENCE.

1. We can add **commas** and **coordinating conjunctions** to join the INDEPENDENT CLAUSES together. (see Chapter 4, page 46):

   *The dog barks***, and** *the dog runs home***, and** *the dog stays home***, and**
   *the dog lies on the rug***, and** *the dog laughs.*

We have used the word **"and"** for all the **coordinating conjunctions** above.

3. You can fix the **fused sentence** with a **semi-colon** that keeps the sentence together, but does not fuse the INDEPENDENT CLAUSES (see Chapter 4, page 46):

> *The dog barks; the dog runs home; the dog stays home;*
> *the dog lies on the rug; the dog laughs.*

2. You can fix the **fused sentence** with **periods** to separate the INDEPENDENT CLAUSES into five different sentences. (see Chapter 4, page 46):

> *The dog barks. The dog runs home. The dog stays home.*
> *The dog lies on the rug. The dog laughs.*

comma splice

If you join two **independent clauses** together with **just** a **comma** (and *no* **coordinating conjunction**), you have a COMMA SPLICE. You have *spliced together* two or more **independent clauses** with *just* a **comma**. You have forgotten the **coordinating conjunction.**

> *The dog barks, the dog runs home, the dog stays home,*
> *the dog lies on the rug, the dog laughs.*

All you need to fix the **comma splice** is a **coordinating conjunction:**

> *The dog barks, and the dog runs home, and the dog stays home,*
> *and the dog lies on the rug, and the dog laughs.*

- or –

You can fix a **comma splice** with a **semi-colon:**

> *The dog barks; the dog runs home; the dog stays home;*
> *the dog lies on the rug; the dog laughs.*

- or –

You can fix a **comma splice** with a **period:**

> *The dog barks. The dog runs home. The dog stays home.*
> *The dog lies on the rug. The dog laughs.*

That's it. Fix a **comma splice** with a **coordinating conjunction**, or with a **semi-colon**, or with a **period**.

Chapter Review: Making the Sentence Work Right

The important factors in making your sentences work right include the following:

- all the parts of speech
- noun/verb agreement
- verb tense
- active verbs vs. passive verbs
- punctuation
- coordinating conjunctions

Independent Clause: Any group of words that has a **SUBJECT** and a **PREDICATE** and can stand alone is an **independent clause**.

To join two or more **independent clauses** together:
- we use **coordinating conjunctions** and
- **commas, periods,** and **semi-colons.**

    The two most common coordinating conjunctions are:
    - and
    - but

Two common run-on sentence types of errors when joining two or more independent clauses:

- You have a **fused sentence** when you join two **independent clauses** without a comma and without a coordinating conjunction.
- You have a **comma splice** when you have joined two **independent clauses** with just a comma but without the coordinating conjunction.

Exercises for Chapter 16

I. RUN-ONS: FUSED SENTENCES

a. In the following sentences, identify the **fused sentences** with the proofreading mark *fs* above where the sentences are **fused**, and then correct them. Fix the capitalization where necessary.

1. I went to the baseball game Johnny and Sally came with me.

   _____

2. The pigeon landed on the picnic table we took our food away.

   _____

3. The summer luau begins in August we go every year.

   _____

4. Janet bought her daughter the stickers her daughter wanted at Sticker Planet her daughter cried anyway.

   _____

5. My mom plays the Lottery every week one day she'll win a million dollars we'll all go away for the week-end.

   _____

6. We were going to meet at the yellow umbrellas on the beach everybody went to the lifeguard station.

   _____

7. You're not supposed to barbecue on the beach we'll do it after the guards leave on second thought, we better not.

_____

8. The heat's getting to us we should move inside.

_____

9. Teenagers text-message on average three thousand times a month how do they find the time?

_____

10. I went out with Bob he is a jerk I went out with Bill he is a jerk I went out with Sam he's cool.

_____

b. In the following sentences, identify the **coordinating conjunction** by writing it in the space provided:

THE COORDINATING CONJUNCTION

1. I did not study Chinese in High School, nor did I study Ugaritic in high school. _____

2. I did not study the African language Xhosa in High School, yet I did study the African language Swahili. _____

3. My uncle could not come out to my soccer game, for he was in bed with a bad case of the flu. _____

4. I told you that I want to go bowling, or I want to go fishing. _____

5. I said I would like to go swimming, but I would not like to play tennis. _____

6. My uncle got well suddenly, so he did come to my soccer game after all. _____

7. I went to visit my Grandmother in August, and I went to visit her again in December. _____

8. When I played tennis last week, I got tennis elbow, so I have to wait to play again until it heals.   _____

9. Yesterday I wrote a poem, but not a short story.   _____

10. Today was better, and I wrote a poem and a short story.   _____

II. RUN-ONS: COMMA SPLICES

Identify the **comma splices** in the following sentences by writing *CS* above the **comma splices** and then fix them.

1. I went to the baseball game, Johnny and Sally came with me.

   _____

2. The pigeon landed on the picnic table, we took our food away.

   _____

3. The summer luau begins in August, we go every year.

   _____

4. Janet bought her daughter the stickers her daughter wanted at Sticker Planet, her daughter cried anyway.

   _____

5. My Mom plays the Lottery every week, she's never won.

   _____

6. We were supposed to meet at the yellow umbrellas on the beach, everyone gathered at the lifeguard station.

   _____

   _____

7. You're not supposed to barbecue there, by the yellow umbrellas, we'll do it after the guards leave. On second thought, we better not.

_____

_____

8. The heat was getting to us, we moved inside.

_____

9. Teenagers text-message on average three thousand times a month, how do they find the time?

_____

10. I went out with Bob, he is a jerk, I went out with Bill, he is a jerk, I went out with Sam, he's cool.

_____

III. FUSED SENTENCES AND COMMA SPLICES

Write *fs* above each **fused sentence** below, and *cs* above each **comma splice** below, and then fix each **fused sentence** and each **comma splice** in the text itself. Fix the capitalization where necessary.

Lotería is a children's card game in Mexico similar to Bingo, it uses illustrated pictures fifty-four different images make up the deck some of the symbols include: el pescado, the fish; il ambor, the drum; il mundo, the world; il diablito, the devil; la coron, the crown; la pera, the pear; el arbol, the tree; il orso, the bear the colorful cards have become popular in Mexican culture they are broadly recognized all over Latin America when they win, players shout "Lotería!"

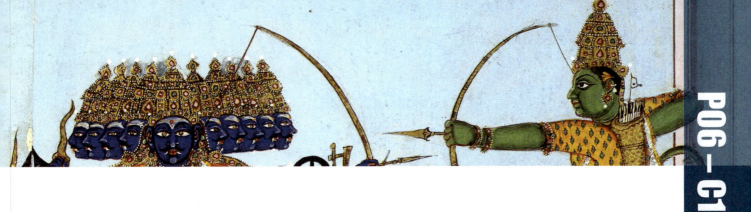

CHAPTER 17

the act of reading | essay as argument

We have said that every reader has a **DIALOGUE** with the text and that every text has a DIALOGUE with its readers. Every text is also in **DIALOGUE** with other texts. The whole process of writing and reading goes over and over in this circle of communication. The reader is in **DIALOGUE** with the text; the text is in **DIALOGUE** with the reader; each text is in **DIALOGUE** with other texts. We might call this a circle of literary communication.

As we participate in this circle of communication, we find that, at the heart of each communication, there is an argument—not in the contrary sense of the word "argument," meaning to disagree, but in the sense that an argument is at the core of what that communication wants to say. The **argument** sets the dialogue in motion.

> **Argument:**
> Latin: *argumentum*
> *Arguare* = to make clear, to prove

Every essay or fiction should make an argument. Your essay should make something clear. It should prove something.

Look at your **THESIS.** There you have your **argument**. The stronger your **argument**, the more you believe in it, the more vividly you will write. Ask yourself: "Why am I writing this essay?" If the answer to that question gives you something you care about, something that raises your passion, then you will write well.

Even *Alice's Adventures in Wonderland* has an **argument**: if a young girl, with a strong imagination, becomes transported to an imaginary, upside-down world, that world could contain all the wild things that this story describes.

215

When we talked about forming a THESIS in Chapter 3, page 31, we saw that a good THESIS cannot just state the obvious. It should also state your **argument**. Read the following essay by William Manchester. His THESIS fits the model we set forth in Chapter 3: it requires **argument**, proof, evidence, and discussion.

Manchester's argument also contains some ambiguity. However, no idea can be all one-sided. We call this "ambiguity," the idea that no viewpoint is one hundred percent true.

Ambiguous:

From the Latin: *Amb* = both ways

agere = to drive

An ambiguous idea or argument can be understood in two or more possible ways.

During World War II[1], Manchester fought as a U.S. Marine in a horrendous battle on the Southern Japanese island of Okinawa. His essay presents us with a difficult ambiguity. On the one hand, he grew up in a patriotic family and in a culture that valued military service and honored both war and those who fought in it. On the other hand, Manchester sees modern warfare, with its machines of destruction, as a meaningless pursuit. While he certainly respects the Marines he served with and honors those who fell in battle, he sees the loss of life in modern warfare as a waste. Manchester has mixed feelings about his subject. Far from being a negative quality of the essay, that ambiguity strengthens the essay, giving us more to think about and challenging us to respond with our own ideas about war. If you can consider all viewpoints in your essay, you will have a stronger piece of work.

Some of the American and Japanese soldiers who fought in the battle of Okinawa organized a memorial service 55 years later. Manchester begins his essay writing about that memorial ceremony.

The Bloodiest Battle of All

ON OKINAWA TODAY, Flag Day will be observed with an extraordinary ceremony: two groups of elderly men, one Japanese, the other American, will gather for a solemn rite. They could scarcely have less in common.

---

[1]World War II, the deadliest conflict in history, with over seven million casualties, took place around the world between 1939–1945. There were two major alliances in the war. The United States fought with the Allies, while Japan fought with the Axis powers.

Their motives are mirror images; each group honors the memory of men who tried to slay the men honored by those opposite them. But theirs is a common grief. After 42 years the ache is still there. They are really united by death, the one great victor in modern war.

They have come to Okinawa to dedicate a lovely monument in remembrance of the Americans, Japanese, and Okinawans killed there in the last and bloodiest battle of the Pacific war. More than 200,000 perished in the 82-day struggle—twice the number of Japanese lost at Hiroshima[2] and more American blood than had been shed at Gettysburg[3]. My own regiment—I was a sergeant in the 29th Marines—lost more than 80 percent of the men who landed on April 1, 1945. Before the battle was over, both the Japanese and American commanding generals lay in shallow graves.

Okinawa lies 330 miles southwest of the southernmost Japanese island of Kyushu; before the war, it was Japanese soil. Had there been no atom bombs—and at that time the most powerful Americans, in Washington and at the Pentagon, doubted that the device would work—the invasion of the Nipponese[4] homeland would have been staged from Okinawa, beginning with a landing on Kyushu to take place Nov. 1. The six Marine divisions, storming ashore abreast, would lead the way. President Truman[5] asked Gen. Douglas MacArthur, whose estimates of casualties on the eve of battles had proved uncannily accurate, about Kyushu. The general predicted a million Americans would die in that first phase.

Given the assumption that nuclear weapons would contribute nothing to victory, the battle of Okinawa had to be fought. No one doubted the need to bring Japan to its knees. But some Americans came to hate the things we had to do, even when convinced that doing them was absolutely necessary; they had never understood the bestial, monstrous and vile means required to reach the objective—an unconditional Japanese surrender. As for me, I could not reconcile the romanticized view of war that runs like a red streak through our literature—and the glowing aura of selfless patriotism that had led us to put our lives at forfeit—with the wet, green hell from which I had barely escaped. Today, I understand. I was there, and was twice wounded. This is the story of what I knew and when I knew it.

***

If all Americans understood the nature of battle, they might be vulnerable to truth. But the myths of warfare are embedded deep in our ancestral memories. By the time children have reached the age of awareness, they regard uniforms, decorations and Sousa marches as exalted, and those who argue otherwise are regarded as unpatriotic.

[2]On August 6, 1945, the Americans dropped the first atomic bomb on the Japanese city Hiroshima, ending World War II.
[3]The Battle of Gettysburg, in the American Civil War, took place July 1–3, 1863. There were over 50,000 casualties in those three days.
[4]Another name for Japan.
[5]Harry S. Truman, 33rd President of the United States, 1945–1953.

General MacArthur, quoting Plato, said: "Only the dead have seen the end of war." One hopes he was wrong, for war, as it had existed for over 4,000 years, is now obsolete. As late as the spring of 1945, it was possible for one man, with a rifle, to make a difference, however infinitesimal, in the struggle to defeat an enemy who had attacked us and threatened our West Coast. The bomb dropped on Hiroshima made that man ludicrous, even pitiful. Soldiering has been relegated to Sartre's theater of the absurd[6]. The image of the man as protector and defender of the home has been destroyed (and I suggest that that seed of thought eventually led women to re-examine their own role in society).

***

dialogue of text with text(s)

We have talked about how you, the reader, have a dialogue with the text that you read. We have talked about how your readers, those who read what you write, have a dialogue with your text. Now, let's look finally at how all texts are always in dialogue with all other texts. Manchester quotes General McArthur, a famous American General who fought in World War II. Gen. McArthur quoted Plato, the 5th–4th Century BCE Greek philosopher, who said, "Only the dead have seen the end of war." These texts from Plato, General McArthur, and William Manchester are all in dialogue with each other.

Manchester, in the full essay reprinted on page 293, recounts some of the history of war, referring to the famous Battle of Agincourt, the Battle of Gettysburg, and others. He got all that information from other texts. Manchester even criticizes the "romanticized view of war that runs like a red streak through our literature," making reference to all American literature, perhaps all of world literature. In his dialogue with those texts that portray a "romanticized view of war that runs like a red streak through our literature," Manchester's dialogue becomes a critique. He disagrees with and criticizes those texts that romanticize war. In the full essay, Manchester gives us an example of this kind of text: John Wayne's 1949 movie about World War II, *The Sands of Iwo Jima,* which glorifies war.

The dialogue among texts is just like the dialogue among people—full of agreement, disagreement, analysis, and discussion. In bringing different texts into his essay, Manchester sustains an active dialogue with other books. Others, in turn, will now quote Manchester in their books/essays, continuing that dialogue into the future.

All texts are in some sense in dialogue with *all other* texts. Let's take an unlikely example to see if this thesis proves true. How can William Manchester's essay "The Bloodiest Battle" enter into a dialogue with, for example, N. Scott Momaday's essay "The Way to Rainy Mountain"? We might, at first glance, say they have nothing in common, nothing to talk about. But, a closer look reveals a different reality. Both write about nature. Momaday writes lovingly about the landscape he comes

---

[6]Jean-Paul Sartre (1905–1980), French writer who, among others, developed the "theater of the absurd" after World War II. Following the immense destruction of WW II, the theater of the absurd represented a view of life that war had made us see that life was meaningless, and that we had to search for new kinds of meaning.

from. "Your imagination comes to life, and this, you think, is where Creation was begun." Momaday portrays nature lovingly, while Manchester, who has a similar reverence for nature, writes about what war does to a beautiful landscape: "All greenery had vanished; as far as one could see, heavy shellfire had denuded the scene of shrubbery. What was left resembled a cratered moonscape. But the craters were vanishing, because the rain had transformed the earth into a thin porridge—too thin even to dig foxholes."

Chapter Review: Essay As Argument

We have a **DIALOGUE WITH THE TEXT** that we read. All texts also carry on a **DIALOGUE** with all other texts. When we read we participate in an ongoing circle of communication.

Every **THESIS** makes an **ARGUMENT.** When you know what the **ARGUMENT** of your essay is, you can write more clearly, and you will write with more passion. But your **ARGUMENT** does not need to be all one-sided; it can be ambiguous, requiring you to write about the different sides of your argument and perhaps incorporating counter-arguments.

Exercises for Chapter 17

I. YOUR THOUGHTS

a. Have you read books or seen films that portray war? Discuss one of these books or films. Does it glorify war? What reactions do you have to the book or film? What images stick with you from that book or film, and why do those images in particular effect you?

b. What images from Manchester's essay stick with you? Why do those images in particular seem important to you?

c. Why did William Manchester write this essay? Remember, we have no "correct" answer to this question. Your thoughts will constitute a "correct" answer.

II. WILLIAM MANCHESTER'S ART

a. To further study William Manchester's style, write *noun* above each **NOUN,** *verb* above each **VERB,** *adjective* above each **ADJECTIVE,** and *adverb* above each **ADVERB.**

1. They have come to Okinawa to dedicate a lovely monument in remembrance of the Americans,

    Japanese, and Okinawans killed there in the last and bloodiest battle of the Pacific war.

2. Before the battle was over, both the Japanese and American commanding generals lay in shallow graves.

3. But some Americans came to hate the things we had to do, even when convinced that doing them was absolutely necessary; they had never understood the bestial, monstrous and vile means required to reach the objective—an unconditional Japanese surrender.

4. One hopes he was wrong, for war, as it had existed for over 4,000 years, is now obsolete.

5. The image of the man as protector and defender of the home has been destroyed (and I suggest that that seed of thought eventually led women to re-examine their own role in society).

6. As for me, I could not reconcile the romanticized view of war that runs like a red streak through our literature—and the glowing aura of selfless patriotism that had led us to put our lives at forfeit—with the wet, green hell from which I had barely escaped.

7. If all Americans understood the nature of battle, they might be vulnerable to truth.

8. Only the dead have seen the end of war.

9. The General predicted a million Americans would die in that first phase.

10. The image of the man as protector and defender of the home has been destroyed.

c. William Manchester uses well-chosen words. List ten words or phrases that strike you as particularly strong and memorable.

1. _____

2. _____

3. _____

4. _____

5. _____

6. _____

7. _____

8. _____

9. _____

10. _____

   b. William Manchester is a great stylist. He writes perfect sentences that establish sounds, rhythms, and patterns in his work that highlight his meaning. But, for the sake of our exercises, we'll give you some William Manchester sentences and ask you to re-write them with different punctuation. Your re-writes may not sound as good as Manchester's writing, but you will have some experience in working with punctuation, and you may come to clearly see just how well Manchester does write.

We will put in **bold type** the part of Manchester's sentences where you might change the punctuation.

Example:

Manchester: On Okinawa today, Flag Day will be observed with an extraordinary ceremony: two groups of elderly men, one Japanese, the other American, will gather for a solemn **rite. They** could scarcely have less in common.

Rewritten: *On Okinawa today, Flag Day will be observed with an extraordinary ceremony: two groups of elderly men, one Japanese, the other American, will gather for a solemn rite, and they could scarcely have less in common.*

1. Manchester: But theirs is a common grief. After 42 years the ache is still there. If all Americans understood the nature of battle, they might be vulnerable to **truth. But the** myths of warfare are embedded deep in our ancestral memories.

   Your re-write: _____

   _____

   _____

2. Manchester: Okinawa lies 330 miles southwest of the southernmost Japanese island of **Kyushu; before** the war, it was Japanese soil.

   Your re-write: _____

   _____

   _____

3. Manchester: President Truman asked Gen. Douglas MacArthur, whose estimates of casualties on the eve of battles had proved uncannily accurate, about **Kyushu. The** general predicted a million Americans would die in that first phase.

   Your re-write: _____

   _____

   _____

4. Manchester: No one doubted the need to bring Japan to its **knees. But** some Americans came to hate the things we had to do, even when convinced that doing them was absolutely **necessary; they** had never understood the bestial, monstrous and vile means required to reach the objective— an unconditional Japanese surrender.

   Your re-write: _____

   _____

   _____

5. Manchester: If all Americans understood the nature of battle, they might be vulnerable to **truth.** **But** the myths of warfare are embedded deep in our ancestral memories.

Your re-write: _____

_____

_____

III. YOUR EXPERIENCE

a. Given what William Manchester has written about war, do you think that war is ever justified? If so, when?

b. William Manchester writes that war is obsolete? Is war obsolete? Why or why not?

c. Would you join the military to fight our country's current wars, in Iraq, Afghanistan, or elsewhere?

IV. ACTIVE READING

a. What is William Manchester's **THESIS?**

_____

_____

b. List three examples of **EVIDENCE** Manchester uses to support his **THESIS.**

1. _____

_____

_____

2. _____

_____

_____

3. _____

_____

_____

c. Manchester writes:

Their motives are mirror images; each group honors the memory of men who tried to slay the men honored by those opposite them. But theirs is a common grief. After 42 years the ache is still there. They are really united by death, the one great victor in modern war.

Explain, in your own words, what Manchester means by this. In other words, interpret it.

_____

_____

_____

_____

_____

CHAPTER18
the act of writing | dialogue with text(s)

Language Expresses Identity

The artists who painted the Cave at Lascaux expressed their identity, their culture, through painting. Even earlier than Lascaux, primitive people expressed their identity through the simple act of putting their hand against a cave wall, and with fingers outspread, splattering paint over their hand. When they took their hand away, an **image** of their hand remained on the wall. In this simple way, they left their mark. Many of us did this in kindergarten. It was the first expression of our identity, of saying who we are, of saying, "I am here."

Throughout our book, we have given you essays by authors who have expressed in language their identity and the identity of their cultures. All of these essays express this kind of identity.

In "The Bloodiest Battle of All," William Manchester sees his own cultural identity as connected to patriotism, and through patriotism, to his heritage of soldiering and war. By the end of the essay, Manchester has come to see war as futile, and patriotism as perhaps a questionable value, but one which he upholds.

From his youth, Manchester remembers the patriotic atmosphere of the Memorial Day parade in his hometown of Attleboro, Mass. He describes all the military pride of that parade, including his own "father, hero of the 5th Marines and Belleau Wood," who "lost his arm in the Argonne." For Manchester, patriotism is rooted in military glory.

Yet, Manchester sees war as miserable and even calls it "obsolete" in modern culture. He criticizes books that see a "romanticized view of war" with the "glowing aura of selfless patriotism." He writes, "Soldiering has been relegated to Sartre's theater of the absurd." If war is obsolete, if soldiering is absurd, is patriotism also dead? Has that patriotism Manchester identified with as a child become no longer a valid identity?

dialogue of the text with the text (s)

If Manchester's essay, "The Bloodiest Battle," is about a search for his own identity as he discusses patriotism, soldiering, family, and warfare, each of the other essays we have read also searches for a personal and cultural identity in some form. All of these texts, M. Scott Momaday's "The Way to Rainy Mountain," Jack London's "The Story of an Eyewitness: The San Francisco Earthquake," Diane Ackerman's "Modern Love," Lewis Carroll's *Alice's Adventures in Wonderland,* John Seabrook's "Renaissance Pears," and William Manchester's "The Bloodiest Battle" carry on a dialogue with each other about identity.

Both Manchester's and London's essays are about the *loss of* some aspect of their identity. Manchester sees his identity as a soldier and a patriot, formed in his youth, fade into insignificance. London sees his identity as he identifies with San Francisco, the city of his youth, destroyed by earthquake and fire. This identification with the city may be why London gives his essay the dramatic title "The Story of an Eyewitness: The San Francisco Earthquake." It may be the reason that he writes in such powerful terms of observation. We could form a **THESIS** from this analysis: William Manchester and Jack London both write about a loss of identity based on historical and natural changes they witness.

Or, we could form a broader **THESIS** and use their pieces as **EVIDENCE** for that **THESIS**:

In our youth, we form personal identities based on the culture around us. As that culture changes, we are challenged to re-think our own identities.

Before we begin writing, let's review the **STEPS FOR DEVELOPING AN ESSAY.**

PARTS OF AN ESSAY: STEPS FOR DEVELOPING YOUR ESSAY

STEP 1. Present your thesis

STEP 2. Present examples as evidence that *prove* your thesis

STEP 3. Discuss the evidence

STEP 4. Discuss *how* the evidence proves your thesis

STEP 5. Move on to further develop your evidence
or
Present new evidence

Writing & Identity

In our youth, we form personal identities based on the culture around us. As that culture changes, we are challenged to re-think our own identities.

William Manchester, who was a "sergeant in the 29th Marines" during World War II, came from a patriotic and military culture in Massachusetts (Manchester). During his childhood, in the town of Attleboro, the whole town "would turn out to cheer the procession on Memorial Day" (Manchester). That procession included the local police and those veterans still living from all the American wars going back to the Civil War of 1860-1865. It also included William Manchester's own father, who, in World War I (1917–1919), was a "hero of the 5th Marines" (Manchester). Manchester's childhood was filled with noble images of patriotism, soldiering, and war.

Jack London was born in a house on 3rd and Brannan Street in San Francisco in 1876 (London), 46 years before William Manchester was born in Massachusetts. As opposed to Manchester's stable youth, drenched in the social values of duty and service, London's turbulent early years began with his birth. When Jack London's unmarried mother, Flora Wellman, became pregnant by William Chaney, Chaney demanded she have an abortion. In despair, Flora Wellman tried to commit suicide by shooting herself. She failed in her suicide attempt, but when she gave birth to Jack, she turned him over for care to an ex-slave, Virginia Prentiss. Eventually, Jack's mother, Flora, took him back to raise him, but Virginia Prentiss remained an important figure in Jack London's life. Jack's mother, Flora, eventually married John London, a partially disabled Civil War veteran, and Jack became Jack London (London).

After living in different parts of San Francisco and the Bay Area, London went to college at the University of California at Berkeley, across the Bay from San Francisco. After finding his biological father through newspaper accounts of his mother's attempted suicide, his biological father, William Cheney, denied that Jack was his son. London, devastated, dropped out of college and traveled north to Alaska ("Jack London").

Eventually, London became a successful journalist and novelist, writing some of the most important stories and novels we have in American Literature. As he grew up, he had little stability. The only thing that remained constant throughout his youth, indeed, throughout his life, was San Francisco, the city in which he was born, and to which he often returned.

Given the stability of William Manchester's childhood, it comes as no surprise that he chose a military life. As he proudly watched his father in his dress uniform march in the Memorial Day parades of Manchester's youth, Manchester's "own military future was already determined" (Manchester). Manchester had formed his identity as a patriot, a soldier, a Marine. After World War II, however, Manchester came to question that identity. Always proud of it, he yet realized that it was an old-fashioned identity of a world gone by. For war, what Winston Churchill had once called "cruel and magnificent," had become just "cruel and squalid." Modern technology, especially the atomic bomb that fell first in World War II at Hiroshima, Japan, had made war "obsolete" (Manchester).

In 1907, 31 years after Jack London's birth in San Francisco, the massive San Francisco earthquake demolished the city that had given him the greatest stability of his youth, it had given him an identity and a sense of himself that he cherished. When called to write about that earthquake, London took the opportunity to express his love for the city. He wrote about the earthquake and about the city with a tremendous power. His gives his piece an almost Biblical title, "The Story of an Eyewitness: The San Francisco Earthquake." He becomes the eyewitness not only to the destruction of San Francisco, in which his house at 3rd and Bannon Street burned down, but to the turbulence of his own origins. His turbulence has now become the chaos of the earthquake. He writes that, "Not in history has a modern imperial city been so completely destroyed. San Francisco is gone. Nothing remains of it but memories and a fringe of dwelling-houses on its outskirts" (London). He writes to salvage his own memories from the ruins of his city.

William Manchester also writes to salvage the memories of his youth from the passing of the values and sense of history and duty that gave him his identity. These essays—"The Bloodiest Battle of All" and "The Story of an Eyewitness: The San Francisco Earthquake"—in dialogue with each other—speak to and with each other. They say to each other: though time changes and disrupts our identities, through writing we can salvage our sense of who we were, and develop a sense of who are.

Works Cited

Manchester, William. "The Bloodiest Battle of All." *New York Times* 14 June 1987. *New York Times.* 21 August 2009. <http://www.nytimes.com/1987/06/14/magazine/the-bloodiest-battle-of-all.html>. 30 May 2010.

----------. "Jack London." *Wikipedia.* 21 August 2009. <http://en.wikipedia.org/wiki/Jack london>. 30 May 2010.

London, Jack. "Story of an Eyewitness: The San Francisco Earthquake." *Collier's* (2006). *The Jack London Online Collection.* Roy Tennant and Clarice Stasz. Web. 30 May 2010. <http://london.sonoma.edu/Writings/Journalism/sfearthquake.html>.

Chapter Review: Dialogue of Text with Text(s)

Language Expresses Identity

We use language as a tool to struggle with and express our identity.

Parts of an Essay: Steps for Developing Your Essay

STEP 1. <u>Present</u> your thesis

STEP 2. <u>Present</u> examples as evidence that *prove* your thesis

STEP 3. <u>Discuss</u> the evidence

STEP 4. <u>Discuss</u> *how* the evidence proves your thesis

STEP 5. Move on to <u>further develop</u> your evidence
or
<u>Present</u> new evidence

Exercises for Chapter 18

I. Language & Identity

a. In what way does N. Scott Momaday seek to discover his own identity in "The Way to Rainy Mountain?"

b. In what way does Diane Ackerman seek to discover her identity in "Modern Love?"

c. In what way does Alice seek to discover her identity in *Alice's Adventures in Wonderland?*

d. What aspect of your own identity, cultural or personal or both, would you most want *not* to lose?

II. Dialogue of Text with Text(s)

a. Pick any two movies you have recently seen. How do they engage in a **DIALOGUE** with each other? What are they both talking about? Even if you choose two movies about different things, you will soon see that they have something to say to each other.

b. Choose any two articles from the front page of today's newspaper. How do they engage in a **DIALOGUE** with each other? Even if you choose two articles that seem to have little in common, you will soon discover that they have something to say to each other.

c. How might the "text" of the Salvador Dalí painting in Chapter 12, page 162, engage in a dialogue with the cave painting from Lascaux in the Origins of Language I on page 1. Let your imagination wander as you put these two artworks, 15,000 years apart, together in dialogue.

Assignment for Chapter 18

Write a paper in which you either:

Look at any two essays in our book and develop a THESIS about the role of identity in those two essays

    - **or** –

Look at any two essays in our book and develop a THESIS about the role in those two essays of either:

- environment and culture;
- time and change;
- war and reflection;
- the meeting of cultures;
- art.

Remember: as always, your essay depends on your THESIS. Make sure you have chosen a good thesis, one that is narrow enough, but requires argument, proof, evidence, and discussion.

APPENDIX
the origins of language vii: a scientific explanation

Linguists, those who study language, generally agree that we cannot know the exact origins of language. We know that we need certain biological features in order to speak—tongue, teeth, voice box, etc.—and that we have also developed mental processes to build language. Some animals have these qualities, but they have not developed language. Certain birds can imitate human sounds but do not have language. Animals do communicate by use of sounds and gestures, but of all the creatures on earth, language belongs to humans alone. When we define language as the invention of words organized into systems of speech and writing by grammar and syntax, we see that we humans have accomplished something remarkable.

Any child can learn to speak any language. Each child will will learn the language of the culture into which he or she is born. This very complex learning process involves highly developed brain capacity and intelligence, yet we all do it naturally.

We have so many languages on earth that it is hardly possible to count them. As the world grows more and more into a global village, some of the languages spoken by small groups of people are disappearing. Our language, English, belongs to the Indo-European group, which stretches all the way from Iceland down through Europe into parts of the Middle East and even into Southeast Asia and China. It is incredible to think that English belongs to this same group of languages, and that we are connected to all these people linguistically.

We divide the Indo-European languages into ten sub-groups, one of which is Torcharian, a now extinct language from China; Greek is an Indo-European language; the Romance languages are all Indo-European (there are about 50 Romance languages, and they include French, Spanish, and Italian); Celtic is an Indo-European language; and the Germanic languages, which include our own English, as well as German, Dutch, Danish, Swedish, Norwegian, and Icelandic are all part of this Indo-European family tree.

If such a large number of languages are all connected, perhaps the myths are true that all humans once spoke the same language. But linguists do not believe we all spoke one original language. Not all languages are connected. But we do all share in common the ownership of language itself. And we do all share the desire and the ability to communicate in language, in speech and in writing.

235

INDEX01

proofreading marks

PROOFREADING MARK	MEANING
ro	run-on sentence
FS	fused sentence
CS	comma splice
P	a punctuation error (used by some proofreaders/Professors to indicate a run-on sentence [instead of *ro*], or a fused sentence [instead of *FS*], or a comma splice [instead of *CS*]; it indicates a punctuation error that needs further looking into)
va	verb agreement error (the verb form does not agree with the subject of the sentence)
t	verb tense error (the verb is in the wrong tense)
sp	spelling error
FRAG	sentence fragment (not a complete sentence: missing a subject or a verb or it is not a complete thought)
ww	wrong word (you have used the wrong word for the meaning you intended)
pref.	pronoun reference error (we don't know to which noun your pronoun refers)

℞	take out the letter(s) or word(s)
( )	suggest that you take out the letter or the word or the phrase or the punctuation mark
⌣	close-up (an extra space between letters or words)
#	insert a space (between letters or words or lines)
¶	begin a new paragraph
‖	phrases or clauses are not parallel
∧	tells you where to insert something as indicated
stet	leave it alone (the proofreader made an error in his/her proofreading mark, so disregard it)
mix	mixed construction
poss	possesive
pv	passive verb

INDEX02

pronouns

PERSONAL PRONOUNS

SUBJECTIVE:

I	We
You	You
She/He/It	They

OBJECTIVE

Me	Us
You	You
Her/Him/Them	Them

We use **SUBJECTIVE PRONOUNS** when the pronoun is the **subject** of the sentence.

You kissed me.

We use **OBJECTIVE PRONOUNS** when the pronoun is the **object** of the sentence.

You kissed **me.**

POSSESSIVE PRONOUNS

My/Mine	Our/Ours
Your/Yours	Your/Yours
Her/Hers/His/Its	Their/Theirs

We use **POSSESSIVE PRONOUNS** when the pronoun indicates possession:

I took **my** bat and went home.

REFLEXIVE PRONOUNS

Myself   Ourselves

Yourself   Yourselves

Herself/Himself/Itself   Themselves

We use **REFLEXIVE PRONOUNS** to emphasize another noun or pronoun:

The mayor **herself** came to the game.

RELEATIVE PRONOUNS

Who

Whom

Whose

Which

That

We use **RELATIVE PRONOUNS** to introduce a subordinate clause that acts as an adjective:

The mayor **who** came to our game wasn't reelected.

INTERROGATIVE PRONOUNS

Who

Whom

Whose

Which

What

We use **INTERROGATIVE PRONOUNS** to introduce a question:

Who came to our game? **Which** mayor came to our game? Was it the mayor who didn't get reelected?

DEMONSTRATIVE PRONOUNS

This

That

These

Those

We use **DEMONSTRATIVE PRONOUNS** to point to a noun:

When the mayor came to our game, she sat in **that** chair.

INDEFINITE PRONOUNS

All	Either	Nobody	Some
Another	Everybody	None	Somebody
Any	Everyone	No one	Someone
Anybody	Everything	No thing	Some thing
Anyone	Few	Nothing	Something
Anything	Many	One	
Each	Neither	Several	

We use **INDEFINITE PRONOUNS** to refer to nonspecific persons or things:

Few people knew it was the mayor when she came to our game. She brought **someone** with her, but **no one** knew who that person was.

RECIPROCAL PRONOUNS

Each other
One another

We use **RECIPROCAL PRONOUNS** to refer to individual parts of a plural noun.

We all helped **each other** to win that game. The mayor and her friend hugged **one another** at our victory. Then I took my bat, and I went home.

INDEX03

conjunctions

I. COORDINATING CONJUNCTIONS

These join things that are grammatically equal. They are:

| and | but | or | nor | for | so | yet |

<u>Some Examples:</u>

I went to the store **and** to my friend's house.

I went to the store **but** not to my friend's house.

I went to the store, and I went to my friend's house.

II. CORRELATIVE CONJUNCTIONS

These *pairs* of conjunctions also connect grammatically equal things, but with a different meaning. They are:

either....or   **whether....or**   **both....and**   **neither....nor**   **not only....but also**

<u>Some Examples:</u>

I went to **either** the store **or** to my friend's house.

I went to **neither** the store **nor** to my friend's house.

I went to **both** the store **and** to my friend's house.

I went **not only** to the store **but also** to my friend's house.

III. Subordinating Conjunctions

These conjunctions join a subordinate clause to the sentence. They are:

after	although	as	as if	because
before	even though	how	if	in order that
once	rather than	since	so that	than
that	though	unless	until	when
where	whether	while	why	

Some Examples:

It was **as if** I were going to the store and to my friend's house.

I went to the store **although** I also went to my friend's house.

I went to the store **rather** than going to my friend's house.

I went to the store **where** I saw my friend, Julie.

I went to the store **before** going to my friend's house.

IV. Conjunctive Adverbs

Conjunctive Adverbs join independent clauses. They are:

accordingly	also	anyway	besides	certainly	consequently
conversely	finally	furthermore	hence	however	incidentally
indeed	instead	likewise	meanwhile	moreover	nevertheless
next	nonetheless	once	otherwise	similarly	specifically
still	subsequently	then	therefore	thus	

Some Examples:

I went to the store; **likewise,** I went to my friend's house.

I went to the store; **nevertheless,** I went to my friend's house.

I went to the store; **still,** I went to my friend's house.

I was going to go to the store; **instead,** I went to my friend's house.

INDEX04
prepositions

I. THE COMMON PREPOSITIONS IN THE ENGLISH LANGUAGE:

about	before	concerning	into	outside
above	behind	considering	like	over
across	below	despite	near	past
after	beneath	down	next	plus
against	beside	during	of	regarding
along	besides	except	off	respecting
among	between	for	on	round
around	beyond	from	onto	since
as	but	in	opposite	than
at	by	inside	out	through
throughout	under	unto	within	till
underneath	up	without	to	unlike
upon	toward	until	with	

A few prepositions are made up of more than one word:

along with

as well as

in addition to

next to

INDEX05

how prepositional phrases work

PREPOSITIONAL PHRASES work in three different ways:

1. As **adjectives**
2. As **adverbs**
3. As **nominals**

As adjectives:

An **adjective** describes a **noun.**

A **PREPOSITIONAL PHRASE** is not an **adjective**, but it can work like an **adjective** when it describes a **noun**:

I saw the guy **with the pony tail** you were talking about.

> guy = **noun**
> with the pony tail = **prepositional phrase** that describes the **noun** (guy)

I saw the horse **beside the barn**.

> horse = **noun**
> beside the barn = **prepositional phrase** that describes the **noun** (horse)

As adverbs:

Adverbs describe **verbs**.

A **PREPOSITIONAL PHRASE** is not an **adverb**, but it can work like an **adverb** when it describes a **verb**:

I played tennis **with my brother**.

> played = **verb**
> with my brother = **prepositional phrase** that describes the **verb** (played)

The car started **after we used** the jumper cables.

> started = **verb**
> after we used = **prepositional phrase** that describes the **verb** (started)

As nominals

- What's a **nominal?**

  A **nominal** is a word—any word or group of words—that *acts like* a noun.

  (A **noun** names a person, place, thing, or idea. So a nominal is any word or group of words that names a person, place, thing, or idea.)

- The **nominal** is a special case of prepositional phrase that we use <u>only</u> with the verb **be**.

A **PREPOSITIONAL PHRASE** is not a **nominal**, but it can work like a **nominal** when we use it with the **verb** *be*, <u>and</u> it takes the place of a **noun**:

The restaurant is on the corner.

> The restaurant = **noun**
> is = **verb** *be*
> on the corner = **prepositional phrase** that stands for the **noun** (restaurant)

The boy is before the girl in line.

> The boy = **noun**
> is = **verb be**
> before the girl = **prepositional phrase** that stands for the **noun** (boy)

INDEX06

irregular verbs

BASE/SIMPLE PRESENT TENSE	SIMPLE PAST TENSE	PAST PARTICIPLE
arise	arose	arisen
awake	awoke	awoken
am / is / are	was, were	been
bear	bore	borne
beat	beat	beaten
become	became	become
begin	began	begun
bend	bent	bent
bet	bet	bet
bind	bound	bound
bite	bit	bitten
bleed	bled	bled
blow	blew	blown
break	broke	broken
breed	bred	bred
bring	brought	brought
build	built	built
burn	burned, burnt	burned, burnt
buy	bought	bought
cast	cast	cast
catch	caught	caught
choose	chose	chosen
cling	clung	clung
come	came	come

cost	cost	cost
creep	crept	crept
cut	cut	cut
deal	dealt	dealt
dig	dug	dug
dive	dived, dove	dived
do	did	done
drag	dragged	dragged
draw	drew	drawn
dream	dreamed, dreamt	dreamed, dreamt
drink	drank	drunk
drive	drove	driven
drown	drowned	drowned
eat	ate	eaten
fall	fell	fallen
feed	fed	fed
feel	felt	felt
fight	fought	fought
find	found	found
fit	fit	fit
flee	fled	fled
fling	flung	flung
fly	flew	flown
forbid	forbade	forbidden
forget	forgot	forgotten, forgot
forgive	forgave	forgiven
forsake	forsook	forsaken
forswear	forswore	forsworn
foretell	foretold	foretold
freeze	froze	frozen
get	got	gotten, got
give	gave	given
go	went	gone
grind	ground	ground
grow	grew	grown
hang (suspend)	hung	hung
have	had	had
hang (execute)	hanged	hanged
hear	heard	heard

hide	hid	hidden
hold	held	held
hurt	hurt	hurt
keep	kept	kept
kneel	knelt, kneeled	knelt, kneeled
knit	knit, knitted	knit, knitted
know	knew	known
lay (put)	laid	laid
lead	led	led
leap	leapt, leaped	leapt, leaped
learn	learnt, learned	learnt, learned
leave	left	left
lend	lent	lent
let	let	let
lie (recline)	lay	lain
light	lighted, lit	lighted, lit
lose	lost	lost
make	made	made
mean	meant	meant
meet	met	met
mislay	mislaid	mislaid
mislead	misled	misled
misspeak	misspoke	misspoken
misspend	misspent	misspent
pay	paid	paid
prove	proved	proved, proven
put	put	put
quit	quit	quit
read	read	read
ride	rode	ridden
ring	rang	rung
rise	rose	risen
run	ran	run
saw	sawed	sawn
say	said	said
see	saw	seen
seek	sought	sought
sell	sold	sold
send	sent	sent

set	set	set
shake	shook	shaken
shed	shed	shed
shine	shone	shone
shoe	shod	shod
shoot	shot	shot
show	showed	shown
shrink	shrank	shrunk, shrunken
shut	shut	shut
sing	sang	sung
sink	sank	sunk
sit	sat	sat
slay	slew	slain
sleep	slept	slept
slide	slid	slid
sling	slung	slung
speak	spoke	spoken
spend	spent	spent
spin	spun	spun
spread	spread	spread
spring	sprang	sprung
stand	stood	stood
steal	stole	stolen
stick	stuck	stuck
sting	stung	stung
stink	stank	stunk
strike	struck	struck, stricken
string	strung	strung
strive	strove	striven
swear	swore	sworn
sweep	swept	swept
swim	swam	swum
swing	swung	swung
take	took	taken
teach	taught	taught
tear	tore	torn
tell	told	told
think	thought	thought
throw	threw	thrown

tread	trod	trodden
wake	woke	woken
wear	wore	worn
understand	understood	understood
win	won	won
wind	wound	wound
wring	wrung	wrung
write	wrote	written

INDEX07

helping verbs

We will give you the basic idea of helping verbs here. As the use of helping verbs gets complicated and extensive, we will let you go to another, more detailed source, such as a grammar handbook, for all the information on helping verbs, all the tenses you can create with them, and how to use them.

When we conjugate verbs (Chapter 10 page 133), we indicate *when* something takes place. If we want more complicated indications of time, we use helping verbs. For example, we might use the simple past tense:

I **worked** in the garden, and then you called on the telephone.—PAST TENSE

But if your friend called *while* you were working in your garden, you would say:

I **had been working** in the garden when you called on the telephone.—PAST PERFECT
CONTINUOUS TENSE

To create that past perfect continuous tense, you need the helping verbs "had been."

Helping verbs help the main verb in the sentence to convey precisely the time something happens.

We have 23 helping verbs in English. We categorize them into two groups:

- Forms of *have, do,* and *be*;
- Modal verbs

Have, do, be

We use *have, do,* and *be* to more precisely define the time we are talking about in the sentence.

When we use *have*, *do,* and *be*, we conjugate them just as we would any other verb.

I have been working in the garden all day.

She has been working in her garden all day.

I had been working in the garden all day.

She had been working in the garden all day.

Modals

The other 9 helping verbs we call modals.

We use modals to express more precisely the meaning of the main verb in the sentence.

We don't conjugate the modals when we use them as helping verbs.

We have nine modals in English:

can	shall
could	should
may	will
might	would
must	

For example:

You should help your sister with her homework.

You must help your sister with her homework.

You will help your sister with her homework.

The main verb in the sentence, "help," needs some help from a helping verb to express more precisely what we are talking about.

INDEX**08**

punctuation

(See Chapter 13 [page 171] for the basic
punctuation marks.)

Further rules for commas

a. To set off NONRESTRICTIVE ELEMENTS.

(A **non-restrictive** element describes a **noun** but does not restrict, or limit, its meaning.)

Don't use commas with restrictive elements.

(A **restrictive** element *limits* the noun it describes: "The pastry I had this morning, with peach filling, was not so good.")

Example:
The pastry I had this morning at the Corner Café, good with coffee, was reasonably priced.

Exercise:
The lion trained by Gustavo Escabaldo escaped from the zoo at about 11:30 this morning, its mane flying in the wind.

b. To set off **transitional expressions**

(A **transitional expression**, which links two ideas in a sentence together, shows the reader how one idea relates to another, so that the sentence is **one thought**, one idea.)

Example:
They had several new pastries on display this morning at the Corner Café, for example, an Italian kind that looked divine!

Exercise:
When the lion escaped, the zoo was open; even so, however, there weren't many guests yet.

c. To set off **parenthetical expressions**

(A **parenthetical expression** adds some extra but non-essential information to the sentence. You could set it off by parentheses, but the commas make it a more casual intrusion into the sentence.)

Example:
Italian pastries, I believe, can be the best in the world.

Exercise:
The lion according to zoo officials eats 20 pounds of meat per day and should not be hungry.

d. To set off contrasted elements

Example:
Italian breakfast pastries, unlike American muffins and donuts, are generally not so sweet.

Exercise:
The lion not the elephant escaped from the zoo this morning.

e. To set off **absolute phrases**

(An **absolute phrase** modifies the whole sentence)

Example:
Italian-style pastries have become more popular here, the Corner Café alone having sold more than a hundred and ten last week.

Exercise:
The lion lay down on the lawn more than 12 miles from the zoo not so far for the lion.

f. To set off nouns of direct address

Example:
Excuse me, Mr. Bonelli, when you get a chance, I'll have a brioche, please.

Exercise:
Look over there Sgt. Battle the lion's lying on that lawn!

g. To set off **interrogative tags**

(You tag an **interrogative tag** on to a previous phrase or sentence, making a question [interrogative] that emphasizes the previous phrase or sentence)

Example:
Have you had the new Italian pastries they are making at the Corner Café? They're terrific, aren't they?

Exercise:
I actually sat down on the lawn with the lion and petted him. It's incredible isn't it?

h. To set off mild interjections (see Chapter 4)

Example:
You like the Corner Café? Well, I'll meet you there tomorrow morning, all right?

Exercise:
I sat down right there on the lawn with the lion. Now isn't that incredible?

i. To set off the words "yes" and "no"

Example:
Yes, I'll have a brioche and a small coffee, please.
No, I don't take cream in my coffee.

Exercise:
Yes the lion escaped from the zoo this morning.
No the giraffe did not escape along with the lion.

j To separate the elements of a <u>complete</u> date

Example:
On December 25, 2010, the Corner Café will deliver a box of pastries to our house.
But not in: In December 2010, I will be twenty-one.

Exercise:
The newspapers mistakenly reported that the lion escaped from the zoo on December 25 2010. Actually, the lion escaped on June 25 2010. We recovered the lion after midnight, on June 26 2010.

k. In addresses

Example:
You can mail the check for the pastries to the Corner Café at 1201 Main Street, Cincinnati, Ohio 45202.

Exercise:
If you want a photograph of me on the lawn with the lion, send me a stamped, self addressed envelope to 22 Main Street Lionsville Ohio.

l. With titles

Example:
Peter Doyle, MD, arrived at the Corner Café just as I was leaving. Priscilla Davis, Ph.D., was also just leaving.

Exercise:
When we walked the lion back to the zoo, Peter Manetti Zoo Director greeted us. He had called in Angeline Azzaro MD for an examination. Dr. Azzaro then called her colleague, Leonard Saltzman DVM to confirm her appraisal of the lion's good health.

m. With numbers (**but not** in years, zip codes, street numbers, telephone numbers)

Example:
The owner of the Corner Café told me he eventually expected to make another $10,000 - $15,000 annually on his new Italian pastries, bringing his total profit to about $200,000 per year. "Not bad," he said. "Not bad," I had to agree, handing him $4.75 for my coffee and brioche.

Exercise:
The zoo offered me a $5000 reward for finding the escaped lion. The newspapers reported that over 4000 people visited the zoo the day after the escape, and that zoo attendance had increased overall by about 15000 visitors over the year.

n. To set off tag lines in direct quotations

Example:
"I'll meet you at the Corner Café at 11:00," he said.

Exercise:
"I'm just glad to be back where I belong to," the lion said. "The streets aren't very exciting for me. And here, they treat me like a prince."

—Dash

Indicates a pause in the sentence to separate parts of the sentence and to give emphasis to the part set off with a dash, or to add something to the end of your sentence that you want to emphasize

Example:
I had the best breakfast this morning—coffee and a great pastry—at the corner café.

Exercise:
The zoo offered me a reward for finding the escaped lion $5,000.

: Colon (Further Uses):

Use the colon to:

• summarize, or restate what you've just written

Example:
The Corner Café is close: right around the block.

Exercise:
The zoo offered me a reward for finding the escaped lion, but I turned it down I didn't want it.

• To add an idea that completes or explains or further describes what you've just written (an appositive).

Example:
The Corner Café just opened: right around the block.

Exercise:
The zoo offered me a reward for finding the escaped lion a big reward!

• To introduce a quote

Example:
When I met him at the Corner Café, he said: "Not bad, not a bad joint."

Exercise:
The zoo Director thanked me profusely "You've done an amazing thing for us!"

- After a salutation in a formal letter:

Example:
Dear Corner Café:

Dear Madam Senator:

Exercise:
Dear Director

Dear Lion

- To indicate hours, minutes, and seconds:

Example:
If you can meet me today, I'll meet you at the Corner Café at 2:30 p.m., or, to be exact, at 2:30:00.

Exercise:
They usually feed the lion every day at exactly 3 25 in the afternoon.

- Or, to separate items such as:
- In math, between the numbers of a ratio:

Example:
This map will show you how to get to the Corner Café. The ratio of miles on the map is 25:1.

Exercise:
I drew this map of our lion-chase. It shows the route we took, including back-turns and retracings. It has a ratio of about 100 1.

'Apostrophe

Use the apostrophe to make a *contraction,* making one word out of two words

Example:
I had the best breakfast this morning at the corner café, but I **can't** remember what I had. I **didn't** have eggs, and I **couldn't** have had bacon, and I **wouldn't** have had granola, so I must have had coffee and a pastry. **I'll** have to play at least one extra set of tennis today to work off the pastry.

Exercise:
I ll tell you all about the lion-chase if you ll promise me to go visit the lion to see for yourself what he looks like.

( ) Parentheses

Use parentheses for two things:

- To add some extra, nonessential thoughts to your sentence

Example:
Early this morning, at the Corner Café, I had a coffee ($2.75), a brioche ($3.25), and a fruit cup ($2.75). I spent ($8.75) more than for lunch ($5.50).

Exercise:
I got home late, after midnight, and my parents were watching TV the Late Night Show but actually anxiously waiting for me.

[ ] Brackets

- Use brackets to set off any words <u>you insert</u> into a direct quote

Example:
As my tennis coach told me: "Play your heart out. Then, whether you win or lose (or draw), you've won." After the game today, he wanted to give me some pointers. "I'll meet you," he said, "in an hour at the usual spot (the Corner Café)."

Exercise:
Later, I told my best friend: "My parents heard a news briefing that some animal a lion had escaped the zoo and that some zoo officials, some police officers, and at least one citizen me were in pursuit."

. . . Ellipsis

- Use an ellipsis to indicate that you've left something out the middle of a direct quote

Example:
After the game today, my tennis coach wanted to give me some pointers. He called after me as I was leaving the court: "I'll meet you … at the usual spot (the Corner Café)."

Exercise:
My parents said, "We'd like to believe you. You're always an honest kid. But to expect us to believe you were chasing a lion well, go get a good night's sleep and we'll talk in the morning."

• To indicate a hesitation or interruption in someone's speech

Example:
"I was at the Corner Café, planning to eat alone, when…well, as you know, George came in."

Exercise:
My friend called me to ask me, "So, are you an official Lion Watcher now   or what?

• To indicate an unfinished thought

Example:
After a restless night, I wanted to have breakfast alone at my favorite spot, the Corner Café, where they know me and always take good care of me, but, well….

Exercise:
I told my friend that I was a   Well, I wasn't sure what I was anymore.

/ Slash

• Use the slash to separate items that go together in a pair

Example:
After a restless night, I wanted to have breakfast alone at my favorite spot, the Corner Café, where they know me and always take good care of me. But when I went to my usual corner window table and saw there were already a knife/fork/napkin placed there, I sat down anyway. No one came in, so I was free to write in my journal and get my act together for the day.

Exercise:
I have now become a great fan of zoos savannahs game reserves, anywhere you might find a lion.

ESSAYS

THE WAY TO RAINY MOUNTAIN

N. Scott Momaday

Navarro Scott Momaday was born on the Kiowa Reservation in Lawton, Oklahoma in 1934. His novel, *House Made of Dawn,* won the Pulitzer Prize for fiction in 1969. Momaday has been featured in television documentaries as a narrator of Native American history and culture (*The West* and *Battle of the Little Bighorn*). As Poet Laureate of Oklahoma from July 2007–January 2009, Momaday wanted to "share my love of poetry…an ancient and wonderful dimension of language…with the people of Oklahoma." In 2007, President George W. Bush awarded Mr. Momaday the National Medal of Arts.

Our selection comes from *The Way to Rainy Mountain* (1969), a book that tells the story of Momaday's own tribe, the Kiowas, from their origins in what is now Canada to their 1867 surrender to the United States Calvary. Under the Treaty of Medicine Lodge, the United States granted the Kiowas land on which they still live near Rainy Mountain, Oklahoma.

———

A single knoll rises out of the plain in Oklahoma, north and west of the Wichita Range. For my people, the Kiowas, it is an old landmark, and they gave it the name Rainy Mountain. The hardest weather in the world is there. Winter brings blizzards, hot tornadic winds arise in the spring, and in summer the prairie is an anvil's edge. The grass turns brittle and brown, and it cracks beneath your feet. There are green belts along the rivers and creeks, linear groves of hickory and pecan, willow and witch hazel. At a distance in July or August the steaming foliage seems almost to writhe in fire. Great green and yellow grasshoppers are everywhere in the tall grass, popping up like corn to sting the flesh, and tortoises crawl about on the red earth, going nowhere in the plenty of time. Loneliness is an aspect of the land. All things in the plain are isolate; there is no confusion of objects in the eye, but *one* hill or tree or *one* man. To look upon that landscape in the early morning, with the sun at your back, is to lose the sense of proportion. Your imagination comes to life, and this, you think, is where Creation was begun.

I returned to Rainy Mountain in July. My grandmother had died in the spring, and I wanted to be at her grave. She had lived to be very old and at last infirm. Her only living daughter was with her when she died, and I was told that in death her face was that of a child.

I like to think of her as a child. When she was born, the Kiowas were living the last great moment of their history. For more than a hundred years they had controlled the open range from the Smoky Hill River to the Red, from the headwaters of the Canadian to the fork of the Arkansas and Cimarron.

In alliance with the Comanches, they had ruled the whole of the southern Plains. War was their sacred business, and they were among the finest horsemen the world has ever known. But warfare for the Kiowas was preeminently a matter of disposition rather than of survival, and they never understood the grim, unrelenting advance of the U.S. Cavalry. When at last, divided and ill-provisioned, they were driven onto the Staked Plains in the cold rains of autumn, they fell into panic. In Palo Duro Canyon they abandoned their crucial stores to pillage and had nothing then but their lives. In order to save themselves, they surrendered to the soldiers at Fort Sill and were imprisoned in the old stone corral that now stands as a military museum. My grandmother was spared the humiliation of those high gray walls by eight or ten years, but she must have known from birth the affliction of defeat, the dark brooding of old warriors.

Her name was Aho, and she belonged to the last culture to evolve in North America. Her forebears came down from the high country in western Montana nearly three centuries ago. They were a mountain people, a mysterious tribe of hunters whose language has never been positively classified in any major group. In the late seventeenth century they began a long migration to the south and east. It was a journey toward the dawn, and it led to a golden age. Along the way the Kiowas were befriended by the Crows, who gave them the culture and religion of the Plains. They acquired horses, and their ancient nomadic spirit was suddenly free of the ground. They acquired Tai-me, the sacred Sun Dance doll, from that moment the object and symbol of their worship, and so shared in the divinity of the sun. Not least, they acquired the sense of destiny, therefore courage and pride. When they entered upon the southern Plains they had been transformed. No longer were they slaves to the simple necessity of survival; they were a lordly and dangerous society of fighters and thieves, hunters and priests of the sun. According to their origin myth, they entered the world through a hollow log. From one point of view, their migration was the fruit of an old prophecy, for indeed they emerged from a sunless world.

Although my grandmother lived out her long life in the shadow of Rainy Mountain, the immense landscape of the continental interior lay like memory in her blood. She could tell of the Crows, whom she had never seen, and of the Black Hills, where she had never been. I wanted to see in reality what she had seen more perfectly in the mind's eye, and traveled fifteen hundred miles to begin my pilgrimage.

Yellowstone, it seemed to me, was the top of the world, a region of deep lakes and dark timber, canyons and waterfalls. But, beautiful as it is, one might have the sense of confinement there. The skyline in all directions is close at hand, the high wall of the woods and deep cleavages of shade. There is a perfect freedom in the mountains, but it belongs to the eagle and the elk, the badger and the bear. The Kiowas reckoned their stature by the distance they could see, and they were bent and blind in the wilderness.

Descending eastward, the highland meadows are a stairway to the plain. In July the inland slope of the Rockies is luxuriant with flax and buckwheat, stonecrop and larkspur. The earth unfolds and the limit of the land recedes. Clusters of trees, and animals grazing far in the distance, cause the vision to reach away and wonder to build upon the mind. The sun follows a longer course in the day, and the sky is immense beyond all comparison. The great billowing clouds that sail upon it are shadows that move upon the grain like water, dividing light. Farther down, in the land of the Crows and Blackfeet, the plain is yellow. Sweet clover takes hold of the hills and bends upon itself to cover and seal the soil. There the Kiowas paused on their way; they had come to the place where they must change their lives. The sun is at home on the plains. Precisely there does it have the certain character of a god. When the Kiowas came to the land of the Crows, they could see the dark lees of the hills at dawn across the Bighorn River, the profusion of light on the grain shelves, the oldest deity ranging after the solstices. Not yet would they veer southward to the caldron of the land that lay below; they must wean their blood from the northern winter and hold the mountains a while longer in their view. They bore Tai-me in procession to the east.

A dark mist lay over the Black Hills, and the land was like iron. At the top of a ridge I caught sight of Devil's Tower upthrust against the gray sky as if in the birth of time the core of the earth had broken though its crust and the motion of the world was begun. There are things in nature that engender an awful quiet in the heart of man; Devil's Tower is one of them. Two centuries ago, because they could not do otherwise, the Kiowas made a legend at the base of the rock. My grandmother said:

> *Eight children were there at play, seven sisters and their brother. Suddenly the boy was struck dumb; he trembled and began to run upon his hands and feet. His fingers became claws, and his body was covered with fur. Directly there was a bear where the boy had been. The sisters were terrified; they ran, and the bear after them. They came to the stump of a great tree, and the tree spoke to them. It bade them climb upon it, and as they did so it began to rise into the air. The bear came to kill them, but they were just beyond its reach. It reared against the tree and scored the bark all around with its claws. The seven sisters were borne into the sky, and they became the stars of the Big Dipper.*

From that moment, and so long as the legend lives, the Kiowas have kinsmen in the night sky. Whatever they were in the mountains, they could be no more. However tenuous their well-being, however much they had suffered and would suffer again, they had found a way out of the wilderness.

My grandmother had a reverence for the sun, a holy regard that now is all but gone out of mankind. There was a wariness in her, and an ancient awe. She was a Christian in her later years, but she had come a long way about, and she never forgot her birthright. As a child she had been to the Sun Dances; she had taken part in those annual rites, and by them she had learned the restoration of her people in the presence of Tai-me. She was about seven when the last Kiowa Sun Dance was held in 1887 on the Washita River above Rainy Mountain Creek. The buffalo were gone. In order to consummate the ancient sacrifice—to impale the head of a buffalo bull upon the medicine tree—a delegation of old men journeyed into Texas, there to beg and barter for an animal from the Goodnight herd. She was ten when the Kiowas came together for the last time as a living Sun Dance culture. They could find no buffalo; they had to hang an old hide from the sacred tree. Before the dance could begin, a company of soldiers rode out from Fort Sill under orders to disperse the tribe. Forbidden without cause the essential act of their faith, having seen the wild herds slaughtered and left to rot upon the ground, the Kiowas backed away forever from the medicine tree. That was July 20, 1890, at the great bend of the Washita. My grandmother was there. Without bitterness, and for as long as she lived, she bore a vision of deicide.

Now that I can have her only in memory, I see my grandmother in the several postures that were peculiar to her: standing at the wood stove on a winter morning and turning meat in a great iron skillet; sitting at the south window, bent above her beadwork, and afterwards, when her vision failed, looking down for a long time into the fold of her hands; going out upon a cane, very slowly as she did when the weight of age came upon her; praying. I remember her most often at prayer. She made long, rambling prayers out of suffering and hope, having seen many things. I was never sure that I had the right to hear, so exclusive were they of all mere custom and company. The last time I saw her she prayed standing by the side of her bed at night, naked to the waist, the light of a kerosene lamp moving upon her dark skin. Her long, black hair, always drawn and braided in the day, lay upon her shoulders and against her breasts like a shawl. I do not speak Kiowa, and I never understood her prayers, but there was something inherently sad in the sound, some merest hesitation upon the syllables of sorrow. She began in a high and descending pitch, exhausting her breath to silence; then again and again—and always the same intensity of effort, of something that is, and is not, like urgency in the human voice. Transported so in the dancing light among the shadows of her room, she seemed beyond the reach of time. But that was illusion; I think I knew then that I should not see her again.

Houses are like sentinels in the plain, old keepers of the weather watch. There, in a very little while, wood takes on the appearance of great age. All colors wear soon away in the wind and rain, and then the wood is burned gray and the grain appears and the nails turn red with rust. The windowpanes are black and opaque; you imagine there is nothing within, and indeed there are many ghosts, bones given up to the land. They stand here and there against the sky, and you approach them for a longer time than you expect. They belong in the distance; it is their domain.

Once there was a lot of sound in my grandmother's house, a lot of coming and going, feasting and talk. The summers there were full of excitement and reunion. The Kiowas are a summer people; they abide the cold and keep to themselves, but when the season turns and the land becomes warm and vital they cannot hold still; an old love of going returns upon them. The aged visitors who came to my grandmother's house when I was a child were made of lean and leather, and they bore themselves upright. They wore great black hats and bright ample shirts that shook in the wind. They rubbed fat upon their hair and wound their braids with strips of colored cloth. Some of them painted their faces and carried the scars of old and cherished enmities. They were an old council of warlords, come to remind and be reminded of who they were. Their wives and daughters served them well. The women might indulge themselves; gossip was at once the mark and compensation of their servitude. They made loud and elaborate talk among themselves, full of jest and gesture, fright and false alarm. They went abroad in fringed and flowered shawls, bright beadwork and German silver. They were at home in the kitchen, and they prepared meals that were banquets.

There were frequent prayer meetings, and great nocturnal feasts. When I was a child I played with my cousins outside, where the lamplight fell upon the ground and the singing of the old people rose up around us and carried away into the darkness. There were a lot of good things to eat, a lot of laughter and surprise. And afterwards, when the quiet returned, I lay down with my grandmother and could hear the frogs away by the river and feel the motion of the air.

Now there is a funeral silence in the rooms, the endless wake of some final word. The walls have closed in upon my grandmother's house. When I returned to it in mourning, I saw for the first time in my life how small it was. It was late at night, and there was a white moon, nearly full. I sat for a long time on the stone steps by the kitchen door. From there I could see out across the land; I could see the long row of trees by the creek, the low light upon the rolling plains, and the stars of the Big Dipper. Once I looked at the moon and caught sight of a strange thing. A cricket had perched upon the handrail, only a few inches away from me. My line of vision was such that the creature filled the moon like a fossil. It had gone there, I thought, to live and die, for there, of all places, was its small definition made whole and eternal. A warm wind rose up and purled like the longing within me.

The next morning I awoke at dawn and went out on the dirt road to Rainy Mountain. It was already hot, and the grasshoppers began to fill the air. Still, it was early in the morning, and the birds sang out of the shadow. The long yellow grass on the mountain shone in the bright light, and a scissortail hied above the land. There, where it ought to be, at the end of a long and legendary way, was my grandmother's grave. Here and there on the dark stones were ancestral names. Looking back once, I saw the mountain and came away.

THE STORY OF AN EYEWITNESS: THE SAN FRANCISCO EARTHQUAKE

Jack London

A journalist, short story writer, novelist, essayist, and political activist, Jack London published eight short story collections, twenty-one novels, two memoirs, and three books of essays, as well as uncollected short stories and journalism articles. He wrote his most famous short story, "To Build a Fire," in 1902 and his most famous novel, *The Call of the Wild,* in 1903.

London was born in San Francisco in 1876, where an ex-slave, Virginia Prentiss, first raised him. He soon returned to live with his mother. London traveled widely throughout the West from California up through Alaska, taking much of his writing from his adventures on these journeys. He later traveled throughout the United States, lecturing on politics.

We have chosen this piece of Jack London's from his journalism career. In it, he returns to his origins in San Francisco to document, in writing, the great earthquake of 1906, still the most destructive earthquake and certainly one of the most calamitous natural disasters in American history.

———

The earthquake shook down in San Francisco hundreds of thousands of dollars worth of walls and chimneys. But the conflagration that followed burned up hundreds of millions of dollars' worth of property There is no estimating within hundreds of millions the actual damage wrought. Not in history has a modern imperial city been so completely destroyed. San Francisco is gone. Nothing remains of it but memories and a fringe of dwelling-houses on its outskirts. Its industrial section is wiped out. Its business section is wiped out. Its social and residential section is wiped out. The factories and warehouses, the great stores and newspaper buildings, the hotels and the palaces of the nabobs, are all gone. Remains only the fringe of dwelling houses on the outskirts of what was once San Francisco.

Within an hour after the earthquake shock the smoke of San Francisco's burning was a lurid tower visible a hundred miles away. And for three days and nights this lurid tower swayed in the sky, reddening the sun, darkening the day, and filling the land with smoke.

On Wednesday morning at a quarter past five came the earthquake. A minute later the flames were leaping upward In a dozen different quarters south of Market Street, in the working-class ghetto, and in the factories, fires started. There was no opposing the flames. There was no organization, no communication. All the cunning adjustments of a twentieth century city had been smashed by the earthquake. The streets were humped into ridges and depressions, and piled with the debris of fallen walls. The steel rails were twisted into perpendicular and horizontal angles. The telephone and telegraph systems were disrupted. And the great water-mains had burst. All the shrewd contrivances and safeguards of man had been thrown out of gear by thirty seconds' twitching of the earth-crust.

The Fire Made Its Own Draft

By Wednesday afternoon, inside of twelve hours, half the heart of the city was gone. At that time I watched the vast conflagration from out on the bay. It was dead calm. Not a flicker of wind stirred. Yet from every side wind was pouring in upon the city. East, west, north, and south, strong winds were blowing upon the doomed city. The heated air rising made an enormous suck. Thus did the fire of itself build its own colossal chimney through the atmosphere. Day and night this dead calm continued, and yet, near to the flames, the wind was often half a gale, so mighty was the suck.

Wednesday night saw the destruction of the very heart of the city. Dynamite was lavishly used, and many of San Francisco's proudest structures were crumbled by man himself into ruins, but there was no withstanding the onrush of the flames. Time and again successful stands were made by the fire-fighters, and every time the flames flanked around on either side or came up from the rear, they turned to defeat the hard-won victory.

An enumeration of the buildings destroyed would be a directory of San Francisco. An enumeration of the buildings undestroyed would be a line and several addresses. An enumeration of the deeds of heroism would stock a library and bankrupt the Carnegie medal fund. An enumeration of the dead-will never be made. All vestiges of them were destroyed by the flames. The number of the victims of the earthquake will never be known. South of Market Street, where the loss of life was particularly heavy, was the first to catch fire.

Remarkable as it may seem, Wednesday night while the whole city crashed and roared into ruin, was a quiet night. There were no crowds. There was no shouting and yelling. There was no hysteria, no disorder. I passed Wednesday night in the path of the advancing flames, and in all those terrible hours I saw not one woman who wept, not one man who was excited, not one person who was in the slightest degree panic stricken.

Before the flames, throughout the night, fled tens of thousands of homeless ones. Some were wrapped in blankets. Others carried bundles of bedding and dear household treasures. Sometimes a whole family was harnessed to a carriage or delivery wagon that was weighted down with their possessions. Baby buggies, toy wagons, and go-carts were used as trucks, while every other person was dragging a trunk. Yet everybody was gracious. The most perfect courtesy obtained. Never in all San Francisco's history, were her people so kind and courteous as on this night of terror.

A Caravan of Trunks

All night these tens of thousands fled before the flames. Many of them, the poor people from the labor ghetto, had fled all day as well. They had left their homes burdened with possessions. Now and again they lightened up, flinging out upon the street clothing and treasures they had dragged for miles.

They held on longest to their trunks, and over these trunks many a strong man broke his heart that night. The hills of San Francisco are steep, and up these hills, mile after mile, were the trunks dragged. Everywhere were trunks with across them lying their exhausted owners, men and women. Before the march of the flames were flung picket lines of soldiers. And a block at a time, as the flames advanced, these pickets retreated. One of their tasks was to keep the trunk-pullers moving. The exhausted creatures, stirred on by the menace of bayonets, would arise and struggle up the steep pavements, pausing from weakness every five or ten feet.

Often, after surmounting a heart-breaking hill, they would find another wall of flame advancing upon them at right angles and be compelled to change anew the line of their retreat. In the end, completely played out, after toiling for a dozen hours like giants, thousands of them were compelled to abandon their trunks. Here the shopkeepers and soft members of the middle class were at a disadvantage. But the working-men dug holes in vacant lots and backyards and buried their trunks.

The Doomed City

At nine o'clock Wednesday evening I walked down through the very heart of the city. I walked through miles and miles of magnificent buildings and towering skyscrapers. Here was no fire. All was in perfect order. The police patrolled the streets. Every building had its watchman at the door. And yet it was doomed, all of it. There was no water. The dynamite was giving out. And at right angles two different conflagrations were sweeping down upon it.

At one o'clock in the morning I walked down through the same section. Everything still stood intact. There was no fire. And yet there was a change. A rain of ashes was falling. The watchmen at the doors were gone. The police had been withdrawn. There were no firemen, no fire-engines, no men fighting with dynamite. The district had been absolutely abandoned. I stood at the corner of Kearny and Market, in the very innermost heart of San Francisco. Kearny Street was deserted. Half a dozen blocks away it was burning on both sides. The street was a wall of flame. And against this wall of flame, silhouetted sharply, were two United States cavalrymen sitting their horses, calming watching. That was all. Not another person was in sight. In the intact heart of the city two troopers sat their horses and watched.

Speed of the Conflagration

Surrender was complete. There was no water. The sewers had long since been pumped dry. There was no dynamite. Another fire had broken out further uptown, and now from three sides conflagrations were sweeping down. The fourth side had been burned earlier in the day. In that direction stood the tottering walls of the Examiner building, the burned-out Call building, the smoldering ruins of the Grand Hotel, and the gutted, devastated, dynamited Palace Hotel.

The following will illustrate the sweep of the flames and the inability of men to calculate their spread. At eight o'clock Wednesday evening I passed through Union Square. It was packed with refugees. Thousands of them had gone to bed on the grass. Government tents had been set up, supper was being cooked, and the refugees were lining up for free meals.

At half past one in the morning three sides of Union Square were in flames. The fourth side, where stood the great St. Francis Hotel, was still holding out. An hour later, ignited from top and sides the St. Francis was flaming heavenward. Union Square, heaped high with mountains of trunks, was deserted. Troops, refugees, and all had retreated.

A Fortune for a Horse!

It was at Union Square that I saw a man offering a thousand dollars for a team of horses. He was in charge of a truck piled high with trunks from some hotel. It had been hauled here into what was considered safety, and the horses had been taken out. The flames were on three sides of the Square and there were no horses.

Also, at this time, standing beside the truck, I urged a man to seek safety in flight. He was all but hemmed in by several conflagrations. He was an old man and he was on crutches. Said he: "Today is my birthday. Last night I was worth thirty thousand dollars. I bought five bottles of wine, some delicate fish and other things for my birthday dinner. I have had no dinner, and all I own are these crutches."

I convinced him of his danger and started him limping on his way. An hour later, from a distance, I saw the truck-load of trunks burning merrily in the middle of the street.

On Thursday morning at a quarter past five, just twenty-four hours after the earthquake, I sat on the steps of a small residence on Nob Hill. With me sat Japanese, Italians, Chinese, and negroes—a bit of the cosmopolitan flotsam of the wreck of the city. All about were the palaces of the nabob pioneers of Forty-nine. To the east and south at right angles, were advancing two mighty walls of flame.

I went inside with the owner of the house on the steps of which I sat. He was cool and cheerful and hospitable. "Yesterday morning," he said, "I was worth six hundred thousand dollars. This morning this house is all I have left. It will go in fifteen minutes. He pointed to a large cabinet. "That is my wife's collection of china. This rug upon which we stand is a present. It cost fifteen hundred dollars. Try that piano. Listen to its tone. There are few like it. There are no horses. The flames will be here in fifteen minutes."

Outside the old Mark Hopkins residence a palace was just catching fire. The troops were falling back and driving the refugees before them. From every side came the roaring of flames, the crashing of walls, and the detonations of dynamite.

The Dawn of the Second Day

I passed out of the house. Day was trying to dawn through the smoke-pall. A sickly light was creeping over the face of things. Once only the sun broke through the smoke-pall, blood-red, and showing quarter its usual size. The smoke-pall itself, viewed from beneath, was a rose color that pulsed and fluttered with lavender shades. Then it turned to mauve and yellow and dun. There was no sun. And so dawned the second day on stricken San Francisco.

An hour later I was creeping past the shattered dome of the City Hall. There was no better exhibit of the destructive force of the earthquake. Most of the stone had been shaken from the great dome, leaving standing the naked framework of steel. Market Street was piled high with the wreckage, and across the wreckage lay the overthrown pillars of the City Hall shattered into short crosswise sections.

This section of the city with the exception of the Mint and the Post-Office, was already a waste of smoking ruins. Here and there through the smoke, creeping warily under the shadows of tottering walls, emerged occasional men and women. It was like the meeting of the handful of survivors after the day of the end of the world.

Beeves Slaughtered and Roasted

On Mission Street lay a dozen steers, in a neat row stretching across the street just as they had been struck down by the flying ruins of the earthquake. The fire had passed through afterward and roasted them. The human dead had been carried away before the fire came. At another place on Mission Street I saw a milk wagon. A steel telegraph pole had smashed down sheer through the driver's seat and crushed the front wheels. The milk cans lay scattered around.

All day Thursday and all Thursday night, all day Friday and Friday night, the flames still raged on.

Friday night saw the flames finally conquered, though not until Russian Hill and Telegraph Hill had been swept and three-quarters of a mile of wharves and docks had been licked up.

The Last Stand

The great stand of the fire-fighters was made Thursday night on Van Ness Avenue. Had they failed here, the comparatively few remaining houses of the city would have been swept. Here were the magnificent residences of the second generation of San Francisco nabobs, and these, in a solid zone, were dynamited down across the path of the fire. Here and there the flames leaped the zone, but these fires were beaten out, principally by the use of wet blankets and rugs.

San Francisco, at the present time, is like the crater of a volcano, around which are camped tens of thousands of refugees At the Presidio alone are at least twenty thousand. All the surrounding cities and towns are jammed with the homeless ones, where they are being cared for by the relief committees.

The refugees were carried free by the railroads to any point they wished to go, and it is estimated that over one hundred thousand people have left the peninsula on which San Francisco stood. The Government has the situation in hand, and, thanks to the immediate relief given by the whole United States, there is not the slightest possibility of a famine. The bankers and business men have already set about making preparations to rebuild San Francisco.

MODERN LOVE

Diane Ackerman

Naturalist, author of children's books, essayist, and poet, Diane Ackerman focuses much of her attention on nature, exploring its mysteries, its beauties, and its powerful potential for healing in our lives. As Ms. Ackerman is often concerned with that arena where nature and human life meet, she published her now most popular book, *A Natural History of the Senses,* in 1990.

We have chosen "Modern Love," an essay from Ms. Ackerman's book, *A Natural History of Love* (1994). That title, with the word "Natural" in it, portrays Ms. Ackerman's vision of love as a part of nature, not apart from nature. Love is in our nature, as we are natural beings. Ms. Ackerman looks at how we have organized love in our social lives, what rules, traditions, and rituals we have created to make our natural instinct for love function within our changing societies.

———

When I think about the essence of being modern, the changes in attitude that led to the life we now know, three things come to mind: choice, privacy, and books. As a child of the seventies, I find it almost impossible to fathom a time when people couldn't make choices in their lives—whimsical choices, let alone solemn ones. Personal freedom has a long, slow history, based in part on the growing size of the world's population, which gave people a chance to be anonymous. If they couldn't be exempt from the moral law, they could at least toy with exemption in private. Despite arranged marriages, people stole the freedom to love whom they chose, without shame; then to choose whom to marry; and in time they even made the shocking leap to wishing to marry someone they loved. As wealth and leisure grew, houses began to have specific rooms for specific uses, including a bedroom where couples could be unobserved. Soon, young marrieds wanted a place of their own, separate from their in-laws. They wanted to be "alone together," a new idea based on a newly won sense of privacy.

The invention of printing aided and abetted lovers. Once people became more literate, they could take a book with them to some quiet place and read to themselves and think. Reading changed society forever. Solitary contemplation began to emerge as commonplace, and readers could discover in romantic and erotic literature what was possible, or at least imaginable. They could dare controversial thoughts and feel bolstered by allies, without telling anyone. Books had to be kept somewhere, and with the library came the idea of secluded hours, alone with one's innermost thoughts. Lovers could blend their hearts by sharing sympathetic authors; what they could not express in person they could at least point to in the pages of a book. A shared book could speak to lovers in confidence, increasing their sense of intimacy even if the loved one was absent or a forbidden companion. Books opened the door to an aviary filled with flights of the imagination, winged fantasies of love; they gave readers a sense of emotional community. Somewhere in another city or state another soul was reading the same words, perhaps dreaming the same dream.

ALICE'S ADVENTURES IN WONDERLAND

Lewis Carroll

Lewis Carroll, the pen name for Charles Lutwidge Dodgson, an English author, logician, Anglican deacon, and photographer, lived from 1832 - 1898. He is best known for *Alice's Adventures in Wonderland* and its sequel *Through the Looking-Glass*.

On a pleasant day in 1862, Dodgson rowed on the River Thames, on the way to a picnic, with the three daughters of a family friend, the Liddel family: Lorina Charlotte Liddell (13), Alice Pleasance Liddell(10), and Edith Mary Liddell (8). During the five-mile journey down the river, Alice asked Dodgson to entertain the three sisters with a story. To answer Alice's request, Dodgson created the story of *Alice's Adventures in Wonderland*.

The following excerpt is from the first chapter of *Alice's Adventures in Wonderland*.

———

Down the Rabbit-Hole

Alice was beginning to get very tired of sitting by her sister on the bank, and of having nothing to do: once or twice she had peeped into the book her sister was reading, but it had no pictures or conversations in it, 'and what is the use of a book,' thought Alice, 'without pictures or conversation?'

So she was considering in her own mind (as well as she could, for the hot day made her feel very sleepy and stupid), whether the pleasure of making a daisy-chain would be worth the trouble of getting up and picking the daisies, when suddenly a White Rabbit with pink eyes ran close by her.

There was nothing so *VERY* remarkable in that; nor did Alice think it so *VERY* much out of the way to hear the Rabbit say to itself, 'Oh dear!' I shall be too late!' (when she thought it over afterwards, it occurred to her that she ought to have wondered at this, but at the time it all seemed quite natural); but when the Rabbit actually **TOOK A WATCH OUT OF ITS WAISTCOAT-POCKET,** and looked at it, and then hurried on, Alice started to her feet, for it flashed across her mind that she had never before seen a rabbit with either a waistcoat-pocket, or a watch to take out of it, and burning with curiosity, she ran across the field after it, and fortunately was just in time to see it pop down a large rabbit-hole under the hedge.

In another moment down went Alice after it, never once considering how in the world she was to get out again.

The rabbit-hole went straight on like a tunnel for some way, and then dipped suddenly down, so suddenly that Alice had not a moment to think about stopping herself before she found herself falling down a very deep well.

Either the well was very deep, or she fell very slowly, for she had plenty of time as she went down to look about her, and to wonder what was going to happen next. First, she tried to look down and make out what she was coming to, but it was too dark to see anything; then she looked at the sides of the well, and noticed that they were filled with cupboards and book-shelves: here and there she saw maps and pictures hung upon pegs. She took down a jar from one of the shelves as she passed; it was labeled 'ORANGE MARMALADE', but to her great disappointment it was empty: she did not like to drop the jar for fear of killing somebody, so managed to put it into one of the cupboards as she fell past it.

'Well!' thought Alice to herself, 'after such a fall as this, I shall think nothing of tumbling down stairs! How brave they'll all think me at home! Why, I wouldn't say anything about it, even if I fell off the top of the house!' (Which was very likely true.)

Down, down, down. Would the fall *NEVER* come to an end! 'I wonder how many miles I've fallen by this time?' she said aloud. 'I must be getting somewhere near the centre of the earth. Let me see: that would be four thousand miles down, I think—' (for, you see, Alice had learnt several things of this sort in her lessons in the schoolroom, and though this was not a *very* good opportunity for showing off her knowledge, as there was no one to listen to her, still it was a good practice to say it over) '—yes, that's about the right distance—but then I wonder what Latitude or Longitude I've got to?' (Alice had no idea what Latitude was, or Longitude either, but thought they were nice grand words to say.)

Presently she began again. 'I wonder if I shall fall right *THROUGH* the earth! How funny it'll seem to come out among the people that walk with their heads downwards! The Antipathies, I think—' (she was rather glad there *was* no one listening, this time, as it didn't sound at all the right word) '—but I shall have to ask them what the name of the country is, you know. Please, Ma'am, is this New Zealand or Australia?' (and she tried to curtsey as she spoke—fancy CURTSEYING as you're falling through the air! Do you think you could manage it?) 'And what an ignorant little girl she'll think me for asking! No, it'll never do to ask: perhaps I shall see it written up somewhere.'

Down, down, down. There was nothing else to do, so Alice soon began talking again. 'Dinah'll miss me very much to-night, I should think!' (Dinah was the cat.) 'I hope they'll remember her saucer of milk at tea-time. Dinah, my dear! I wish you were down here with me! There are no mice in the air, I'm afraid, but you might catch a bat, and that's very like a mouse, you know. But do cats eat bats, I wonder?' And here Alice began to get rather sleepy, and went on saying to herself, in a dreamy sort of way, 'Do cats eat bats? Do cats eat bats?' and sometimes, 'Do bats eat cats?' for, you see, as she couldn't answer either question, it didn't much matter which way she put it. She felt that she was dozing off, and had just begun to dream that she was walking hand in hand with Dinah, and saying to her very earnestly, 'Now, Dinah, tell the truth: did you ever eat a bat?' when suddenly, thump! thump! Down she came upon a heap of sticks and dry leaves, and the fall was over.

Alice was not a bit hurt, and she jumped up on to her feet in a moment: she looked up, but it was all dark overhead; before her was another long passage, and the White Rabbit was still in sight, hurrying down it. There was not a moment to be lost: away went Alice like the wind, and was just in time to hear it say, as it turned a corner, 'Oh my ears and whiskers, how late it's getting!' She was close behind it when she turned the corner, but the Rabbit was no longer to be seen: she found herself in a long, low hall, which was lit up by a row of lamps hanging from the roof.

There were doors all round the hall, but they were all locked; and when Alice had been all the way down one side and up the other, trying every door, she walked sadly down the middle, wondering how she was ever to get out again.

Suddenly she came upon a little three-legged table, all made of solid glass; there was nothing on it except a tiny golden key, and Alice's first thought was that it might belong to one of the doors of the hall; but, alas! either the locks were too large, or the key was too small, but at any rate it would not open any of them. However, on the second time round, she came upon a low curtain she had not noticed before, and behind it was a little door about fifteen inches high: she tried the little golden key in the lock, and to her great delight it fitted!

Alice opened the door and found that it led into a small passage, not much larger than a rat-hole: she knelt down and looked along the passage into the loveliest garden you ever saw. How she longed to get out of that dark hall, and wander about among those beds of bright flowers and those cool fountains, but she could not even get her head through the doorway; 'and even if my head would go through,' thought poor Alice, 'it would be of very little use without my shoulders. Oh, how I wish I could shut up like a telescope! I think I could, if I only knew how to begin.' For, you see, so many out-of-the-way things had happened lately, that Alice had begun to think that very few things indeed were really impossible.

There seemed to be no use in waiting by the little door, so she went back to the table, half hoping she might find another key on it, or at any rate a book of rules for shutting people up like telescopes: this time she found a little bottle on it, ('which certainly was not here before,' said Alice,) and round the neck of the bottle was a paper label, with the words 'DRINK ME' beautifully printed on it in large letters.

It was all very well to say 'Drink me,' but the wise little Alice was not going to do THAT in a hurry. 'No, I'll look first,' she said, 'and see whether it's marked "*poison*" or not'; for she had read several nice little histories about children who had got burnt, and eaten up by wild beasts and other unpleasant things, all because they WOULD not remember the simple rules their friends had taught them: such as, that a red-hot poker will burn you if you hold it too long; and that if you cut your finger VERY deeply with a knife, it usually bleeds; and she had never forgotten that, if you drink much from a bottle marked 'poison,' it is almost certain to disagree with you, sooner or later.

However, this bottle was *NOT* marked 'poison,' so Alice ventured to taste it, and finding it very nice, (it had, in fact, a sort of mixed flavour of cherry-tart, custard, pine-apple, roast turkey, toffee, and hot buttered toast,) she very soon finished it off.

* * *

'What a curious feeling!' said Alice; 'I must be shutting up like a telescope.'

And so it was indeed: she was now only ten inches high, and her face brightened up at the thought that she was now the right size for going through the little door into that lovely garden. First, however, she waited for a few minutes to see if she was going to shrink any further: she felt a little nervous about this; 'for it might end, you know,' said Alice to herself, 'in my going out altogether, like a candle. I wonder what I should be like then?' And she tried to fancy what the flame of a candle is like after the candle is blown out, for she could not remember ever having seen such a thing.

After a while, finding that nothing more happened, she decided on going into the garden at once; but, alas for poor Alice! When she got to the door, she found she had forgotten the little golden key, and when she went back to the table for it, she found she could not possibly reach it: she could see it quite plainly through the glass, and she tried her best to climb up one of the legs of the table, but it was too slippery; and when she had tired herself out with trying, the poor little thing sat down and cried.

'Come, there's no use in crying like that!' said Alice to herself, rather sharply; 'I advise you to leave off this minute!' She generally gave herself very good advice, (though she very seldom followed it), and sometimes she scolded herself so severely as to bring tears into her eyes; and once she remembered trying to box her own ears for having cheated herself in a game of croquet she was playing against herself, for this curious child was very fond of pretending to be two people. 'But it's no use now,' thought poor Alice, 'to pretend to be two people! Why, there's hardly enough of me left to make ONE respectable person!'

Soon her eye fell on a little glass box that was lying under the table: she opened it, and found in it a very small cake, on which the words, 'EAT ME' were beautifully marked in currants. 'Well, I'll eat it,' said Alice, 'and if it makes me grow larger, I can reach the key; and if it make me grow smaller, I can creep under the door; so either way I'll get into the garden, and I don't care which happens!'

She ate a little bit, and said anxiously to herself, 'Which way? Which way?' holding her hand on the top of her head to feel which way it was growing, and she was quite surprised to find that she remained the same size: to be sure, this generally happens when one eats cake, but Alice had got so much into the way of expecting nothing but out-of-the-way things to happen, that it seemed quite dull and stupid for life to go on in the common way.

So she set to work, and very soon finished off the cake.

RENAISSANCE PEARS

John Seabrook

John Seabrook, a staff writer on *The New Yorker* magazine, writes on technology, the media, personal life, and culture. His latest book, *Flash of Genius and Other True Stories of Invention* (2008), became a movie, *Flash of Genius.*

In this article, "Renaissance Pears," Seabrook weaves together a number of subjects, including nature and ecology, art, history, and travel. He presents a personal narrative of his encounter with preserving ecological masterpieces of nature in Italy.

———

The Fiorentina is a squat and hippy pear, its dark-green skin blemished with black freckles. It is to supermarket fruit as real people are to supermodels. Until recently, the pear was thought to have disappeared from central Italy, where it once flourished. But Isabella Dalla Ragione, a forty-seven-year-old agronomist in Perugia, continued to look for it.

Dalla Ragione has straight brown hair and crooked teeth; she can look twenty years younger than her age or ten years older, depending on the angle of her head. She is a fast driver and an even faster talker, with a gift for making *archeologia arborea,* as she calls her vocation—the pursuit and recovery of old varieties of fruit—sound thrilling. She finds clues in many places: Renaissance paintings, obscure books, and the records that were kept by former estate owners in Umbria and Tuscany, where the climate is peculiarly advantageous for many kinds of fruit. Last year, while studying the catalogue of a large estate that once belonged to the Bufalini family, on the northern tip of Umbria, she came across a reference to the Fiorentina. The Bufalini maintained villas with extensive gardens and orchards, from the fifteenth century on up to the nineteen-eighties, when the final landlord left the property to the state.

Pear trees can live for more than two hundred and fifty years—among fruit trees, only olives live longer—and so Isabella thought a Fiorentina might remain on the former Bufalini lands. She knew what the pear looked like, thanks to a memoir left by an itinerant early-twentieth-century musician, Archimede Montanelli, whose travels had taken him all over Umbria. She also happened to have an uncle, Alvaro, who hunted in that part of Umbria and was acquainted with some of the farmers who lived there. Eventually, one of them told Alvaro that a Fiorentina remained on his farm.

Earlier this summer, I accompanied Isabella on a trip to visit the old pear tree. We drove into a mountainous region above the town of Pietralunga, a land of thick woods with small farms in the valleys. Stone houses where the landowners had once lived, many of them now abandoned, sit on the tops of hills. The old orchards are gone, but the landscape is dotted with a few rugged arboreal survivors: almonds, olives, and pears.

The Fiorentina was growing in the Valdescura, the Valley of Darkness. When we arrived, relatives of several families, spanning four generations, were sitting under the big shade trees outside the farmhouse. The matriarch was an eighty-four-year-old woman named Sergia. She wore a ragged shift and filthy slippers, and carried a long walking stick. Hearing my accent, she recalled the Americans who had escaped from a nearby Fascist prison and turned up one night in 1943; she had given them shelter and something to eat.

There was a cherry tree beside the house, and Isabella walked with Sergia to gather some cherries. Or, rather, Isabella gathered them; Sergia ate them, the pits tumbling down her whiskery chin as more cherries went into her mouth.

Then the farmer, a nephew of Sergia's, led us through a potato field to the Fiorentina, which was growing next to a rutted old road. Its black bark had deep crevices, and the trunk and lower branches were covered with scabrous white lichen. Isabella fought through the high weeds around the tree and patted its trunk. "Sometimes when I find one of these old trees I feel like weeping," she said. "If only they could talk—what a story they could tell." Then she frowned, and said, "But I think, Maybe it is better they cannot talk. They would probably curse us."

For thousands of years, peasants in Umbria and Tuscany cultivated fruit trees. Most tended small *pomari,* or family orchards, with no more than ten trees. A fruit tree provided food, shade in summer, fuel in winter, furniture, and children's shoes, which were made from the wood of fig trees. Fruit was also a staple of the cooking of the region, in dishes like salt cod with roasted pears, and pork with plums; whole cherries in *agrodolce*—pickled in vinegar and sugar—were served as a chutney with roasted meat. The farmers planted as many varieties as possible, because the different trees would bear fruit at different times over the growing season. The mountainous topography of Umbria, and its lack of roads, insured that varieties common to one valley were unknown in the next. When a woman married, she often carried seeds from her family's farm with her, in order to prepare her mother's recipes, which were based on the particular varieties of fruit in her home valley.

This feudal way of life endured, more or less unbroken, for two thousand years, until it abruptly ended in the two decades following the Second World War. Nine million Italians, about a sixth of the population at that time, left their rural homes and went to the cities. They acquired Fiats, Vespas, televisions, and fashionable clothes—all the trappings of modern Italian identity. The old fruit trees were among the things they left behind.

The varieties eaten in Umbria and Tuscany were replaced, first, by generic fruit grown in the Emilia-Romagna region, where much of Italy's agricultural industry is concentrated, and, more recently, by fruit from other countries—peaches and cherries from Spain, pears from Argentina, and apples from China. In most markets in Italy you can find only three kinds of apple (Golden Delicious, Stark Delicious, Rome Beauty), and lately the Fuji apple, from China, has begun to replace those. It's not hard to imagine a day when there will be only one kind of apple for sale in the whole industrial world.

The Dalla Ragiones' orchard is an open-air museum of Old World fruit. It was begun by Isabella's father, Livio, forty years ago, on his land in northwestern Umbria, and is now maintained by Isabella. The trees grow on a hilltop in San Lorenzo di Lerchi, a hamlet about seventy miles southeast of Florence and thirty miles northwest of Perugia; Livio lives in a stone farmhouse that overlooks the orchard. There are about four hundred trees in the collection: pears, apples, plums, cherries, peaches, quinces, and medlars. Most were common in Umbria as recently as sixty years ago; now they have all but disappeared. Some of the Dalla Ragiones' specimens are believed to be the last examples of that variety.

Livio Dalla Ragione was born in Pieve Santo Stefano, about twenty miles north of San Lorenzo; his father was a railroad worker. When Italy entered the war, on the German side, in 1940, Livio, then nineteen, was conscripted. In old photographs, one can see a very tall, handsome young man in military uniform. But he soon became disillusioned with Fascism, and in the summer of 1943, not long before Italy signed an armistice with the Allies, he and a few friends were arrested for singing a song called "Death to the House of Savoy" during an inspection by King Vittorio Emanuele III. Livio escaped from a train taking him to prison, and made his way back to northwestern Umbria, where he joined the partisans. He was a lieutenant in the Gruppo San Faustino, one of several partisan bands that managed to keep the Germans from securing positions in central Italy until the Allies arrived in Rome, in June, 1944.

Livio played a leading role in several celebrated *partigiani* actions, including an ambush on an armored German column near the ancient walls of Citta di Castello, an attack on a German arms depot at Gubbio, and the defense of the town of Pianello against a force of some five hundred S.S. troops, in which the Germans lost more than a hundred men and the *partigiani* lost only three. The rugged terrain was ideal for guerrilla warfare. The partisans could carry out operations east toward Gubbio or northwest toward Florence, then disappear into the remote high valleys and the barns and farmhouses of the local farmers, who sometimes lost their farms, and their lives, in German reprisals. Livio was eventually awarded one of Italy's highest citations for valor, the Silver Medal, for his actions during these years. His exploits are recounted in "Guerrilla in Striped Pants," a memoir by Walter W. Orebaugh, an American diplomat who fought alongside him.

After the war, Livio moved to Rome. In the nineteen-fifties, he was part of an important Roman abstract-art scene, centered on the Via Margutta, which included the sculptor Ettore Colla. Livio worked in a style called *informale,* which emphasized the use of collage and found objects; his paintings often included pieces of wood or metal from old tools that were used by the peasants he had come to know during the war. Other paintings featured the colorful droppings of an owl called an *allocco.* Livio participated in a number of exhibitions in Rome, and in the early sixties he received an offer to be part of a show in Chicago, but he turned it down, and after that his career as a painter began to decline.

Around this time, Livio began collecting the *cultura materiale* of the Umbrian peasantry. He picked up tools in abandoned farmhouses—knives for harvesting olives, pitchforks made out of forked branches—and rescued larger mechanical pieces as well, such as presses for olive oil and looms for weaving linen (for the landowners) and hemp (for the peasants). Just as the farmers had succored him and his partisan comrades, so Livio intended to save the farmers from the American-style consumer culture that Italy embraced after the war, or at least to preserve the memory of their way of life. He took over the house at San Lorenzo, which had been empty for years and was falling into ruin, and gradually restored it, filling it with his found farm objects. Eventually, he accumulated so many things that he moved most of them into a former farm building just outside Citta di Castello. This collection is now a museum, the Folk Traditions Center, run by the city. Arboreal archeology was one aspect of Livio's larger obsession with Italy's prewar past. "I had these tools, all these things," he told me, "but I also wanted to save the smells and tastes of those times. So I began trying to save the trees."

Isabella was born in 1957, the second of Livio's two daughters; her older sister, Laura, is a psychiatrist specializing in children's eating disorders. When the girls were small, they and their mother, Rosa, spent the summers in a cabin in the woods, without electricity or running water. Isabella remembers making a *favola*—a fairy house—inside the hollow trunk of a chestnut tree. "My idea of the world as green comes from seeing the sun come through the thin bark of my chestnut tree," she told me.

At the time, Livio's celebration of the culture of the peasants stopped short of wanting to live like one. In the late fifties and early sixties, he rarely stayed with his family in the country; he preferred Rome. When Isabella was still young, she became aware that her father was living, as she called it, "a double life." By the time she was eighteen, and studying for a degree in agronomy at the University of Perugia, she had become interested in theatre, and joined an experimental acting troupe that embraced the improvisational principles of the Polish playwright and director Jerzy Grotowski. "I think I just wanted to get as far away from my father's world as I could," Isabella told me. "It was not easy to have that kind of man as a father—a great man, a strong, important man. It is hard to find your own way."

After ten years of acting and sporadic studies, Isabella finished her master's degree. She found a job with the city of Perugia, working on its trees. She married Leonardo Tei, a master builder, and they have two daughters, Costanza, who is eleven, and Matilde, who is nine. Livio, in the meantime, had been teaching drawing and painting at two small art schools near Perugia and planting the orchard at San Lorenzo. "It was natural," Isabella says, "with my degree and knowledge, that I started to go with my father, to find fruits and plants." She was skilled at grafting—a technique that involves taking a living piece of the plant one wants to reproduce (known as the "scion"), inserting it into a cleft in the stalk of an already established plant (the "rootstock"), and tying the two plants together. Grafting was practiced by peasants for centuries, and it is the reason that so many old varieties could be preserved for so long. It is a quicker and more reliable way of reproducing trees than growing them from seed, because the rootstock is already established and is known to be compatible with the soil. Because grafting is an asexual form of reproduction, the new tree is not a cross between the rootstock and the scion but a copy of the scion.

As the collection grew, Isabella's relationship with her father improved. The trees helped. She has written several books about her work, including an illustrated catalogue of the collection. As Livio has grown older and more infirm, Isabella has taken on more of the daily maintenance of the orchard: pruning, fertilizing, and grafting. The hardest work comes in the late winter and early spring, when the grass is cut, the soil prepared, paths cleared, and the trees treated with copper, to inhibit the growth of fungi. Isabella and Livio get occasional help from volunteers, but they can't afford to hire a full-time assistant, and they have distanced themselves from the Slow Food movement, an Italian association that promotes and preserves the artisanal production of food, because Isabella dislikes its politics. ("They really only exist to promote themselves," she told me.) The Dalla Ragiones don't sell fruit, but they do sell saplings grafted from trees in the collection. Isabella charges thirteen to fifteen euros for each sapling, and last year she sold about two hundred. Three years ago, they received a grant of fifteen thousand euros for *archeologia arborea* from the Umbrian regional government, and Isabella and Livio were able to print two thousand brochures, create labels for the trees, and launch a Web site. But that money ran out in May, and there will be no more, Isabella said, because "biodiversity is not a political priority in Italy." From now on, the Dalla Ragiones' only source of funding will be from tourists, who may visit the orchard by appointment and are encouraged to contribute to the cost of maintaining it by adopting a tree.

The idea of using still-life paintings as forensic tools occurred to Isabella in the early nineteen-nineties. Italian Renaissance and Baroque *natura morta* painting is distinguished from much of the Northern European tradition of still-life by its naturalism. Generally, the fruit in Italian paintings is not treated symbolically or didactically, as it is in Flemish and Dutch painting. "The natural fecundity of the fruit itself was symbolism enough in Italian still-lifes," Larry Feinberg, the Ryan Curator in the Department of European Painting at the Art Institute of Chicago, says. "If the fruit was a symbol of anything, it was of abundance, richness, good fortune." In Caravaggio's work, the fruit often has wormholes and looks a little too soft, Feinberg added. It has become a symbol of "*vanitas*—of overripeness, or sensuality."

Three of the most useful artists for identifying old varieties of fruit are Jacopo Ligozzi (1547-1627), Giovanna Garzoni (1600-70), and Bartolomeo Bimbi (1648-1729), all of whom worked for Medici Grand Dukes—Francesco I, Ferdinand II, and Cosimo III, respectively—recording the flowers and fruits that grew in their gardens. Ligozzi was the most botanically correct of the artists, as interested in root systems as in surface texture. Garzoni was a miniaturist who painted with gouache on vellum; her masterly series of fruits and flowers that grew in the Medici gardens now hangs in the Galleria Palatina in Florence's Pitti Palace, where Isabella has consulted it many times. Bimbi, who came a generation later, was a very different kind of painter: a creator of epic, almost bombastic still-lifes, done in oil on huge canvases.

The Medici gardens were begun by Lorenzo, and maintained, with varying degrees of enthusiasm, by his successors, most avidly by Cosimo I, an ardent naturalist who established the first botanical garden in Europe, in Pisa. Keeping a large orchard was a way of showing one's allegiance to "scientific humanism," a core principle of the Renaissance. In an orchard, the most sensuous pleasures of the natural world are carefully constrained by planning, pruning, and cultivating—resulting in a synthesis of nature and science. The orchard's civilizing effect seems to have diminished over time. The virtues of the humanistic gardens had little influence, for example, over the notoriously depraved Gian Gastone, the last of the Medici. After one banquet, having eaten and drunk to gross excess, as Christopher Hibbert relates in "The House of Medici: Its Rise and Fall," Gian Gastone vomited into his napkin and then wiped his mouth with his wig.

Bimbi's fruit paintings hang in the Medici villa at Poggio a Caiano, about fifteen miles west of Florence, a property that now belongs to the state. I asked Isabella to come with me to see them. We met at her house, in the oldest part of Perugia; the stones in the foundations are Etruscan. The autostrada was crowded, and Isabella drove aggressively, cursing the slower drivers in colorful Italian. After exiting, we drove through an ugly industrial area, where most of the roadside signs were in Chinese, because so many of the workers were from China. When we finally got to the villa, the custodian said that the Bimbi rooms were closed. However, since there were few other visitors, he shrugged and said that he supposed he could open them for us.

The paintings occupied two rooms. There were twelve big canvases of fruit grouped by type—citrus, cherries, plums, apples—all captured in the fleeting moment of perfect ripeness, fresh forever. The largest and most astonishingly detailed of the works was "Pears," which depicts a hundred and fifteen different varieties, collected in six baskets labeled by the month in which they ripen, June through December. In the background, there are classical columns and a stormy twilight sky. The artist, denied all but the visual sense to convey the essence of the fruit, concentrated on the texture and color of the skin. The result is not so much a still-life as a psychological portrait of fruit. These are the pears in the Wallace Stevens poem "Study of Two Pears":

The pears are not viols,

Nudes or bottles.

They resemble nothing else.

Bimbi thoughtfully numbered the pears, and provided a key at the bottom of the canvas, so that they can be identified by name. As we were standing in front of the painting, Isabella pointed out that he must have worked on the painting periodically over the growing season, as the different varieties ripened; otherwise the early-summer pears would have rotted by the time the winter pears were ripe.

Afterward, we walked around the galleries, looking at the other paintings.

"Wait," she said, noticing that one of the fruits in "Lemons" was actually a *mela rosa*—a rose apple. Was this a hidden symbol or a mistake? "I think he must have put it there for a reason," Isabella said. It was another mystery for an arboreal archeologist.

San Lorenzo is in the part of northern Umbria known as the Alta Valle del Tevere—the Upper Tiber Valley. The source of Rome's river is nearby. The Dalla Ragiones' trees grow on the southern slopes of the hill. The ground drops steeply away. The sound of rushing water comes up from below, but the valley is so deep that the stream can't be seen.

In past centuries, there were orchards on the hill, but the fruit trees had nearly all died by the time Livio started planting, in the early nineteen-sixties. Now the only old trees in the orchard are some olives and almonds. His house is larger than it looks, with additions built over the centuries; the original part is a thousand years old. A church near the house, where the bones of some eighteenth-century nobles are buried under the floor, now serves as a fruit warehouse. Old tools and weapons and farm implements hang everywhere, rusty and vaguely menacing, suggestive of hard work and poverty and struggle.

Livio lives alone, although his lady friend, Miriam Fiorellino, comes up from Rome for the weekend. (His wife, Rosa, died three years ago.) Laura, Isabella's sister, visits infrequently, but Isabella makes the forty-five-minute drive from Perugia two or three times a week. She checks on her grafts, and then walks around the hillside with a straightened-out paper clip, killing caterpillars that have bored into the tree trunks. The orchard is watched over by Livio's colorful scarecrows, one of which is decked out in a flashy car-racing suit and helmet (in the winter, skis are added), but they seem intended as much to keep away people as birds. Anyway, the birds somehow know exactly when the cherries will turn from white to red, and they often devour them before Isabella can gather the crop.

Meals at San Lorenzo are usually simple, cooked by Miriam and Isabella, who employ as many homegrown ingredients as possible. They use fruit in much of their cooking. Their wine, made by stomping red and white grapes together in the big wooden vats downstairs in the cantina, is a light, fruity rose; Livio drinks it cold, diluting it with water. (Isabella doesn't drink.) A typical meal begins with a soup made from local wild mushrooms, served with bread baked with chestnut flour in a corner of the huge fireplace in the kitchen and followed by a casserole of artichoke, potato, and prosciutto, with chestnut and rosemary cookies or a fruit tart for dessert. The Dalla Ragiones keep many of the traditional Umbrian festivals, and at the end of the year they burn La Vecchia, the effigy of an old woman made of rags and straw, and Livio curses— *"Vaffanculo, anno vecchio!"* ("Up your ass, old year!")—and spits into the fire.

When I visited San Lorenzo in January, we ate the last of the winter pears. They had a sharp, challenging flavor, and were firm and crisp and cold. (The fireplace and a wood-burning stove provide the only heat in the house, and last winter there was three feet of snow on the ground.) The taste was so clean—not buttery, which is the standard by which the commercial pear is bred—that it was almost metallic. "I am convinced that people's taste has changed as a result of the industrialization of fruit production," Isabella said. "The *mela rustica,* for example, which is described in old travellers' accounts as tasting like vinegar, now tastes rather sweet."

Livio is still the genius loci, as Isabella calls him, of the orchard, but, at eighty-four, he is much diminished from his prime. "He is like the Babbo Natale and I am like the elf who makes the toys," Isabella said. Livio has a long white fringe of hair around his bald, speckled, Shakespearean dome, and he has the hopeful expression that very old men get in their eyes. He is gruff and blustery, and Isabella treats him as she does the fruit trees—tenderly but firmly. She worries about his health. "The time is coming," Isabella said, "when we must think about the end—and what this project of ours will be without my father." She was feeling overwhelmed, she added, by caring for the four hundred trees, with little help, knowing that a lost tree might mean the end of that variety forever. "Lately, I have come to feel that the life I have chosen is not my own," she said.

None of Livio's paintings are on view in the house, and when I asked him where they were he told me he had burned them all years ago, adding that the only remaining painting was in the collection of the wife of Jean Arp, the French Dadaist. (Actually, Isabella told me that he had a couple of paintings squirrelled away inside the house, although I saw only photographs of them.) One day, when we were having lunch under the big olive trees, I asked Livio why he had burned his paintings, and he barked, *"Perche tutto quello era finito"* ("Because all that was finished") and did not elaborate. He had not only stopped painting; he had turned against the whole practice of making art and become what he calls *un'artista del pensiero*—an artist of thought. The orchard is his *natura morta*.

Last September, Isabella staged a *mostra pomologica*—a fruit show—in the center of Perugia, in an old palazzo that now belongs to the Bank of Umbria. It featured fruit from the collection—plums, quinces, medlars, apples, and pears—arranged in palm-frond baskets, in the casually sensuous style of Garzoni. Each basket was illuminated by an overhead light. Most of the visitors assumed that the fruit was made of marble or wax—the flyers that Isabella had put up around town had been intentionally ambiguous about whether this was to be a produce fair or an art exhibit.

Many of the younger people laughed when they discovered that the fruit was real. Perhaps the musky, slightly too fecund scent of ripe fruit made them giddy, or maybe the fruit was just funny-looking. The seeds rattled inside some of the apples, like natural castanets. Isabella, however, was more interested in the reactions of the elderly visitors, who are the last living link to the old trees. She was hoping that they would provide some clues to fruit she still hasn't found—perhaps the variety of fig called Fico Rondinino San Sepolcro, which she has been seeking for years.

The elderly people were mostly former sharecroppers, who had dressed formally for their trip to the city. At first, they were inclined to be circumspect and seemed reluctant to answer Isabella's questions. "In many of their memories, the fruit is connected to hunger and hardship," Isabella said. "They aren't good memories." However, the smell and the texture of the fruit soon dissolved their inhibitions. One old woman, from Gualdo Tadino, near Gubbio, remembered how she and her husband used to keep fruit under their bed, where it was cool; the thought made her blush. A farmer remembered how the landowner he worked for had told him he didn't want a particular kind of pear tree growing on his land, and the man had said he would get rid of it. But that night he went to the tree and whispered, "Don't worry, I didn't mean it."

The most exciting piece of arboreal information came from a former nun, who told Isabella she remembered a Fico Rondinino San Sepolcro growing in the convent in Bevagna, near Assisi. Isabella visited the convent as soon as she could, but she was too late. The sisters had cut the old figs down and replaced them with a healthy young kiwi tree.

THE BLOODIEST BATTLE

William Manchester

William Manchester served in the Marine Corps during World War II. Rising to the rank of Sergeant, Manchester fought, and was severely wounded, in the final American military campaign of the war, on the Japanese island of Okinawa. Both a reporter and a Professor of journalism, Mr. Manchester wrote a biography of Gen. Douglas MacArthur and partially completed a biography of Prime Minister Winston Churchill.

Manchester, who was born in Springfield, Massachusetts on April 1, 1922, came from a military family. His father served in the Marine Corps during World War I. Manchester died on June 1, 2004.

In the essay that follows, Mr. Manchester writes about a gathering of American and Japanese soldiers to commemorate the bloody battles that took place on Okinawa. It is a troubled event, raising difficult and powerful emotions in the veterans from both sides. Mr. Manchester takes the occasion of this essay, however, to expand his observations and to write about the nature of war, historically and in modern times.

————

On Okinawa today, Flag Day will be observed with an extraordinary ceremony: two groups of elderly men, one Japanese, the other American, will gather for a solemn rite. They could scarcely have less in common.

Their motives are mirror images; each group honors the memory of men who tried to slay the men honored by those opposite them. But theirs is a common grief. After forty-two years the ache is still there. They are really united by death, the one great victor in modern war.

They have come to Okinawa to dedicate a lovely monument in remembrance of the Americans, Japanese, and Okinawans killed there in the last and bloodiest battle of the Pacific war. More than 200,000 perished in the 82-day struggle—twice the number of Japanese lost at Hiroshima and more American blood than had been shed at Gettysburg. My own regiment—I was a sergeant in the 29th Marines—lost more than 80 percent of the men who had landed on April 1, 1945. Before the battle was over, both the Japanese and American commanding generals lay in shallow graves.

Okinawa lies 330 miles southwest of the southernmost Japanese island of Kyushu; before the war, it was Japanese soil. Had there been no atom bombs—and at that time the most powerful Americans, in Washington and at the Pentagon, doubted that the device would work—the invasion of the Nipponese homeland would have been staged from Okinawa, beginning with a landing on Kyushu to take place November 1. The six Marine divisions, storming ashore abreast, would lead the way. President Truman asked Gen. Douglas MacArthur, whose estimates of casualties on the eve of battles had proved uncannily accurate, about Kyushu. The general predicted a million Americans would die in that first phase.

Given the assumption that nuclear weapons would contribute nothing to victory, the battle of Okinawa had to be fought. No one doubted the need to bring Japan to its knees. But some Americans came to hate the things we had to do, even when convinced that doing them was absolutely necessary; they had never understood the bestial, monstrous and vile means required to reach the objective—an unconditional Japanese surrender. As for me, I could not reconcile the romanticized view of war that runs like a red streak through our literature—and the glowing aura of selfless patriotism that had led us to put our lives at forfeit—with the wet, green hell from which I had barely escaped. Today, I understand. I was there, and was twice wounded. This is the story of what I knew and when I knew it.

To our astonishment, the Marine landing on April 1 was uncontested. The enemy had set a trap. Japanese strategy called first for kamikazes to destroy our fleet, cutting us off from supply ships; then Japanese troops would methodically annihilate the men stranded ashore using the trench-warfare tactics of World War I—cutting the Americans down as they charged heavily fortified positions. One hundred and ten thousand Japanese troops were waiting on the southern tip of the island. Intricate entrenchments, connected by tunnels, formed the enemy's defense line, which ran across the waist of Okinawa from the Pacific Ocean to the East China Sea.

By May 8, after more than five weeks of fighting, it became clear that the anchor of this line was a knoll of coral and volcanic ash, which the Marines christened Sugar Loaf Hill. My role in mastering it—the crest changed hands more than eleven times—was the central experience of my youth, and of all the military bric-a-brac that I put away after the war, I cherish most the Commendation from General Lemuel C. Shepherd Jr., U.S.M.C., our splendid division commander, citing me for "gallantry in action and extraordinary achievement," adding, "Your courage was a constant source of inspiration . . . and your conduct throughout was in keeping with the highest tradition of the United States Naval Service."

The struggle for Sugar Loaf lasted ten days; we fought under the worst possible conditions—a driving rain that never seemed to slacken, day or night. (I remember wondering, in an idiotic moment—no man in combat is really sane—whether the battle could be called off, or at least postponed, because of bad weather.) *Newsweek* called Sugar Loaf "the most critical local battle of the war." *Time* described a company of Marines—270 men—assaulting the hill. They failed; fewer than 30 returned. Fletcher Pratt, the military historian, wrote that the battle was unmatched in the Pacific war for "closeness and desperation." Casualties were almost unbelievable. In the 22d and 29th Marine regiments, two out of every three men fell. The struggle for the dominance of Sugar Loaf was probably the costliest engagement in the history of the Marine Corps. But by early evening on May 18, as night thickened over the embattled armies, the 29th Marines had taken Sugar Loaf, this time for keeps.

On Okinawa today, the ceremony will be dignified, solemn, seemly. It will also be anachronistic. If the Japanese dead of 1945 were resurrected to witness it, they would be appalled by the acceptance of defeat, the humiliation of their Emperor—the very idea of burying Japanese near the barbarians from across the sea and then mourning them together. Americans, meanwhile, risen from their graves, would ponder the evolution of their own society, and might wonder, What ever happened to patriotism?

When I was a child, a bracket was screwed to the sill of a front attic window; its sole purpose was to hold the family flag. At first light, on all legal holidays—including Election Day, July 4, Memorial Day and, of course, Flag Day—I would scamper up to show it. The holidays remain, but mostly they mean long weekends.

In the late 1920's, during my childhood, the whole town of Attleboro, Massachussettes, would turn out to cheer the procession on Memorial Day. The policemen always came first, wearing their number-one uniforms and keeping perfect step. Behind them was a two-man vanguard—the mayor and, at his side, my father, hero of the 5th Marines and Belleau Wood, wearing his immaculate dress blues and looking like a poster of a Marine, with one magnificent flaw: the right sleeve of his uniform was empty. He had lost the arm in the Argonne. I now think that, as I watched him pass by, my own military future was already determined.

The main body of the parade was led by five or six survivors of the Civil War, too old to march but sitting upright in open Pierce-Arrows and Packards, wearing their blue uniforms and broad-brimmed hats. Then, in perfect step, came a contingent of men in their fifties, with their blanket rolls sloping diagonally from shoulder to hip—the Spanish-American War veterans. After these—and anticipated by a great roar from the crowd—came the doughboys of World War I, some still in their late twenties. They were acclaimed in part because theirs had been the most recent conflict, but also because they had fought in the war that—we then thought—had ended all wars.

Americans still march in Memorial Day parades, but attendance is light. One war has led to another and another and yet another, and the cruel fact is that few men, however they die, are remembered beyond the lifetimes of their closest relatives and friends. In the early 1940's, one of the forces that kept us on the line, under heavy enemy fire, was the conviction that this battle was of immense historical import, and that those of us who survived it would be forever cherished in the hearts of Americans. It was rather diminishing to return in 1945 and discover that your own parents couldn't even pronounce the names of the islands you had conquered.

But what of those who do remain faithful to patriotic holidays? What are they commemorating? Very rarely are they honoring what actually happened, because only a handful know, and it's not their favorite topic of conversation. In World War II, 16 million Americans entered the armed forces. Of these, fewer than a million saw action. Logistically, it took nineteen men to back up one man in combat. All who wore uniforms are called veterans, but more than 90 percent of them are as uninformed about the killing zones as those on the home front.

If all Americans understood the nature of battle, they might be vulnerable to truth. But the myths of warfare are embedded deep in our ancestral memories. By the time children have reached the age of awareness, they regard uniforms, decorations and Sousa marches as exalted, and those who argue otherwise are regarded as unpatriotic.

General MacArthur, quoting Plato, said: "Only the dead have seen the end of war." One hopes he was wrong, for war, as it had existed for over four thousand years, is now obsolete. As late as the spring of 1945, it was possible for one man, with a rifle, to make a difference, however infinitesimal, in the struggle to defeat an enemy who had attacked us and threatened our West Coast. The bomb dropped on Hiroshima made that man ludicrous, even pitiful. Soldiering has been relegated to Sartre's theater of the absurd. The image of the man as protector and defender of the home has been destroyed (and I suggest that that seed of thought eventually led women to re-examine their own role in society).

Until nuclear weapons arrived, the glorifying of militarism was the nation's hidden asset. Without it, we would almost certainly have been defeated by the Japanese, probably by 1943. In 1941 American youth was isolationist and pacifist. Then war planes from Imperial Japan destroyed our fleet at Pearl Harbor on December 7, and on December 8 recruiting stations were packed. Some of us later found fighting rather different from what had been advertised. Yet in combat these men risked their lives—and often lost them—in hope of winning medals. There is an old soldier's saying: "A man won't sell you his life, but he'll give it to you for a piece of colored ribbon."

Most of the men who hit the beaches came to scorn eloquence. They preferred the 130-year-old "Word of Cambronne." As dusk darkened the Waterloo battlefield, with the French in full retreat, the British sent word to Gen. Pierre Cambronne, commander of the Old Guard. His position, they pointed out, was hopeless, and they suggested he capitulate. Every French textbook reports his reply as "The Old Guard dies but never surrenders." What he actually said was "Merde."

If you mention this incident to members of the U.S. 101st Airborne Division, they will immediately understand. "Nuts" was not Brigadier General Anthony C. McAuliffe's answer to the Nazi demand that he hoist a white flag over Bastogne. Instead, he quoted Cambronne.

The character of combat has always been determined by the weapons available to men when their battles were fought. In the beginning they were limited to hand weapons—clubs, rocks, swords, lances. At the Battle of Camlann in 539, England's Arthur—a great warrior, not a king—led a charge that slew 930 Saxons, including their leader.

It is important to grasp the fact that those 930 men were not killed by snipers, grenades or shells. The dead were bludgeoned or stabbed to death, and we have a pretty good idea how this was done. One of the facts withheld from civilians during World War II was that Kabar fighting knives, with seven-inch blades honed to such precision that you could shave with them, were issued to Marines and that we were taught to use them. You never cut downward. You drove the point of your blade into a man's lower belly and ripped upward. In the process, you yourself became soaked in the other man's gore. After that charge at Camlann, Arthur must have been half-drowned in blood.

The Battle of Agincourt, fought nearly one thousand years later, represented a slight technical advance: crossbows and longbows had appeared. All the same, Arthur would have recognized the battle. Like all engagements of the time, this one was short. Killing by hand is hard work, and hot work. It is so exhausting that even men in peak condition collapse once the issue of triumph or defeat is settled. And Henry V's spear carriers and archers were drawn from social classes that had been undernourished for as long as anyone could remember. The duration of medieval battles could have been measured in hours, even minutes.

The Battle of Waterloo, fought exactly four hundred years later, is another matter. By 1815, the Industrial Revolution had begun cranking out appliances of death, primitive by today's standards, but revolutionary for infantrymen of that time. And Napoleon had formed mass armies, pressing every available man into service. It was a long step toward total war, and its impact was immense. Infantrymen on both sides fought with single-missile weapons—muskets or rifles—and were supported by (and were the target of) artillery firing cannonballs.

The fighting at Waterloo continued for three days; for a given regiment, however, it usually lasted one full day, much longer than medieval warfare. A half-century later, Gettysburg lasted three days and cost 43,497 men. Then came the marathon slaughters of 1914–1918, lasting as long as ten months (Verdun) and producing hundreds of thousands of corpses lying, as F. Scott Fitzgerald wrote afterward, "like a million bloody rugs." Winston Churchill, who had been a dashing young cavalry officer when Victoria was Queen, said of the new combat: "War, which was cruel and magnificent, has become cruel and squalid."

It may be said that the history of war is one of men packed together, getting closer and closer to the ground and then deeper and deeper into it. In the densest combat of World War I, battalion frontage—the length of the line into which the 1,000-odd men were squeezed—had been 800 yards. On Okinawa, on the Japanese fortified line, it was less than 600 yards—about 18 inches per man. We were there and deadlocked for more than a week in the relentless rain. During those weeks we lost nearly 4,000 men.

And now it is time to set down what this modern battlefield was like.

All greenery had vanished; as far as one could see, heavy shellfire had denuded the scene of shrubbery. What was left resembled a cratered moonscape. But the craters were vanishing, because the rain had transformed the earth into a thin porridge—too thin even to dig foxholes. At night you lay on a poncho as a precaution against drowning during the barrages. All night, every night, shells erupted close enough to shake the mud beneath you at the rate of five or six a minute. You could hear the cries of the dying but could do nothing. Japanese infiltration was always imminent, so the order was to stay put. Any man who stood up was cut in half by machine guns manned by fellow Marines.

By day, the mud was hip-deep; no vehicles could reach us. As you moved up the slope of the hill, artillery and mortar shells were bursting all around you, and, if you were fortunate enough to reach the top, you encountered the Japanese defenders, almost face to face, a few feet away. To me, they looked like badly wrapped brown paper parcels someone had soaked in a tub. Their eyes seemed glazed. So, I suppose, did ours.

Japanese bayonets were fixed; ours weren't. We used the knives, or, in my case, a .45 revolver and M1 carbine. The mud beneath our feet was deeply veined with blood. It was slippery. Blood is very slippery. So you skidded around, in deep shock, fighting as best you could until one side outnumbered the other. The outnumbered side would withdraw for reinforcements and then counterattack.

During those ten days I ate half a candy bar. I couldn't keep anything down. Everyone had dysentery, and this brings up an aspect of war even Robert Graves, Siegfried Sassoon, Edmund Blunden and Ernest Hemingway avoided. If you put more than a quarter million men in a line for three weeks, with no facilities for the disposal of human waste, you are going to confront a disgusting problem. We were fighting and sleeping in one vast cesspool. Mingled with that stench was another—the corrupt and corrupting odor of rotting human flesh.

My luck ran out on June 5, more than two weeks after we had taken Sugar Loaf Hill and killed the seven thousand Japanese soldiers defending it. I had suffered a slight gunshot wound above the right knee on June 2, and had rejoined my regiment to make an amphibious landing on Oroku Peninsula behind enemy lines. The next morning several of us were standing in a stone enclosure outside some Okinawan tombs when a six-inch rocket mortar shell landed among us.

The best man in my section was blown to pieces, and the slime of his viscera enveloped me. His body had cushioned the blow, saving my life; I still carry a piece of his shinbone in my chest. But I collapsed, and was left for dead. Hours later corpsmen found me still breathing, though blind and deaf, with my back and chest a junkyard of iron fragments—including, besides the piece of shinbone, four pieces of shrapnel too close to the heart to be removed. (They were not dangerous, a Navy surgeon assured me, but they still set off the metal detector at the Buffalo airport.) Between June and November I underwent four major operations and was discharged as 100 percent disabled. But the young have strong recuperative powers. The blindness was caused by shock, and my vision returned. I grew new eardrums. In three years I was physically fit. The invisible wounds remain.

Most of those who were closest to me in the early 1940s had left New England campuses to join the Marines, knowing it was the most dangerous branch of the service. I remember them as bright, physically strong and inspired by an idealism and love of country they would have been too embarrassed to acknowledge. All of us despised the pompousness and pretentiousness of senior officers. It helped that, almost without exception, we admired and respected our commander in chief. But despite our enormous pride in being Marines, we saw through the scam that had lured so many of us to recruiting stations.

Once we polled a rifle company, asking each man why he had joined the Marines. A majority cited *To the Shores of Tripoli,* a marshmallow of a movie starring John Payne, Randolph Scott and Maureen O'Hara. Throughout the film the uniform of the day was dress blues; requests for liberty were always granted. The implication was that combat would be a lark, and when you returned, spangled with decorations, a Navy nurse like Maureen O'Hara would be waiting in your sack. It was peacetime again when John Wayne appeared on the silver screen as Sergeant Stryker in *Sands of Iwo Jima,* but that film underscores the point; I went to see it with another ex-Marine, and we were asked to leave the theater because we couldn't stop laughing.

After my evacuation from Okinawa, I had the enormous pleasure of seeing Wayne humiliated in person at Aiea Heights Naval Hospital in Hawaii. Only the most gravely wounded, the litter cases, were sent there. The hospital was packed, the halls lined with beds. Between Iwo Jima and Okinawa, the Marine Corps was being bled white.

Each evening, Navy corpsmen would carry litters down to the hospital theater so the men could watch a movie. One night they had a surprise for us. Before the film the curtains parted and out stepped John Wayne, wearing a cowboy outfit—ten-gallon hat, bandanna, checkered shirt, two pistols, chaps, boots and spurs. He grinned his aw-shucks grin, passed a hand over his face and said, "Hi ya, guys!" He was greeted by a stony silence. Then somebody booed. Suddenly everyone was booing.

This man was a symbol of the fake machismo we had come to hate, and we weren't going to listen to him. He tried and tried to make himself heard, but we drowned him out, and eventually he quit and left. If you liked *Sands of Iwo Jima,* I suggest you be careful. Don't tell it to the Marines.

And so we weren't macho. Yet we never doubted the justice of our cause. If we had failed—if we had lost Guadalcanal, and the Navy's pilots had lost the Battle of Midway—the Japanese would have invaded Australia and Hawaii, and California would have been in grave danger. In 1942 the possibility of an Axis victory was very real. It is possible for me to loathe war—and with reason—yet still honor the brave men, many of them boys, really, who fought with me and died beside me. I have been haunted by their loss these forty-two years, and I shall mourn them until my own death releases me. It does not seem too much to ask that they be remembered on one day each year. After all, they sacrificed their futures that you might have yours.

Yet I will not be on Okinawa for the dedication today. I would enjoy being with Marines; the ceremony will be moving, and we would be solemn, remembering our youth and the beloved friends who died there.

Few, if any, of the Japanese survivors agreed to attend the ceremony. However, Edward L. Fox, chairman of the Okinawa Memorial Shrine Committee, capped almost six years' campaigning for a monument when he heard about a former Japanese naval officer, Yoshio Yazaki—a meteorologist who had belonged to a 4,000-man force led by Rear Adm. Minoru Ota—and persuaded him to attend.

On March 31, 1945, Yazaki-san had been recalled to Tokyo, and thus missed the battle of Okinawa. Ten weeks later—exactly 42 years ago today—Admiral Ota and his men committed seppuku, killing themselves rather than face surrender. Ever since then Yazaki has been tormented by the thought that his comrades have joined their ancestors and he is here, not there.

Finding Yazaki was a great stroke of luck for Fox, for whom an Okinawa memorial had become an obsession. His own division commander tried to discourage him. The Japanese could hardly be expected to back a memorial on the site of their last great military defeat. But Yazaki made a solution possible.

If Yazaki can attend, why can't I? I played a role in the early stages of Buzz Fox's campaign and helped write the tribute to the Marines that is engraved on the monument. But when I learned that Japanese were also participating, I quietly withdrew. There are too many graves between us, too much gore, too many memories of too many atrocities.

In 1978, revisiting Guadalcanal, I encountered a Japanese businessman who had volunteered to become a kamikaze pilot in 1945 and was turned down at the last minute. Mutual friends suggested that we meet. I had expected no difficulty; neither, I think, did he. But when we confronted each other, we froze.

I trembled, suppressing the sudden, startling surge of primitive rage within. And I could see, from his expression, that this was difficult for him, too. Nations may make peace. It is harder for fighting men. On simultaneous impulse we both turned and walked away.

I set this down in neither pride nor shame. The fact is that some wounds never heal. Yazaki, unlike Fox, is dreading the ceremony. He does not expect to be shriven of his guilt. He knows he must be there but can't say why. Men are irrational, he explains, and adds that he feels very sad.

So do I, Yazaki-san, so do I.

20 DAYS IN THE CITY OF ANGELS: THE 12TH DAY (GETTING ALONG)

Douglas Messerli

Douglas Messerli, the founder, editor, and publisher of Sun & Moon Press and Green Integer Press, is the author of numerous books, including plays, novels, poetry, memoir and essays. He has edited some of the most important anthologies of our time in poetry (*From the Other Side of the Century* and *PIP [The Project for Innovative Poetry]*), fiction (*Great Stories, Volumes I & II*), and drama (*From the Other Side of the Century: A New American Drama 1960–1995*).

Messerli has been writing his cultural memoirs—memoirs based on art and cultural life—in yearly volumes, each entitled *My Year _____*. This piece comes from his collection *My Year 2010*. As social commentary, it deals with the Rodney King police beating and the aftermath of riots that followed in Los Angeles in 1991–1992. Mr. Messerli, repulsed by the inhumanity of those events, joins Rodney King's own plea for harmony and civility and mutual respect among all, at the same time that he reminds us of those many African-Americans who worked to heal the community.

———

Certainly the city of Los Angles and its hundreds of suburban communities were aware of the April 1992 trials, held in the outlying community of Simi Valley, concerning the four Los Angeles Police Department officers accused of beating Rodney King on March 3, 1991. We had all watched the tapes, played over and over in the public media, of King's 1991 beating, and almost everyone I knew was outraged by the police brutality. Although the police and their lawyers declared that King was violent, resisting arrest, and insisted that not everything occurred as it seemed on George Holliday's amateur camcorder, we felt it represented a truth that was hard to erase. Both the tape and pictures of King after the incident testified to the outrageous anger of the police.

It came as somewhat of a shock, accordingly, when, on the afternoon of April 29th, 17 years ago from today, the jury decision came down at 3:15, acquitting all four officers of assault and acquitting three of the four of using excessive force.

That night, however, was something that few of us could have imagined. It began at about a quarter of seven as many in the city were watching the evening news. At the corner of Florence and South Normandie Avenues, in South Central Los Angeles, crowds had been dragging a white driver, Reginald Denny, from his vehicle, beating him, and culminating in someone throwing a concrete fragment at Denny's head as he lay unconscious in the street. News helicopters hovered over the entire scene, and dinnertime watchers were forced to witness not only the beating but the horrible whoop and dance of derision by one of Denny's attackers. Police stayed back from the scene, and Denny was saved only by an African-American, Bobby Green, Jr., who, watching the scene on television, rushed to the location and drove Denny, in his own truck, to the hospital.

Other beatings followed, including that of a local construction worker, Fidel Lopez, a Guatemalan immigrant who was pulled from his truck and robbed of almost $2,000, while Damian Williams slammed a stereo into Lopez's head and another rioter tried to slice off Lopez's ear. Upon losing consciousness, Lopez was spray-painted by members of the crowd across his chest, torso, and genitals.

The terrifying savagery of these events, witnessed by millions of viewers, horrified the city. Within about an hour and a half, the entire area near Florence and Normandie had been looted and burned, and rioters began moving into other neighborhoods, torching cars, beating drivers, looting stores, and burning homes and offices; even a Black bookstore was destroyed. Protestors at the police headquarters, Parker Center, began to throw rocks at the entryway to the building. Responding firefighters throughout the city were met with rocks and gun-fire. Some flights at Los Angeles International Airport were cancelled or diverted. The police seemed to have disappeared as a mad and frenzied lawlessness had exploded into the streets.

By the morning of April 30th, Los Angeles mayor, Tom Bradley, declared a state of emergency, and California Governor Pete Wilson activated the National Guard.

That same morning, I received a call from my shipper, Reggie Jones, a Black man who lived in South Central. In a hurried and near-breathless tone he recounted the horrors of the night, how numerous homes near where he and his family lived had burned to the ground, how intense the noise had been, and how he had spent much of the night attempting to put out local fires, which the Fire Department were unable to reach. "I feel like I'm sort of a reporter calling in from the war zone of some foreign country," he gasped.

"Reggie, I think it may be safer if you don't try to come in today, particularly since you do it on bicycle." He agreed, but, by about noon, Reggie arrived, almost out of breath.

"I just couldn't stay there anymore. It was just too difficult to remain," he explained.

At 12:15, Bradley announced a dusk-to-dawn curfew, and Reggie and I began talking about possibly closing the office—located on one of the major thoroughfares of Los Angeles—Wilshire Boulevard—early. Soon after, I received a call from my companion, Howard, a curator at the Los Angeles County Museum of Art, who reported that the museum had suggested its employees leave for the day. As he crossed the street to go home, he'd encountered a long line of cars and trucks, each filled with shouting beings, armed with long sticks and guns. I ran to the porch of my office and saw the procession moving toward us. Together, Reggie and I watched as they jumped from the cars, vandalizing and looting the May Company department store (now part of the Los Angeles County Museum of Art), located a block from the Sun & Moon offices. Again, there were no police in sight.

I quickly demanded that Reggie come inside with me, locking the doors. As the angry procession passed us without incident, I told him we should both leave while we could. He agreed but was determined to stay a bit longer, hinting that he had nowhere else to go. As I left, I told him to keep the doors locked.

I quickly walked home, looking back only to see the violent revelers attacking a small shopping mall west of me. We later heard that the cars and rioters had been turned back at the edge of Beverly Hills, a few blocks further west. The police there were evidently not intimidated. But the gang, in turning, attacked a sports shop, loading up, so I heard, with guns and other weapons. Fifty-three people died over the six days of the riot.

At home, everything was eerily quiet, but as I sat watching the television set in horror, I suddenly told Howard that I was afraid that Reggie left without locking the door. He had forgotten the keys to the building before, and there was every reason that he might have forgotten today.

Howard and I began to drive toward the office using the back way, taking Eighth Street instead of Wilshire. Not a soul was in sight. But suddenly out of nowhere a car came racing toward us, almost forcing us to take to the sidewalk, the driver and passengers screaming obscenities to us as they passed.

The building was wide open. I quickly locked it and returned to the car, and we rushed back home again.

As the sun began its slow set, the television helicopters revealed hundreds of fires throughout the city. At times, it looked as if the entire metropolis was ablaze, and we could see the sky over our courtyard lit up with yellow and orange flames. Curls of papery ash fell to our balconies and walkways. Yet a few minutes later it seemed that every child in our building was in the pool, which our windows overlook. "Why are all the children suddenly swimming?" asked Howard.

"I think their parents were probably afraid of their watching any more television, and sent them out so they could play."

"That seems reasonable," Howard answered. But as we turned our eyes from the flaming city upon the television set to the screaming and shouting children frolicking in those blue waters, the scene seemed surreal, as if somehow all those in our building could not comprehend the severity of the situation.

Finally, as darkness prevailed, and the children returned to their apartments, a strange quiet overcame everything as we listened to the newscasters softly echoing their dismay from nearly all the units of our condominium building.

Our cleaning woman, Ana-Maria Abraham, recently reminded me that I had called to check on her and her husband. They lived near Pico Boulevard, where many of the fires burned late into the night. One person was shot in her neighborhood. She recalls packing all of her important documents into a suitcase and attempting to leave the area by foot, but she was stopped by the police and told to return home. Ana, who has a history of chest infections, later was so affected by the surrounding smoke, that she went to a hospital. The staff there were so overwhelmed, however, they could not admit her, and she was sent home again, unable to sleep because of noise and fear.

By the morning of May 1st, the National Guard units had reached the size of 4,000, moving throughout the city in Humvees. Rodney King appeared on television asking his simple but profound question that would haunt the city for years: "People, I just want to say, you know, can we all get along?"

Reggie called in, reporting that he and his girlfriend had spent much of the night helping to fight fires in our neighborhood, including the Los Angeles County Museum of Art's warehouse, near Pico.

Although no one could condone the acts going on about us, many of us also recognized the extreme bigotry of the community. While Los Angeles is always proud to boast that it is one of the most diverse places on earth, we also know that the layout of the city is a jigsaw puzzle of segregation, with the Hispanics clustered in the East, Blacks restricted to South Central, and vast areas to the West and North of these communities of Central Los Angeles populated by Japanese and, particularly, Korean immigrants. Hundreds of small Koreatown stores and shops had been hit by the virulent wave of riots, and Asians were particularly outraged by the absence of the police to protect their "American Dreams."

Despite a blackout in areas that had been hardest hit, the night of May 1st was calmer. Sports games and other events had been cancelled. Public figures began to speak out, some, like Bill Cosby, attempting to alleviate the hostilities, while others like George H.W. Bush, seemingly stirring them up by denouncing what he described as "random terror and lawlessness." Still other figures attempted to explain the African-American anger and resentment, pent up for years after the 1965 Watts Riots.

In some respects, all who spoke were right. The actions of the rioters were ugly and violent and demonstrated some of the terrors we might expect when the city is hit by a strong earthquake—which will inevitably happen. But the police, long profiling individuals from the Black and Hispanic communities, needed to change their behavior and attitudes. It's hard to know whether those changes were ever thoroughly effected, even though Los Angeles Police Chief, Daryl Gates, lost his job because of police irresponsibility and inaction.

At the time, I attempted to put down some of my feeling and reactions in a letter I sent to a few friends, most notably to poet Lyn Hejinian. Lyn seemed a little overwhelmed by what she read; I think she thought I had been a bit melodramatic. But even now, as I relive those awful few days, my eyes begin to tear.

Order was finally restored on the fifth day, and the curfew lifted on Monday, May 4th.

Can we all get along? Some weeks it appears that we have wonderfully achieved that goal, but at other times it seems we still have a long ways to go. But the answer is "yes," if only we seriously try.

Los Angeles, April 29, 2009
Reprinted from Green Integer Blog (April 2009)

Describing this planned essay to my dear friend poet Will Alexander he noted that he experienced both the Watts Riot and the Rodney King Riot at "ground zero," and suggested that he also planned to write about his experiences. I strongly encouraged him to do so. We need a large number of re-countings of those events, I argued, if we are to release ourselves from the hateful past these events represent and remind ourselves of the changes still necessary to bring this vast, disparate community of Los Angeles into a caring and shared future.

Los Angeles, April 20, 2009

OUR VANISHING NIGHT

Verlyn Klinkenborg

In this article from *National Geographic,* journalist Verlyn Klinkenborg takes on one of his prime subjects: nature and our interrelationship with it. Klinkenborg, born in 1952 in Colorado, was raised on his family's farm in Iowa. His connection to nature comes from his roots in rural, agricultural life. While he writes regularly for *The New Yorker*, his work also often appears in other journals.

The National Geographic Society first published the *National Geographic* magazine in 1888. Since then, *National Geographic* has become the most popular magazine in the world, translated into thirty-two languages. More than 50 million people worldwide receive *National Geographic* each month. Throughout its one hundred twenty-two year history, *National Geographic* has dedicated itself to articles about nature and worldwide civilizations. Famous and revered not only for its in-depth articles, *National Geographic* publishes extraordinary photographs, which have won hundreds of awards.

This piece, on the importance of darkness in human life, comes from the November 2008 issue.

———

If humans were truly at home under the light of the moon and stars, we would go in darkness happily, the midnight world as visible to us as it is to the vast number of nocturnal species on this planet. Instead, we are diurnal creatures, with eyes adapted to living in the sun's light. This is a basic evolutionary fact, even though most of us don't think of ourselves as diurnal beings any more than we think of ourselves as primates or mammals or Earthlings. Yet it's the only way to explain what we've done to the night: We've engineered it to receive us by filling it with light.

This kind of engineering is no different than damming a river. Its benefits come with consequences—called light pollution—whose effects scientists are only now beginning to study. Light pollution is largely the result of bad lighting design, which allows artificial light to shine outward and upward into the sky, where it's not wanted, instead of focusing it downward, where it is. Ill-designed lighting washes out the darkness of night and radically alters the light levels—and light rhythms—to which many forms of life, including ourselves, have adapted. Wherever human light spills into the natural world, some aspect of life—migration, reproduction, feeding—is affected.

For most of human history, the phrase "light pollution" would have made no sense. Imagine walking toward London on a moonlit night around 1800, when it was Earth's most populous city.

Nearly a million people lived there, making do, as they always had, with candles and rushlights and torches and lanterns. Only a few houses were lit by gas, and there would be no public gaslights in the streets or squares for another seven years. From a few miles away, you would have been as likely to *smell* London as to see its dim collective glow.

Now most of humanity lives under intersecting domes of reflected, refracted light, of scattering rays from over-lit cities and suburbs, from light-flooded highways and factories. Nearly all of nighttime Europe is a nebula of light, as is most of the United States and all of Japan. In the south Atlantic the glow from a single fishing fleet—squid fishermen luring their prey with metal halide lamps—can be seen from space, burning brighter, in fact, than Buenos Aires or Rio de Janeiro.

In most cities the sky looks as though it has been emptied of stars, leaving behind a vacant haze that mirrors our fear of the dark and resembles the urban glow of dystopian science fiction. We've grown so used to this pervasive orange haze that the original glory of an unlit night—dark enough for the planet Venus to throw shadows on Earth—is wholly beyond our experience, beyond memory almost. And yet above the city's pale ceiling lies the rest of the universe, utterly undiminished by the light we waste—a bright shoal of stars and planets and galaxies, shining in seemingly infinite darkness.

We've lit up the night as if it were an unoccupied country, when nothing could be further from the truth. Among mammals alone, the number of nocturnal species is astonishing. Light is a powerful biological force, and on many species it acts as a magnet, a process being studied by researchers such as Travis Longcore and Catherine Rich, co-founders of the Los Angeles-based Urban Wildlands Group. The effect is so powerful that scientists speak of songbirds and seabirds being "captured" by searchlights on land or by the light from gas flares on marine oil platforms, circling and circling in the thousands until they drop. Migrating at night, birds are apt to collide with brightly lit tall buildings; immature birds on their first journey suffer disproportionately.

Insects, of course, cluster around streetlights, and feeding at those insect clusters is now ingrained in the lives of many bat species. In some Swiss valleys the European lesser horseshoe bat began to vanish after streetlights were installed, perhaps because those valleys were suddenly filled with light-feeding pipistrelle bats. Other nocturnal mammals—including desert rodents, fruit bats, opossums, and badgers—forage more cautiously under the permanent full moon of light pollution because they've become easier targets for predators.

Some birds—blackbirds and nightingales, among others—sing at unnatural hours in the presence of artificial light. Scientists have determined that long artificial days—and artificially short nights—induce early breeding in a wide range of birds. And because a longer day allows for longer feeding, it can also affect migration schedules. One population of Bewick's swans wintering in England put on fat more rapidly than usual, priming them to begin their Siberian migration early. The problem, of course, is that migration, like most other aspects of bird behavior, is a precisely timed biological behavior. Leaving early may mean arriving too soon for nesting conditions to be right.

Nesting sea turtles, which show a natural predisposition for dark beaches, find fewer and fewer of them to nest on. Their hatchlings, which gravitate toward the brighter, more reflective sea horizon, find themselves confused by artificial lighting behind the beach. In Florida alone, hatchling losses number in the hundreds of thousands every year. Frogs and toads living near brightly lit highways suffer nocturnal light levels that are as much as a million times brighter than normal, throwing nearly every aspect of their behavior out of joint, including their nighttime breeding choruses.

Of all the pollutions we face, light pollution is perhaps the most easily remedied. Simple changes in lighting design and installation yield immediate changes in the amount of light spilled into the atmosphere and, often, immediate energy savings.

It was once thought that light pollution only affected astronomers, who need to see the night sky in all its glorious clarity. And, in fact, some of the earliest civic efforts to control light pollution—in Flagstaff, Arizona, half a century ago—were made to protect the view from Lowell Observatory, which sits high above that city. Flagstaff has tightened its regulations since then, and in 2001 it was declared the first International Dark Sky City. By now the effort to control light pollution has spread around the globe. More and more cities and even entire countries, such as the Czech Republic, have committed themselves to reducing unwanted glare.

Unlike astronomers, most of us may not need an undiminished view of the night sky for our work, but like most other creatures we do need darkness. Darkness is as essential to our biological welfare, to our internal clockwork, as light itself. The regular oscillation of waking and sleep in our lives—one of our circadian rhythms—is nothing less than a biological expression of the regular oscillation of light on Earth. So fundamental are these rhythms to our being that altering them is like altering gravity.

For the past century or so, we've been performing an open-ended experiment on ourselves, extending the day, shortening the night, and short-circuiting the human body's sensitive response to light. The consequences of our bright new world are more readily perceptible in less adaptable creatures living in the peripheral glow of our prosperity. But for humans, too, light pollution may take a biological toll. At least one new study has suggested a direct correlation between higher rates of breast cancer in women and the nighttime brightness of their neighborhoods.

In the end, humans are no less trapped by light pollution than the frogs in a pond near a brightly lit highway. Living in a glare of our own making, we have cut ourselves off from our evolutionary and cultural patrimony—the light of the stars and the rhythms of day and night. In a very real sense, light pollution causes us to lose sight of our true place in the universe, to forget the scale of our being, which is best measured against the dimensions of a deep night with the Milky Way—the edge of our galaxy—arching overhead.

WORLD MAKING & HUNGER

Ursula Le Guin

Ursula Le Guin, born October 21, 1929, has written numerous books, including fiction, short stories, poetry, books for children, and essays. While known as a science fiction or fantasy writer, her books address issues of human ethics in both our relations to our environment and our relations to each other and society. Among her many awards and achievements, the Library of Congress honored Ms. Le Guin with the *Living Legends* award in 2000 for her important contributions to American culture.

"World Making" comes from a 1981 speech Ursula Le Guin gave, by invitation, to a Stanford University symposium called "Lost Worlds and Future Worlds." "Hunger" comes from a speech Le Guin gave in 1981 at a Portland Food Bank event to publicize the Oxfam America Fast for the Hungry. Le Guin, both a writer and a public figure, has spoken out often on important causes. In these short pieces, Ms. Le Guin addresses two of her passions: creativity and social justice.

Film and television productions have adapted much of Ms. Le Guin's work.

————

World-Making

We're supposed to be talking about world-making. The idea of making makes me think of making new. Making a new world: a different world: Middle Earth, say, or the planets of science fiction. That's the work of the fantastic imagination. Or there's making the world new: making the world different: a utopia or dystopia, the work of the political imagination.

But what about making the world, this world, the old one? That seems to be the province of the religious imagination, or of the will to survive (they may be the same thing). The old world is made new at the birth of every baby, and every New Year's Day, and every morning, and the Buddhist says at every instant.

That, in every practical sense, we make the world we inhabit is pretty well beyond question, but I leave it to the philosophers to decide whether we make it all from scratch—mmmm! tastes like a scratch world! But it's Bishop Berkeley's Cosmo-Mix!—or whether we patch it together by a more or less judicious selection of what strikes us as useful or entertaining in the inexhaustible chaos of the real.

In either case, what artists do is make a particularly skillful selection of fragments of cosmos, unusually useful and entertaining bits chosen and arranged to give an illusion of coherence and duration amidst the uncontrollable streaming of events. An artist makes the world her world. An artist makes her world the world. For a little while. For as long as it takes to look at or listen to or watch or read the work of art. Like a crystal, the work of art seems to contain the whole, and to imply eternity. And yet all it is is an explorer's sketch-map. A chart of shorelines on a foggy coast.

To make something is to invent it, to discover it, to uncover it, like Michelangelo cutting away the marble that hid the statue. Perhaps we think less often of the proposition reversed, thus: To discover something is to make it. As Julius Caesar said, "The existence of Britain was uncertain, until I went there." We can safely assume that the ancient Britons were perfectly certain of the existence of Britain, down to such details as where to go for the best woad. But, as Einstein said, it all depends on how you look at it, and as far as Rome, not Britain, is concerned, Caesar invented (*invenire*, "to come into, to come upon") Britain. He made it be, for the rest of the world.

Alexander the Great sat down and cried, somewhere in the middle of India, I think, because there were no more new worlds to conquer. What a silly man he was. There he sits sniveling, halfway to China! A conqueror. Conquistadores, always running into new worlds, and quickly running out of them. Conquest is not finding, and it is not making. Our culture, which conquered what is called the New World, and which sees the world of nature as an adversary to be conquered: look at us now. Running out of everything.

The name of our meeting is Lost Worlds and Future Worlds. Whether our ancestors came seeking gold, or freedom, or as slaves, we are the conquerors, we who live here now, in possession, in the New World. We are the inhabitants of a Lost World. It is utterly lost. Even the names are lost. The people who lived here, in this place, on these hills, for tens of thousands of years, are remembered (when they are remembered at all) in the language of the conquistadores: the "Costanos," the "Santa Claras," the "San Franciscos," names taken from foreign demigods. Sixty-three years ago, in the *Handbook of the Indians of California,* my father wrote:

> The Costanoan group is extinct so far as all practical purposes are concerned. A few scattered individuals survive....The larger part of a century has passed since the missions were abolished, and nearly a century and a half since they commenced to be founded. These periods have sufficed to efface even traditional recollections of the forefathers' habits, except for occasional fragments.

Here is one such fragment, a song; they sang it here, under the lives oaks, but there weren't any wild oats here then, only the Californian bunch-grasses. The people sang:

> I dream of you,
> I dream of you jumping,
> Rabbit, jackrabbit, and quail.

And one line is left of a dancing song:

> Dancing on the brink of the world.

With such fragments I might have shored my ruin, but I didn't know how. Only knowing that we must have a past to make a future with, I took what I could from the European-based culture of my own forefathers and mothers. I learned, like most of us, to use whatever I could, to filch an idea from China and steal a god from India, and so patch together a world as best I could. But still there is a mystery. This place where I was born and grew up and love beyond all other, my world, my California, still needs to be made. To make a new world you start with an old one, certainly. To find a world, maybe you have to have lost one. Maybe you have to be lost. The dance of renewal, the dance that made the world, was always danced here at the edge of things, on the brink, on the foggy coast.

Hunger

You probably didn't expect to hear anything about Macchu Picchu today—that lost city high in the Andes, built a thousand years ago—but the Chilean poet Pablo Neruda wrote a book about it, and I could find nothing to offer you that came closer to the heart of our subject here today. He describes the wonderful place in a long series of images—this is my own rather wild translation.

> Then up the ladder of the earth I climbed
> through the terrible mazes of lost jungles
> to reach you, Macchu Picchu.
>
> Tall city of stepped stone
>
> in you two lineages meet,
> the cradle of man, the cradle of light,
> rock together in the thorny wind.
>
> Mother of stone, foam of the condor,
> high reef of the human dawn…

And then the poet begins to ask who, in fact, built the city.

Ancient America, bride of the depths,

did you too, did your hands

up from the forests to the high void of the gods,

under the marriage-day banners of light and order,

mixed with the thunder of drums and lances,

did you too, did your hands

that wove the mind's rose and the snowline

and the blood-red grain of the furrows

into the web of shining matter, into the hollows of stone,

O buried America, did you too, did your hands hold down

in the under-depths, in the bitter pit, the eagle, hunger?

Hunger, coral of mankind,

hunger, did your steep reefs rise

as high as those high, ill-founded towers?

Macchu Picchu, did you build

stone upon stone, and the foundation, hunger?

diamond on diamond, and the foundation, tears?

That says to me what we have come here for. It says that so long as the beautiful towers of stone, of concrete, of glass, are not well founded, they are not habitable. No house worth living in has for its cornerstone the hunger of those who built it. We in America now raise our cities taller even than Macchu Picchu. But along with what they call the "real" city, the "real estate," there is an invisible city. It is to the stones of the city as the soul is to the body. And that's what we're talking about. That is the city we're trying to build, to found, not on hoarding and moneymaking and hunger, but on sharing and on justice. A house that deserves its children.

We don't live in such a house. We never have, no doubt we never will. But that doesn't matter. Whoever helps to build that house, to lay a single stone of it, may feel that they've done more in their life and with their life than all the Kings and Incas in all their power ever did.

THE DISCOVERY OF WHAT IT MEANS TO BE AN AMERICAN

James Baldwin

Born in Harlem, New York in 1924, James Baldwin lived with his mother, Emma Berdis Joynes and his adoptive father, the Harlem preacher David Baldwin. Author of twenty-four books, Baldwin writes fiction, plays, poetry, and essays that cover topics from growing up in Harlem to racial and sexual conflicts within society. As a political activist, Baldwin worked for the civil rights of African-Americans and social equality for all Americans. The thoughtfulness, clarity, and directness of Baldwin's writing style brought his work to the attention of a wide audience. As an important intellectual of our time, Mr. Baldwin had the wisdom and the insight to speak to us all. Mr. Baldwin died in November 1987.

In this well-known piece, "The Discovery of What It Means to Be An American," Baldwin describes for all of America what it means to be an African-American, how an African-American writer views the world and American culture, and what place an African-American might find in contemporary America.

———

"It is a complex fate to be an American," Henry James observed, and the principal discovery an American writer makes in Europe is just how complex this fate is. America's history, her aspirations, her peculiar triumphs, her even more peculiar defeats, and her position in the world—yesterday and today—are all so profoundly and stubbornly unique that the very word "America" remains a new, almost completely undefined and extremely controversial proper noun. No one in the world seems to know exactly what it describes, not even we motley millions who call ourselves Americans.

I left America because I doubted my ability to survive the fury of the color problem here. (Sometime I still do.) I wanted to prevent myself from becoming *merely* a Negro; or, even, merely a Negro writer. I wanted to find out in what way the *specialness* of my experience could be made to connect me with other people instead of dividing me from them. (I was as isolated from Negroes as I was from whites, which is what happens when a Negro begins, at bottom, to believe what white people say about him.)

In my necessity to find the terms on which my experience could be related to that of others, Negroes and whites, writers and non-writers, I proved, to my astonishment, to be as American as any Texas G.I. And I found my experience was shared by every American writer I knew in Paris. Like me, they had been divorced from their origins, and it turned out to make very little difference that the origins of white Americans were European and mine were African—they were no more at home in Europe than I was.

The fact that I was the son of a slave and they were the sons of free men meant less, by the time we confronted each other on European soil, than the fact that we were both searching for our separate identities. When we had found these, we seemed to be saying, why, then, we would no longer need to cling to the shame and bitterness which had divided us so long.

It became terribly clear in Europe, as it never had been here, that we knew more about each other than any European ever could. And it also became clear that, no matter where our fathers had been born, or what they had endured, the fact of Europe had formed us both was part of our identity and part of our inheritance.

I had been in Paris a couple of years before any of this became clear to me. When it did, I, like many a writer before me upon the discovery that his props have all been knocked out from under him, suffered a species of breakdown and was carried off to the mountains of Switzerland. There, in that absolutely alabaster landscape, armed with two Bessie Smith records and a typewriter, I began to try to re-create the life that I had first known as a child and from which I had spent so many years in flight.

It was Bessie Smith, through her tone and her cadence, who helped me to dig back to the way I myself must have spoken when I was a pickaninny, and to remember the things I had heard and seen and felt. I had buried them very deep. I had never listened to Bessie Smith in America (in the same way that, for years, I would not touch watermelon), but in Europe she helped to reconcile me to being a "nigger."

I do not think that I could have made this reconciliation here. Once I was able to accept my role—as distinguished, I must say, from my "place"—in the extraordinary drama which is America, I was released from the illusion that I hated America.

The story of what can happen to an American Negro writer in Europe simply illustrates, in some relief, what can happen to any American writer there. It is not meant, of course, to imply that it happens to them all, for Europe can be very crippling, too; and, anyway, a writer, when he has made his first breakthrough, has simply won a crucial skirmish in a dangerous, unending and unpredictable battle. Still, the breakthrough is important, and the point is that an American writer, in order to achieve it, very often has to leave this country.

The American writer, in Europe, is released, first of all, from the necessity of apologizing for himself. It is not until he *is* released from the habit of flexing his muscles and proving that he is just a "regular guy" that he realizes how crippling this habit has been. It is not necessary for him, there, to pretend to be something he is not, for the artist does not encounter in Europe the same suspicion he encounters here. Whatever the Europeans may actually think of artists, they have killed enough of them off by now to know that they are as real—and as persistent—as rain, snow, taxes or businessmen.

Of course, the reason for Europe's comparative clarity concerning the different functions of men in society is that European society has always been divided into classes in a way that American society never has been. A European writer considers himself to be part of an old and honorable tradition—of intellectual activity, of letters—and his choice of a vocation does not cause him any uneasy wonder as to whether or not it will cost him all his friends. But this tradition does not exist in America.

On the contrary, we have a very deep-seated distrust of real intellectual effort (probably because we suspect that it will destroy, as I hope it does, that myth of America to which we cling so desperately). An American writer fights his way to one of the lowest rungs on the American social ladder by means of pure bull-headedness and an indescribable series of odd jobs. He probably *has* been a "regular fellow" for much of his adult life, and it is not easy for him to step out of that lukewarm bath.

We must, however, consider a rather serious paradox: though American society is more mobile than Europe's, it is easier to cut across social and occupational lines there than it is here. This has something to do, I think, with the problem of status in American life. Where everyone has status, it is also perfectly possible, after all, that no one has. It seems inevitable, in any case, that a man may become uneasy as to just what his status is.

But Europeans have lived with the idea of status for a long time. A man can be as proud of being a good waiter as of being a good actor, and, in neither case, feel threatened. And this means that the actor and the waiter can have a freer and more genuinely friendly relationship in Europe than they are likely to have here. The waiter does not feel, with obscure resentment, that the actor has "made it," and the actor is not tormented by the fear that he may find himself, tomorrow, once again a waiter.

This lack of what may roughly be called social paranoia causes the American writer in Europe to feel—almost certainly for the first time in his life—that he can reach out to everyone, that he is accessible to everyone and open to everything. This is an extraordinary feeling. He feels, so to speak, his own weight, his own value.

It is as though he suddenly came out of a dark tunnel and found himself beneath the open sky. And, in fact, in Paris, I began to see the sky for what seemed to be the first time. It was borne in on me—and it did not make me feel melancholy—that this sky had been there before I was born and would be there when I was dead. And it was up to me, therefore, to make of my brief opportunity the most that could be made.

I was born in New York, but have lived only in pockets of it. In Paris, I lived in all parts of the city—on the Right Bank and the Left, among the bourgeoisie and among *les misérables,* and knew all kinds of people, from pimps and prostitutes in Pigalle to Egyptian bankers in Neuilly. This may sound extremely unprincipled or even obscurely immoral: I found it healthy. I love to talk to people, all kinds of people, and almost everyone, as I hope we still know, loves a man who loves to listen.

This perpetual dealing with people very different from myself caused a shattering in me of preconceptions I scarcely know I held. The writer is meeting in Europe people who are not American, whose sense of reality is entirely different from his own. They may love or hate or admire or fear or envy this country—they see it, in any case, from another point of view, and this forces the writer to reconsider many things he had always taken for granted. This reassessment, which can be very painful, is also very valuable.

This freedom, like all freedom, has its dangers and its responsibilities. One day it begins to be borne in on the writer, and with great force, that he is living in Europe as an American. If he were living there as a European, he would be living on a different and far less attractive continent.

This crucial day may be the day on which an Algerian taxi-driver tells him how it feels to be an Algerian in Paris. It may be the day on which he passes a café terrace and catches a glimpse of the tense, intelligent and troubled face of Albert Camus. Or it may be the day on which someone asks him to explain Little Rock and he begins to feel that it would be simpler—and, corny as the words may sound, more honorable—to *go* to Little Rock than sit in Europe, on an American passport, trying to explain it.

This is a personal day, a terrible day, the day to which his entire sojourn has been tending. It is the day he realizes that there are no untroubled countries in this fearfully troubled world; that if he has been preparing himself for anything in Europe, he has been preparing himself—for America. In short, the freedom that the American writer finds in Europe brings him, full circle, back to himself, with the responsibility for his development where it always was: in his own hands.

Even the most incorrigible maverick has to be born somewhere. He may leave the group that produced him—he may be forced to—but nothing will efface his origins, the marks of which he carries with him everywhere. I think it is important to know this and even find it a matter for rejoicing, as the strongest people do, regardless of their station. On this acceptance, literally, the life of a writer depends.

The charge has often been made against American writers that they do not describe society, and have no interest in it. They only describe individuals in opposition to it, or isolated from it. Of course, what the American writer is describing is his own situation. But what is *Anna Karenina* describing if not the tragic fate of the isolated individual, at odds with her time and place?

The real difference is that Tolstoy was describing an old and dense society in which everything seemed—to the people in it, though not to Tolstoy—to be fixed forever. And the book is a masterpiece because Tolstoy was able to fathom, and make us see, the hidden laws which really governed this society and made Anna's doom inevitable.

American writers do not have a fixed society to describe. The only society they know is one in which nothing is fixed and in which the individual must fight for his identity. This is a rich confusion, indeed, and it creates for the American writer unprecedented opportunities.

That the tensions of American life, as well as the possibilities, are tremendous is certainly not even a question. But these are dealt with in contemporary literature mainly compulsively; that is, the book is more likely to be a symptom of our tension than an examination of it. The time has come,

God knows, for us to examine ourselves, but we can only do this if we are willing to free ourselves of the myth of America and try to find out what is really happening here.

Every society is really governed by hidden laws, by unspoken but profound assumptions on the part of the people, and ours is no exception. It is up to the American writer to find out what these laws and assumptions are. In a society much given to smashing taboos without thereby managing to be liberated from them, it will be no easy matter.

It is no wonder, in the meantime, that the American writer keeps running off to Europe. He needs sustenance for his journey and the best models he can find. Europe has what we do not have yet, a sense of the mysterious and inexorable limits of life, a sense, in a word, of tragedy. And we have what they sorely need: a new sense of life's possibilities.

In this endeavor to wed the vision of the Old World with that of the New, it is the writer, not the statesman, who is our strongest arm. Though we do not wholly believe it yet, the interior life is a real life, and the intangible dreams of people have a tangible effect on the world.

BURIED ALIVE BY LANGUAGE

Helen Barolini

Helen Barolini, an Italian-American writer, was born in Syracuse, New York in 1925. Barolini's writings explore the connections between the United States and Italy and between Americans and Italian-Americans, revolving around questions of culture and identity. Ms. Barolini is the author of nine books, which include numerous short stories and essays.

The following essay, taken from Ms. Barolini's book *Chiaorscuro: Essays of Identity*, looks at how language marks and defines individual identities in cultural forms.

———

I remembered two seemingly incongruous things when I first heard about the racial murder of the Black youth Yusuf Hawkins in August, 1989 in the Bensonhurst section of Brooklyn by a gang of mostly Italian American young men. I remembered a friend telling me of being in Louisiana and finding "Wop Salad" featured on a menu. "What was that?" I asked. He laughed and said, salad with Italian dressing. "Didn't anyone care about the language," I wondered. No, he said, it was a joke. But language is no joke. And racial murder starts with racial intolerance that arises and spreads from such apparently innocuous jokes.

The second thing I remembered was hearing Lynn Samuels's talk show on radio WOR when a listener called in and said, "How come I'm called anti-Semitic if I make a remark, but Jews can get away with calling the rest of us goyim, schwartzer, wop, or whatever it is?"

Samuels, who is Jewish herself, answered unhesitatingly, "They're politically organized."

And that, I told myself, is why there'll never be a kike salad on any menu.

I think that Italian Americans are too easily used as objects of ridicule and scorn. It has been said that anti-Catholicism is the prejudice of choice of the liberal intellectual. That could be expanded to include Italian Americans, as reflected in the reportage of the Bensonhurst affair in the *New York Times*. What happened was a tragedy of far greater ramifications than reported in the news media. What also is tragic is the insularity and backwardness of the Italian Americans. "Niggers, stay out of our neighborhoods!" they shouted to Black marchers protesting the Hawkins murder. Their language was shocking, arresting. Worse, it was uninformed and unformed. Listen to their voices, as quoted on the murder in their neighborhood, by the *Times* reporter: "This wasn't racial and I've never been racial in my life. But white people should stick together for ourselves," says a young woman. And an old woman in a Bensonhurst candy store speaking of the murdering gang, adds, "These were good boys… they were defending the neighborhood."

"We don't go to Harlem; the kids were in the wrong spot," says an eighteen-year-old youth. "This is Bensonhurst. It's all Italian. We don't need these niggers."

These Americans of Italian descent spoke haltingly when interviewed on television; they groped for words to express themselves, their constructions were ear-grating, their words defamatory, racist, pathetically ignorant. They were people imprisoned by being closed off from education, from wide social interaction, from knowledge of broader values than those of their Old World village. As their pastor, Father Fermeglia of St. Dominic's Church in Bensonhurst, explains, "This is a very provincial neighborhood . . . everyone knows each other. . . . People get the meaning of their lives from their relationships."

What they also get is an inbred, self-perpetuating inability to think, and hence to speak in an informed way; they are buried alive in the low language of insularity.

Like illiterates using picture language, they hold up emblems of the intolerance, watermelons are raised as a racial taunt against the Blacks marching in protest of the Yusuf Hawkins murder. Ludicrously, they hold up an Italian flag. What they can't express verbally, they show. Show and Tell: that is the level of a people in a linguistic backwater, in a backwater of old outdated attitudes; of a people uneducated in values beyond the blatant materialistic one that seduces so many new comers to America: get rich and make good, defend your property values.

"It is an old truth that if we do not have mastery over our language, language itself will master us . . . it is through language that we control and create the world. We discover life through language, and that—as all great writers have told us—is why we must master it," Malcolm Bradbury wrote in another context.

Language *is* relevant. The racial outbursts that have taken place in Howard Beach, Staten Island, Bensonhurst are committed by young white men who are both poorly educated and socially marginal. They are feeling what it is to be outcasts in a society which promised them that if they made it materially, that would be what mattered. They are outraged because society lied; they are looking for scapegoats to take their rage out on, they are responsible for the reprehensible attacks on Blacks (and more recently, Jews). As the anthropologist and writer Thomas Belmonte has said, "We ignore their yearning and waste their fierce energies at our peril."

Along with the tragedy of the murdered Yusuf Hawkins is the tragedy of a whole community locked in extreme xenophobia and doing, wrongfully, to others what was done to them. It is useful to review the discrimination perpetrated against Italian Americans themselves in order to put into context some of the motivation for their current antisocial behavior. They, too, were once victimized by those who got here before they did and so "owned" their neighborhoods and didn't want the wops in them. Did Italian American learn another American lesson as well as materialism—that violence is a means of expression, and the last one in gets it? They got it, now they'll give it to the Blacks who move into "the Italian neighborhood."

In an ironic synchronization, Black filmmaker Spike Lee's film, *Do the Right Thing*, about Blacks in Brooklyn hanging out at Sal's pizza parlor, came out just at the time of the Bensenhurst murders, and addressed racial violence. What, in fact, is the right thing to do? Is it, as in the film, for Blacks to take out resentments and rage on white society by attacking and destroying their pizza parlor? Is it, as the last scene of the film shows, for the Black pillagers to remove from Sal's ruined walls the photographic totems of his Italian American allegiance—Sinatra, DiMaggio, Perry Como, et al.—and to replace them with photos of Martin Luther King, Jr., and Malcolm X?

Symbolically that is a masterful statement. The leaders of the Black movement, who have powerfully and eloquently spoken for their people and have had broad social influence, will in the end replace the meager idols of Italian Americans, for whom the inadequate message has been: make a pile, keep it in the family, aim for material satisfactions. What do the "famous" Italian Americans stand for? Money and celebrity status. Not much uplift there, not much for the soul of an alienated and ambivalent people to feed on. No gut nourishment.

Take this exchange between Sal's son Vinnie and Moukie, the Black youth who works as a delivery boy at the pizza parlor. When Moukie says, "Hey, Vinnie, how come you're always talking of Black baseball stars and singers? I think you want to be Black." Vinnie, who is imprisoned as much by inadequate language (the reflection of inadequate thought) as by his restrictive social attitudes, gropes to express what he has never thought out. "They're not Black," he finally mumbles, "they're famous."

Vinnie thus not only unconsciously identifies the un-illustrious (including himself) with the—to him—demeaning connotation of Black, but must painfully grasp for words and meaning in order to speak at all. The scene is a graphic illustration of what it is to be without articulation because the language of thought has never been fully absorbed or respected, only the language of money.

Thus, "Black" is code for poor, deprived, ignorant, the dregs; it's nigger and wop all over again. And that includes all who have believed only in the commercial opportunities of this country and haven't educated themselves in the language of other values or in what America most hopefully signifies.

It's the triumph of materialist views and Sal's narrow sense of property rights (not exclusively an Italian American attitude, as we recall the actions of Southern Anglo-Americans) that contribute to racial tensions. Rather than recognize the interdependence between his business and the exclusively Black clientele who eat his pizza, Sal insists on making his place a fortress of his Italian background. And the Blacks, too, like Moukie, look for the differences, not the commonality between them. Just as the Power Structure intends.

"Break the Power" is the theme song of the film which is dedicated to the Black or Hispanic victims of police brutality. It is powerful music, and the words are aimed at the structure of a society that abuses people, makes them violent and filled with rage, makes them drown each other out with shouts and curses and shrieking radio music, and ultimately causes them to turn on each other in their frustration.

The police in their patrol car who go up and down the streets of the Black neighborhood where Sal's pizza parlor is located look malevolent as they view the scene through cold, suspicious slit-eyes. Their counterpart is the striking arrangement of three Black men under a bright umbrella against a red wall who are laid-back, benevolent, and the wise commentators on what they observe. They spurn a boycott against Sal, as do others in the neighborhood ("I was born and brought up on Sal's pizza," says a Black girl). And yet in the anguish of their powerlessness, the Blacks will, reacting to police violence, vent their fury against Sal rather than against the societal attitudes that keep them *all* down.

With two eloquent and effective metaphors, *Do the Right Thing* depicts the futility of racial war. One is the wall of photos that provokes one Black youth to ask why, since all of Sal's customers are Black, he doesn't have Martin Luther King and Malcolm X up there, too. Sal says it's his place and he's Italian and he'll have who he wants, showing remarkable insensitivity and stupidity all at once.

The other symbolic device used by director Spike Lee is the shrieking radio music that prevents spoken communication between people as talk becomes a duel of shouts and curses, each attempting to drown the other out. The blaring music is the final provocation that incites Sal to throw a Black kid and his radio out of his place. This precipitates a police action that ends in the youth's death at the hands of the police. Moukie then leads a riot destroying not only Sal's place but his own livelihood and something of value to the neighborhood. The Blacks will be as much kept down by their more overt and mindless violence as Sal and sons by their impoverished social attitudes and lack of self-knowledge.

Blindly, not even noticing the friction between them, Sal had extolled to his sons the money that can be made in a business when families are in it together. He tells them (to their horror) that he'll pass the business on to them. Feeling trapped in the alien territory of a Black neighborhood, all the sons want to do is get out.

But what will get them out? Sal is blind in his defense of a lost cause: his family, his business, his property rights, his pathetic Italian pride, as manifested on his wall by Sinatra & Co., none of whom has the stature of the Black leaders. Sal has not awakened to reality, he lives in a time warp of old, played-out, irrelevant allegiances and chauvinism. He's a decent, hardworking guy, and his sense of responsibility and kindness are well contrasted with the fecklessness of Moukie who has fathered a son and left him, and seems to have no aim in life. But Sal has not evolved with the times. He is harboring a narrow, limited mentality in a time and place that urgently calls for more expansiveness. Are the Koreans across the street, whose place is spared by the rioting Blacks, meant to be Sal's smart counterpart? At least they understand the reality of their situation and are not spinning pipe dreams based on spurious values.

Chauvinistically, Sal has defended a wall of false images. In the end, the photos of Martin Luther King, Jr., and Malcolm X, with their two different messages, get pinned to Sal's burned-out wall which no longer can mark the bounds of narrow territoriality. That, Spike Lee's film seems to say, is the right thing to do. It's a lesson, like language, still to be learned in some insular Italian American city enclaves.

A young man in Bensenhurst, again quoted in the *Times*, spoke an American fact of life that many harbor, few speak: "No one likes no one if they don't look the same. Everybody's prejudiced. And that's the way it is."

He is confirmed, sadly, by Adele Dutton Terrell, program director of the National Institute against Prejudice and Violence, who adds, "Every day we have incidents...the sad lesson is that in America we have neighborhoods where people do and don't belong."

But *Do the Right Thing* tells clearly that such narrow territoriality is doomed.

"Go home," call the Italian American taunters of Bensonhurst to the protestors who march through their blocks. "We are home," the Black marchers call back.

THE DAY OF THE DEAD

Octavio Paz

Translated by Sander Kemp

Mexican diplomat and writer of poetry and essays, Octavio Paz won the Nobel Prize for Literature in 1990. As a social activist, he founded two political journals. In 1977, the Jerusalem Prize honored Mr. Paz for his writings on individual freedom.

We have taken Paz's essay "The Day of the Dead" from his book *The Labyrinth of Solitude.* Throughout the chapters in that text, Paz analyzes Mexican culture in its many guises, concluding that the Mexican persona lives in solitude, hidden behind masks and caught in a never-land between the Mayan culture of ancient Mexico and the modern Mexican culture resulting from the Spanish conquest.

In all the pieces in *The Labyrinth of Solitude*, Mr. Paz investigates Mexican cultural practices, rites, and rituals as they impact the individual in her/his psychological life and cultural identity. Here, Paz looks at the celebration of the holiday that Mexicans call The Day of the Dead.

———

The solitary Mexican loves fiestas and public gatherings. Any occasion for getting together will serve, any pretext to stop the flow of time and commemorate men and events with festivals and ceremonies. We are a ritual people, and this characteristic enriches both our imaginations and our sensibilities, which are equally sharp and alert. The art of the fiesta has been debased almost everywhere else, but not in Mexico. There are few places in the world where it is possible to take part in a spectacle like our great religious fiestas with their violent primary colors, their bizarre costumes and dances, their fireworks and ceremonies, and their inexhaustible welter of surprises: the fruit, candy, toys and other objects sold on these days in the plazas and open-air markets.

Our calendar is crowded with fiestas. There are certain days when the whole country, from the most remote villages to the largest cities, prays, shouts, feasts, gets drunk and kills, in honor of the Virgin of Guadalupe or Benito Juárez. Each year on the fifteenth of September, at eleven o'clock at night, we celebrate the fiesta of the *Grito*[1] in all the plazas of the Republic, and the excited crowds actually shout for a whole hour…the better, perhaps, to remain silent for the rest of the year. During the days before and after the twelfth of December,[2] time comes to a full stop, and instead of pushing us toward a deceptive

[1] Padre Hidalgo's call-to-arms against Spain, 1810.—Tr.
[2] Fiesta of the Virgin of Guadalupe.—Tr.

tomorrow that is always beyond our reach, offers us a complete and perfect today of dancing and revelry, of communion with the most ancient and secret Mexico. Time is no longer succession, and becomes what it originally was and is: the present, in which past and future are reconciled.

But the fiestas which the Church and State provide for the country as a whole are not enough. The life of every city and village is ruled by a patron saint whose blessing is celebrated with devout regularity. Neighborhoods and trades also have their annual fiestas, their ceremonies and fairs. And each one of us—atheist, Catholic, or merely indifferent—has his own saint's day, which he observes every year. It is impossible to calculate how many fiestas we have and how much time and money we spend on them. I remember asking the mayor of a village near Mitla, several years ago, "What is the income of the village government?" "About 3,000 pesos a year. We are very poor. But the Governor and the Federal Government always help us to meet our expenses." "And how are the 3,000 pesos spent?" "Mostly on fiestas, señor. We are a small village, but we have two patron saints."

This reply is not surprising. Our poverty can be measured by the frequency and luxuriousness of our holidays. Wealthy countries have very few: there is neither the time nor the desire for them, and they are not necessary. The people have other things to do, and when they amuse themselves they do so in small groups. The modern masses are agglomerations of solitary individuals. On great occasions in Paris or New York, when the populace gathers in the squares or stadiums, the absence of people, in the sense of *a* people, is remarkable: there are couples and small groups, but they never form a living community in which the individual is at once dissolved and redeemed. But how could a poor Mexican live without the two or three annual fiestas that make up for his poverty and misery? Fiestas are our only luxury. They replace, and are perhaps better than, the theater and vacations, Anglo-Saxon weekends and cocktail parties, the bourgeois reception, the Mediterranean café.

In all of these ceremonies—national or local, trade or family—the Mexican opens out. They all give him a chance to reveal himself and to converse with God, country, friends or relations. During these days the silent Mexican whistles, shouts, sings, shoots off fireworks, discharges his pistol into the air. He discharges his soul. And his shout, like the rockets we love so much, ascends to the heavens, explodes into green, red, blue, and white lights, and falls dizzily to earth with a trail of golden sparks. This is the night when friends who have not exchanged more than the prescribed courtesies for months get drunk together, trade confidences, weep over the same troubles, discover that they are brothers, and sometimes, to prove it, kill each other. The night is full of songs and loud cries. The lover wakes up his sweetheart with an orchestra. There are jokes and conversations from balcony to balcony, sidewalk to sidewalk. Nobody talks quietly. Hats fly in the air. Laughter and curses ring like silver pesos. Guitars are brought out. Now and then, it is true, the happiness ends badly, in quarrels, insults, pistol shots, stabbings. But these too are part of the fiesta, for the Mexican does not seek amusement: he seeks to escape from himself, to leap over the wall of solitude that confines him during the rest of the year. All are possessed by violence and frenzy. Their souls explode like the colors and voices and emotions. Do they forget themselves and show their true faces? Nobody knows. The important thing is to go out, open a way, get drunk on noise, people, colors. Mexico is celebrating a fiesta. And this fiesta, shot through with lightning and delirium, is the brilliant reverse to our silence and apathy, our reticence and gloom.

According to the interpretation of French sociologists, the fiesta is an excess, an expense. By means of this squandering the community protects itself against the envy of the gods or of men. Sacrifices and offerings placate or buy off the gods and the patron saints. Wasting money and expending energy affirms the community's wealth in both. This luxury is a proof of health, a show of abundance and power. Or a magic trap. For squandering is an effort to attract abundance by contagion. Money calls to money. When life is thrown away it increases; the orgy, which is sexual expenditure, is also a ceremony of regeneration; waste gives strength. New Year celebrations, in every culture, signify something beyond the mere observance of a date on the calendar. The day is a pause: time is stopped, is actually annihilated. The rites that celebrate its death are intended to provoke its rebirth, because they mark not only the end of an old year but also the beginning of a new. Everything attracts its opposite. The fiesta's function, then, is more utilitarian than we think: waste attracts or promotes wealth, and is an investment like any other, except that the returns on it cannot be measured or counted. What is sought is potency, life, health. In this sense the fiesta, like the gift of the offering, is one of the most ancient of economic forms.

This interpretation has always seemed to me to be incomplete. The fiesta is by nature sacred, literally or figuratively, and above all it is the advent of the unusual. It is governed by its own special rules, that set it apart from other days, and it has a logic, an ethic and even an economy that are often in conflict with everyday norms. It all occurs in an enchanted world: time is transformed to a mythical past or a total present; space, the scene of the fiesta, is turned into a gaily decorated world of its own; and the persons taking part cast off all human or social rank and become, for the moment, living images. And everything takes place as if it were not so, as if it were a dream. But whatever happens, our actions have a greater lightness, a different gravity. They take on other meanings and with them we contract new obligations. We throw down our burdens of time and reason.

In certain fiestas the very notion of order disappears. Chaos comes back and license rules. Anything is permitted: the customary hierarchies vanish, along with all social, sex, caste, and trade distinctions. Men disguise themselves as women, gentlemen as slaves, the poor as the rich. The army, the clergy, and the law are ridiculed. Obligatory sacrilege, ritual profanation is committed. Love becomes promiscuity. Sometimes the fiesta becomes a Black Mass. Regulations, habits and customs are violated. Respectable people put away the dignified expressions and conservative clothes that isolate them, dress up in gaudy colors, hide behind a mask, and escape from themselves.

Therefore the fiesta is not only an excess, a ritual squandering of the good painfully accumulated during the rest of the year; it is also a revolt, a sudden immersion in the formless, in pure being. By means of the fiesta society frees itself from the norms it has established. It ridicules its gods, its principles, and its laws: it denies its own self.

The fiesta is a revolution in the most literal sense of the word. In the confusion that it generates, society is dissolved, is drowned, insofar as it is an organism ruled according to certain laws and principles. But it drowns in itself, in its own original chaos or liberty. Everything is united: good and evil, day and night, the sacred and the profane. Everything merges, loses shape and individuality and returns to the primordial mass. The fiesta is a cosmic experiment, an experiment in disorder, reuniting contradictory elements and principles in order to bring about a renascence of life. Ritual death promotes a rebirth; vomiting increases the appetite; the orgy, sterile in itself, renews the fertility of the mother or of the earth. The fiesta is a return to a remote and undifferentiated state, prenatal or presocial. It is a return that is also a beginning, in accordance with the dialectic that is inherent in social processes. The group emerges purified and strengthened from this plunge into chaos. It has immersed itself in its own origins, in the womb from which it came. To express it in another way, the fiesta denies society as an organic system of differentiated forms and principles, but affirms it as a source of creative energy. It is a true "re-creation," the opposite of the "recreation" characterizing modern vacations, which do not entail any rites or ceremonies whatever and are as individualistic and sterile as the world that invented them.

Society communes with itself during the fiesta. Its members return to original chaos and freedom. Social structures break down and new relationships, unexpected rules, capricious hierarchies are created. In the general disorder everybody forgets himself and enters into otherwise forbidden situations and places. The bounds between audience and actors, officials and servants, are erased. Everybody takes part in the fiesta, everybody is caught up in its whirlwind. Whatever its mood, its character, its meaning, the fiesta is participation, and this trait distinguishes it from all other ceremonies and social phenomena. Lay or religious, orgy or saturnalia, the fiesta is a social act based on the full participation of all its celebrants.

Thanks to the fiesta the Mexican opens out, participates, communes with his fellows and with the values that give meaning to his religious or political existence. And it is significant that a country as sorrowful as ours should have so many and such joyous fiestas. Their frequency, their brilliance and excitement, the enthusiasm with which we take part, all suggest that without them we would explode. They free us, if only momentarily, from the thwarted impulses, the inflammable desires that we carry within us. But the Mexican fiesta is not merely a return to an original state of formless and normless liberty: the Mexican is not seeking to return, but to escape from himself, to exceed himself. Our fiestas are explosions. Life and death, joy and sorrow, music and mere noise are united, not to re-create or recognize themselves, but to swallow each other up. There is nothing so joyous as a Mexican fiesta, but there is also nothing so sorrowful. Fiesta night is also a night of mourning.

If we hide within ourselves in our daily lives, we discharge ourselves in the whirlwind of the fiesta. It is more than an opening out: we rend ourselves open. Everything—music, love, friendship—ends in tumult and violence. The frenzy of our festivals shows the extent to which our solitude closes us off from communication with the world. We are familiar with delirium, with songs and shouts, with the monologue…but not with the dialogue. Our fiestas, like our confidences, our loves, our attempts to reorder our society, are violent breaks with the old or the established. Each time we try to express ourselves we have to break with ourselves. And the fiesta is only one example, perhaps the most typical, of this violent break. It is not difficult to name others, equally revealing: our games, which are always a going to extremes, often mortal; our profligate spending, the reverse of our timid investments and business enterprises; our confessions. The somber Mexican, closed up in himself, suddenly explodes, tears open his breast and reveals himself, though not without a certain complacency, and not without a stopping place in the shameful or terrible mazes of his intimacy. We are not frank, but our sincerity can reach extremes that horrify a European. The explosive, dramatic, sometimes even suicidal manner in which we strip ourselves, surrender ourselves, is evidence that something inhibits and suffocates us. Something impedes us from being. And since we cannot or dare not confront our own selves, we resort to the fiesta. It fires us into the void; it is a drunken rapture that burns itself out, a pistol shot in the air, a skyrocket.

Death is a mirror which reflects the vain gesticulations of the living. The whole motley confusion of acts, omissions, regrets and hopes which is the life each one of us finds in death, not meaning or explanation, but an end. Death defines life; a death depicts a life in immutable forms; we do not change except to disappear. Our deaths illuminate our lives. If our deaths lack meaning, our lives also lacked it. Therefore we are apt to say, when somebody has died a violent death, "He got what he was looking for." Each of us dies the death he is looking for, the death he has made for himself. A Christian death or a dog's death are ways of dying that reflect ways of living. If death betrays us and we die badly, everyone laments the fact, because we should die as we have lived. Death, like life, is not transferable. If we do not die as we lived, it is because the life we lived was not really ours: it did not belong to us, just as the bad death that kills us does not belong to us. Tell me how you die and I will tell you who you are.

The opposition between life and death was not so absolute to the ancient Mexicans as it is to us. Life extended into death, and vice versa. Death was not the natural end of life but one phase of an infinite cycle. Life, death and resurrection were stages of a cosmic process which repeated itself continuously. Life had no higher function than to flow into death, its opposite and complement; and death, in turn, was not an end in itself; man fed the insatiable hunger of life with his death. Sacrifices had a double purpose: on the one hand man participated in the creative process, at the same time paying back to the gods the debt contracted by his species; on the other hand he nourished cosmic life and also social life, which was nurtured by the former.

Perhaps the most characteristic aspect of this conception is the impersonal nature of the sacrifice. Since their lives did not belong to them, their deaths lacked any personal meaning. The dead—including warriors killed in battle and women dying in childbirth, companions of Huitzilopochtli the sun god—disappeared at the end of a certain period, to return to the undifferentiated country of the shadows, to be melted into the air, the earth, the fire, the animating substance of the universe. Our indigenous ancestors did not believe that their deaths belonged to them, just as they never thought that their lives were really theirs in the Christian sense. Everything was examined to determine, from birth, the life and death of each man: his social class, the year, the place, the day, the hour. The Aztec was as little responsible for his actions as for his death.

Space and time were bound together and formed an inseparable whole. There was a particular "time" for each place, each of the cardinal points and the center in which they were immobilized. And this complex of space-time possessed its own virtues and powers, which profoundly influenced and determined human life. To be born on a certain day was to pertain to a place, a time, a color and a destiny. All was traced out in advance. Where we dissociate space and time, mere stage sets for the actions of our lives, there were as many "space-times" for the Aztecs as there were combinations in the priestly calendar, each one endowed with a particular qualitative significance, superior to human will.

Religion and destiny ruled their lives, as morality and freedom rule ours. We live under the sign of liberty, and everything—even Greek fatality and the grace of the theologians—is election and struggle, but for the Aztecs the problem reduced itself to investigating the never-clear will of the gods. Only the gods were free, and only they had the power to choose—and therefore, in a profound sense, to sin. The Aztec religion is full of great sinful gods—Quetzalcóatl is the major example—who grow weak and abandon their believers, in the same way that Christians sometimes deny God. The conquest of Mexico would be inexplicable without the treachery of the gods, who denied their own people.

The advent of Catholicism radically modified this situation. Sacrifice and the idea of salvation, formerly collective, became personal. Freedom was humanized, embodied in man. To the ancient Aztecs the essential thing was to assure the continuity of creation; sacrifice did not bring about a salvation in another world, but cosmic health; the universe, and not the individual, was given life by the blood and death of human beings. For Christians it is the individual who counts. The world—history, society—is condemned beforehand. The death of Christ saved each man in particular. Each one of us is Man, and represents the hopes and possibilities of the species. Redemption is a personal task.

Both attitudes, opposed as they may seem, have a common note: life, collective or individual, looks forward to a death that in its way is a new life. Life only justifies and transcends itself when it is realized in death, and death is also a transcendence, in that it is a new life. To Christians death is a transition, a somersault between two lives, the temporal and the otherworldly; to the Aztecs it was the profoundest way of participating in the continuous regeneration of the creative forces, which were always in danger of being extinguished if they were not provided with blood, the sacred food. In both systems life and death lack autonomy, are the two sides of a single reality. They are references to the invisible realities.

Modern death does not have any significance that transcends it or that refers to other values. It is rarely anything more than the inevitable conclusion of a natural process. In a world of facts, death is one more fact. But since it is such a disagreeable fact, contrary to all our concepts and to the very meaning of our lives, the philosophy of progress ("Progress toward what, and from what?" Scheler asked) pretends to make it disappear, like a magician palming a coin. Everything in the modern world functions as if death did not exist. Nobody takes it into account, it is suppressed everywhere: in political pronouncements, commercial advertising, public morality and popular customs; in the promise of cut-rate health and happiness offered to all of us by hospital, drugstores and playing fields. But death enters into everything we undertake, and it is no longer a transition but a great gaping mouth that nothing can satisfy. The century of health, hygiene and contraceptives, miracle drugs and synthetic foods, is also the century of the concentration camp and the police state, Hiroshima and the murder story. Nobody thinks about death, about his own death, as Rilke asked us to do, because nobody lives a personal life. Collective slaughter is the fruit of a collectivized way of life.

Death also lacks meaning for the modern Mexican. It is no longer a transition, an access to another life more alive than our own. But although we do not view death as a transcendence, we have not eliminated it from our daily lives. The word death is not pronounced in New York, in Paris, in London, because it burns the lips. The Mexican, in contrast, is familiar with death, jokes about it, caresses it, sleeps with it, celebrates it; it is one of his favorite toys and his most steadfast love. True, there is perhaps as much fear in his attitude as in that of others, but at least death is not hidden away: he looks at it face to face, with impatience, disdain or irony. "If they are going to kill me tomorrow, let them kill me right away."[3]

The Mexican's indifference toward death is fostered by his indifference toward life. He views not only death but also life as non-transcendent. Our songs, proverbs, fiestas and popular beliefs show very clearly that the reason death cannot frighten us is that "life has cured us of fear." It is natural, even desirable, to die, and the sooner the better. We kill because life—our own or another's—is of no value. Life and death are inseparable, and when the former lacks meaning, the latter becomes equally meaningless. Mexican death is the mirror of Mexican life. And the Mexican shuts himself away and ignores both of them.

Our contempt for death is not at odds with the cult we have made of it. Death is present in our fiestas, our games, our loves and our thoughts. To die and to kill are ideas that rarely leave us. We are seduced by death. The fascination it exerts over us is the result, perhaps, of our hermit-like solitude and of the fury with which we break out of it. The pressure of our vitality, which can only express itself in forms that betray it, explains the deadly nature, aggressive or suicidal, of our explosions. When we explode we touch against the highest point of that tension, we graze the very zenith of life. And there, at the height of our frenzy, suddenly we feel dizzy: it is then that death attracts us.

Another factor is that death revenges us against life, strips it of all its vanities and pretensions and converts it into what it really is: a few neat bones and a dreadful grimace. In a closed world where everything is death, only death has value. But our affirmation is negative. Sugar-candy skulls, and tissue-paper skulls and skeletons strung with fireworks…our popular images always poke fun at life,

---

[3]From the popular folk song *La Valentina*.—Tr.

affirming the nothingness and insignificance of human existence. We decorate our houses with death's heads, we eat bread in the shape of bones on the Day of the Dead, we love the songs and stories in which death laughs and cracks jokes, but all this boastful familiarity does not rid us of the question we all ask: What is death? We have not thought up a new answer. And each time we ask, we shrug our shoulders: Why should I care about death if I have never cared about life?

Does the Mexican open out in the presence of death? He praises it, celebrates it, cultivates it, embraces it, but he never surrenders himself to it. Everything is remote and strange to him, and nothing more so than death. He does not surrender himself to it because surrender entails a sacrifice. And a sacrifice, in turn, demands that someone must give and someone receive. That is, someone must open out and face a reality that transcends him. In a closed, non-transcendent world, death neither gives nor receives: it consumes itself and is self-gratifying. Therefore our relations with death are intimate—more intimate, perhaps, than those of any other people—but empty of meaning and devoid of erotic emotion. Death in Mexico is sterile, not fecund like that of the Aztecs and the Christians.

Nothing is more opposed to this attitude than that of the Europeans and North Americans. Their laws, customs and public and private ethics all tend to preserve human life. This protection does not prevent the number of ingenious and refined murders, of perfect crimes and crime-waves, from increasing. The professional criminals who plot their murders with a precision impossible to a Mexican, the delight they take in describing their experiences and methods, the fascination with which the press and public follow their confessions, and the recognized inefficiency of the systems of prevention, show that the respect for life of which Western civilization is so proud is either incomplete or hypocritical.

The cult of life, if it is truly profound and total, is also the cult of death, because the two are inseparable. A civilization that denies death ends by denying life. The perfection of modern crime is not merely a consequence of modern technical progress and the vogue of the murder story: it derives from the contempt for life which is inevitably implicit in any attempt to hide death away and pretend it does not exist. It might be added that modern technical skills and the popularity of crime stories are, like concentration camps and collective extermination, the results of an optimistic and unilateral conception of existence. It is useless to exclude death from our images, our words, our ideas, because death will obliterate all of us, beginning with those who ignore it or pretend to ignore it.

When the Mexican kills—for revenge, pleasure or caprice—he kills a person, a human being. Modern criminals and statesmen do not kill: they abolish. They experiment with beings who have lost their human qualities. Prisoners in the concentration camps are first degraded, changed into mere objects; then they are exterminated en masse. The typical criminal in the large cities—beyond the specific motives for his crimes—realizes on a small scale what the modern leader realizes on a grand scale. He too experiments, in his own way: he poisons, destroys corpses with acids, dismembers them, converts them into objects. The ancient relationship between victim and murderer, which is the only thing that humanizes murder, that makes it even thinkable, has disappeared. As in the novels of Sade, there is no longer anything except torturers and objects, instruments of pleasure and destruction.

And the nonexistence of the victim makes the infinite solitude of the murderer even more intolerable. Murder is still a relationship in Mexico, and in this sense it has the same liberating significance as the fiesta or the confession. Hence its drama, its poetry and—why not say it?—its grandeur. Through murder we achieve a momentary transcendence.

At the beginning of his eighth Duino Elegy, Rilke says that the "creature," in his condition of animal innocence, "beholds the open"…unlike ourselves, who never look forward, toward the absolute. Fear makes us turn our backs on death, and by refusing to contemplate it we shut ourselves off from life, which is totality that includes it. The "open" is where contraries are reconciled, where light and shadow are fused. This conception restores death's original meaning: death and life are opposites that complement each other. Both are halves of a sphere that we, subjects of time and space, can only glimpse. In the prenatal world, life and death are merged; in ours, opposed; in the world beyond, reunited again, not in the animal innocence that precedes sin and the knowledge of sin, but as in innocence regained. Man can transcend the temporal opposition separating them (and residing not in them but in his own consciousness) and perceive them as a superior whole. This recognition can take place only through detachment: he must renounce his temporal life and his nostalgia for limbo, for the animal world. He must open himself out to death if he wishes to open himself out to life. Then he will be "like the angels."

Thus there are two attitudes toward death: one, pointing forward, that conceives of it as creation; the other, pointing backward, that expresses itself as a fascination with nothingness or as a nostalgia for limbo. No Mexican or Spanish-American poet, with the possible exception of César Vallejo, approaches the first of these two concepts. The absence of a mystic—and only a mystic is capable of offering insights like those of Rilke—indicates the extent to which modern Mexican culture is insensible to religion. But two Mexican poets, José Gorostiza and Xavier Villaurrutia, represent the second of these two attitudes. For Gorostiza life is a "death without end," a perpetual falling into nothingness; for Villaurrutia it is no more than a "nostalgia for death."

The phrase that Villaurrutia chose for his book, *Nostalgia de la Muerte,* is not merely a lucky hit. The author has used it in order to tell us the ultimate meaning of his poetry. Death as nostalgia, rather than as the fruition or end of life, is death as origin. The ancient, original sourse is a bone, not a womb. This statement runs the risk of seeming either an empty paradox or an old commonplace: "For thou art dust, and unto dust shalt thou return." I believe that the poet hopes to find in death (which is, in effect, our origin) a revelation that his temporal life has denied him: the true meaning of life. When we die,

> The second hand
>
> will race around its dial,
>
> all will be contained in an instant…
>
> and perhaps it will be possible
>
> to live, even after death.

A return to original death would be a return to the life before life, the life before death: to limbo, to the maternal source.

Muerte sin Fin, the poem by José Gorostiza, is perhaps the best evidence we have in Latin America of a truly modern consciousness, one that is turned in upon itself, imprisoned in its own blinding clarity. The poet, in a sort of lucid fury, wants to rip the mask off existence in order to see it as it is. The dialogue between man and the world, which is as old as poetry and love, is transformed into a dialogue between the water and the glass that contains it, between the thought and the form into which it is poured and which it eventually corrodes. The poet warns us from his prison of appearances— trees and thought, stones and emotions, days and nights and twilights are all simply metaphors, mere colored ribbons—that the breath which informs matter, shaping it and giving it form, is the same breath that corrodes and withers and defeats it. It is a drama without personae, since all are merely reflections, the various disguises of a suicide who talks to himself in a language of mirrors and echoes, and the mind also is nothing more than a reflection of death, of death in love with itself. Everything is immersed in its own clarity and brilliance, everything is directed toward this transparent death: life is only a metaphor, an invention with which death—death too!—wants to deceive itself. The poem is a variation on the old theme of Narcissus, although there is no allusion to it in the text. And it is not only the consciousness that contemplates itself in its empty, transparent water (both mirror and eye at the same time, as in the Valéry poem): nothingness, which imitates form and life, which feigns corruption and death, strips itself naked and turns in upon itself, loves itself, falls into itself: a tireless death without end.

If we open out during fiestas, then, or when we are drunk or exchanging confidences, we do it so violently that we wound ourselves. And we shrug our shoulders at death, as at life, confronting it in silence or with a contemptuous smile. The fiesta, the crime of passion and the gratuitous crime reveal that the equilibrium of which we are so proud is only a mask, always in danger of being ripped off by a sudden explosion of our intimacy.

All of these attitudes indicate that the Mexican senses the presence of a stigma both on himself and on the flesh of his country. It is diffused but none the less living, original, and ineradicable. Our gestures and expressions all attempt to hide this wound, which is always open, always ready to catch fire and burn under the rays of a stranger's glance.

Now, every separation causes a wound. Without stopping to investigate how and when the separation is brought about, I want to point out that any break (with ourselves or those around us, with the past or the present) creates a feeling of solitude. In extreme cases—separation from one's parents, matrix or native land, the death of the gods or a painful self-consciousness—solitude is identified with orphanhood. And both of them generally manifest themselves as a sense of sin. The penalties and guilty feelings inflicted by a state of separation can be considered, thanks to the ideas of expiation and redemption, as necessary sacrifices, as pledges or promises of a future communion that will put an end to the long exile. The guilt can vanish, the wound heal over, the separation resolve itself in communion. Solitude thus assumes a purgative, purifying character. The solitary or isolated individual transcends his solitude, accepting it as a proof or promise of communion.

The Mexican does not transcend his solitude. On the contrary, he locks himself up in it. We live in our solitude like Philoctetes on his island, fearing rather than hoping to return to the world. We cannot bear the presence of our companions. We hide within ourselves—except when we rend ourselves open in our frenzy—and the solitude in which we suffer has no reference either to a redeemer or a creator. We oscillate between intimacy and withdrawal, between a shout and a silence, between a fiesta and a wake, without ever truly surrendering ourselves. Our indifference hides life behind a death mask; our wild shout rips off this mask and shoots into the sky, where it swells, explodes, and falls back in silence and defeat. Either way, the Mexican shuts himself off from the world: from life and from death.

A MOMENT OF SILENCE

Steve Friedman

In an article taken from the magazine, *Runner's World,* editor and journalist Steve Friedman, finds a broad context for the sport of running by connecting it to 9/11, that date in 2001 when Al-Qaeda terrorists attacked the United States by hijacking four commercial airplanes in suicide missions: two planes attacked the two World Trade Center towers in New York, one plane attacked the Pentagon, in Virginia, while a third plane, headed for the White House, crashed in Pennsylvania. In all, 2,993 people died in the 9/11 attacks, including the Al-Qaeda suicide attackers, all of the passengers aboard all four planes, many of those working in and around the World Trade Center on that day when the two towers collapsed, and New York City police and firemen who tried to rescue as many people as possible from the burning towers.

Steve Friedman writes about John Moylan, who worked in the World Trade Center and was there on the morning of 9/11. Moylan escaped the collapsing towers. Mr. Friedman conveys to us the tragedy of that day, focusing in detail on the aftereffects of terrorism on one man trying to recover his life.

———

He will wake at 4:00 A.M., as he does every weekday, except Monday. He'll wear shorts and a T-shirt, even in the rain, unless it's winter, when he might pull on a Gore-Tex jacket and pants. When it snows and the snow is heavy enough, he'll stretch thin rubber sandals with metal spikes over his running shoes. He'll grab a small canister of pepper spray. Three seasons out of the year, he'll lace up one of his six pairs of "active" size 13 Souconys that he keeps in a closet underneath his one hundred hanging T-shirts, and in the winter he'll wear one of his half-dozen pairs of active Nikes from the same closet, because the layer of air in them doesn't seem to compress in cold weather as much as the foam in the Sauconys. He'll be out his front door at 4:15, back inside at 5:05. Then he'll shower, eat a bowl of instant oatmeal, make himself a lunch of a peanut butter and jelly sandwich or pack a cup of yogurt, and leave his house in Warwick, New York, at 6:10 to drive to the train station in Harriman for the 6:42 train to Hoboken, New Jersey. The trip will take a little over an hour, and in Hoboken he'll board a 7:55 underground train bound for Manhattan. Once there, he'll walk fifteen minutes to his office at an insurance company at Madison Avenue and Thirty-Sixth Street.

John Moylan is a man of habit and routine and caution, and for much of his life attention to detail has served him well. Some mornings, when he's feeling adventurous or wild, he'll make a little extra noise between 4:00 A.M. and 4:15 A.M., just to see if his wife of thirty years, Holly, will wake up. She hasn't yet.

His running route starts outside his front door, and it hasn't varied for six years, since he and Holly and their two daughters moved from Crystal Lake, Illinois, when his then-employer, Kemper Insurance, transferred him to New York City. Down Kings Highway, through the small village, up a small hill, and by the time he passes the Mobile gasoline station at the end of the first mile, he'll know if the run will be easy or hard, and if it's hard, he'll remind himself to eat healthier that day, to make sure to get to sleep by 9:00 P.M. At one and a half miles, he might pass a gaggle of geese that like to waddle near the black granite memorial to the seven people from Warwick who died on September 11, 2001. He'll run past one dairy farm and its herd of cows, and he'll make mooing sounds and wonder why they never moo back. Later, he'll pass another dairy farm and moo at those cows, who always moo back. One of life's mysteries. He'll run past what's really no more than a giant puddle next to the road that he thinks of as the turtle pond, because he once saw a turtle waddling across the concrete toward the water. He'll run four to five miles, ten or twelve on Saturday, and on Sunday anywhere from ten to sixteen. Mondays, he rests.

Moylan is by nature conservative, by profession cautious. He has been in the insurance business for thirty-three years and has spent much of his life calculating risk, calibrating the costs of bad planning and devastating whim. Men who worry about the future can guard against the worst sorts of accidents. Men who look ahead can avoid life's greatest dangers. Even when running, even during the time of his life that is devoted to release and escape from daily tallies and concerns, he can't quite escape the principles that have guided him for so long.

"What do I think about?" he says. "God, just about everything. Am I on target for my marathon goal? How am I going to pay my daughters' college tuition? Do I have good retirement plans?"

Some days—one of life's mysteries—he thinks of that terrible morning five years ago.

The Simple Things

He and one of his coworkers, Jill Steidel, had just arrived at their office on the thirty-sixth floor of the north tower at the World Trade Center in downtown Manhattan. They were carrying coffee they had picked up from the Starbucks in the building's atrium. He had his usual—a grande-size cup of the breakfast blend, black. It was 8:46 A.M., and Moylan was standing at his window, looking west, gazing at the ferries on the Hudson River. It was one of his great pleasures, what he called "one of the simple things in life." That's when he felt the building shake and heard a loud "thwaaang." He had heard longtime employees talk about the 1993 bombing in the building's parking garage, and now he thought the building might be collapsing as a result of residual structural damage. Then he heard screaming. He was one of the fire marshals on his floor, so he rounded up his employees—there were about twenty-five of them—and herded them to the stairs. As a longtime runner, he checked his watch as the group entered the stairwell. It was 8:48 A.M.

The stairwell was packed, but orderly. He remembers two "nice, neat rows" of people, scared but polite. He remembers many breathing hard and sweating, wide-eyed. He remembers thinking that his experience as a runner helped him stay calm. "What was it?" someone asked. "It wasn't a bomb," someone else said.

The people in front of his group would sometimes stop suddenly, which made his group stop. That didn't make sense. Neither did the smell. Moylan had been in the Air Force as a young man, and it was a familiar odor. "I thought, *What the hell is jet fuel doing here?*"

It took twenty-eight minutes to get to the ground floor. Moylan left the building at 9:16 A.M. He turned to his right and looked east, just as two bodies hit the ground. He saw other bodies on the ground, realized that's why firefighters had kept people from exiting the doors in a constant flow. He saw greasy puddles of blazing jet fuel, huge chunks of twisted metal. He saw more bodies falling. (It's estimated that of the more than twenty-five hundred people who died in the twin towers, two hundred had jumped.)

He and the others were marshaled to the overpass that stretched over the West Side Highway and to the marina next to the Hudson River. At the marina, he looked back. People on the higher floors were waving pieces of clothing and curtains from the windows. There were helicopters—he thought there were eight or ten—circling. He could see that the helicopters couldn't get through the fire and smoke, and he knew that the people in the windows could see it too. He was used to synthesizing facts quickly, and it didn't take long to comprehend the horrible calculus confronting the people in the window: be burned alive or jump. He wondered what he would have done.

Thousands of people were on the marina. Some stared upwards. Others walked north, toward Midtown. The Kemper employees for whom Moylan was responsible had all gotten out safely; now Moylan needed to get home. The subway was shut down, as was the underground train to New Jersey, so he boarded a ferry to Hoboken. When he got to Hoboken at 9:59, he looked back, and as he did so, the south tower, which had been hit at 9:02 A.M., crumbled. The north tower, his tower, would fall at 10:28 A.M.

In Hoboken he boarded a train for home, but first he tried to call Holly and his daughters, Meredith and Erin. He had left his cell phone in his office, so he borrowed one, but it wasn't working. Neither, he remembers, were the landlines.

He remembers the hour-long train ride to Harriman, and from there the drive to Warwick. He remembers with absolute clarity walking through his door at 4:00 P.M., covered in soot, smelling of fire and death. Five years later, the memory still troubles him.

"The home office had called, looking for me, which just scared my wife even more. My suit was ruined. I was reeking. I scared the living daylights out of them. My daughters especially were emotionally ruined, or disturbed....When your family thinks you're dead and you walk in your house and surprise them . . ."

He stayed up all night, watching television. In the morning, he knew what he had to do. He rose from the bed where he had failed to sleep. "I wanted desperately to go out running," he says. He just couldn't get his shoes on.

Accidents Happen

Moylan knows better than most men how accidents can shape a life. He had been working in the East Norwich, Long Island, post office in the summer of 1970 when he learned he had drawn the eleventh spot in one of this country's last drafts. He had always thought how neat it would be to fly planes, so he enrolled in the U.S. Air Force. And that's how he got to Iceland.

There he was, in the summer of 1971, a cop's son from East Norwich, playing softball at midnight, soaking afterward in thermal hot springs, gorging on fresh salmon, drinking beer with pretty girls who spoke another language. Forget planning. He couldn't have dreamed that summer— "one of the best years of my life." Pure chance. Then another one of life's mysteries. Late one night, in April of 1972, there was a knock on his barrack's door. It was the chaplain. Moylan's father had died; he was only forty-six. After the funeral, Moylan asked his mother how she was going to hold on to the house. She told him not to worry, but he pressed. Did she need his help?

The Air Force gave him an honorable hardship discharge, and he went back to the post office, and he might still be there if his mother hadn't insisted that he go talk to one of the leaders of the church she attended. He was an insurance executive, and he was always looking for bright young men.

So in 1973, Moylan became a company man, a trainee for Crum & Forster, a salaried student of chance and fate. Every morning, he waited for the 7:00 A.M. Manhattan-bound train from the station in Syosset, Long Island, and every morning he stood in the same spot and walked through the same door and sat in the same seat. And every afternoon, he did the same thing at Pennsylvania Station, when the 5:06 eastbound train pulled in. Then one afternoon, the train stopped twenty feet short of its usual spot and people pushed and shoved and Moylan's seat was taken and he had no choice, there was only one empty seat left. He found himself sitting next to a pretty blond dress designer from Huntington. Her name was Holly.

Accidents happen, and it's one of life's mysteries the effect they'll have, and all you can do is try to control what's controllable. And that's how a young, married company man started running. It was 1979, and Moylan had gone from a lean, 180-pound military man to a 220-pound, twenty-eight-year-old, pudgy, listless suit. He needed to do something. He had read an article about Bill Rodgers and the New York City Marathon, and he decided that running sounded like fun.

Moylan is not a man to make a big deal out of things, and he doesn't make a big deal about that decision. But two years later, in the spring of 1981, he ran the Long Island Marathon. He ran it in just under four hours. In the fall, he ran the New York City marathon, and did even better, finishing in 3:51.

He cut out junk food, started eating lean meats. He woke early, ran before the sun rose. He experimented with equipment and distance and learned "to not let my mind get in front of my body. I learned that patience is a virtue."

He wore his running shoes when he walked from the train to his office building, and he wore them when he took his midday forty-five-minute walks around Manhattan. He always worried that people thought he looked funny.

By 2001, by the time he was fifty, he had run fourteen marathons, many half-marathons, countless 10-Ks and 5-Ks. Running helped him reduce his blood pressure from 120/90 to 110/60, helped him reduce his weight from 220 to anywhere from 180 to 195, depending on where he was in his training cycle. His resting pulse is 50 now, and when he gives blood, Red Cross officials routinely question him to make sure he's not a fainter. Running helped him cope when his mother died in 1985 at age fifty-nine, with the birth of his daughters in 1982 and 1985, with the demands of being a middle-age father and husband and provider and company man. He ran because he didn't want to die young, as his parents had, and because it relaxed him and was part of his life. Accidents would happen, and there were some things a man couldn't do anything about, terrible things. But with discipline and attention and will, a man could carve out a safe place, a part of life that was predictable, calming in its sameness. Half an hour or so in the early morning stillness could help a man deal with almost anything.

It was Tuesday, five years ago, the week after Labor Day, and warm for that time of year, in that part of the country. A morning like this was rare and precious. It would be a good run. It felt like it would be a good day. At the Mobil station, Moylan picked up his pace.

He ran past the cows and the geese and the turtle pond. He thought about his retirement fund, even though he had many years to go before needing it. He worried about his daughters' college tuition, even though he had been saving for years. He wondered if he would run as swiftly as he wanted to in the New York City Marathon, even though it was still two months away. He was back at home at 5:05 A.M., and showered and had his instant oatmeal and caught his train and met Jill Steidel at Starbucks, and they rode the elevator up to the thirty-sixth floor, and less than a minute later, he felt the building shake. And the next day, he couldn't get his running shoes on. He couldn't put them on the next day either. He woke at four each day, got out of bed, thought about running, got his shoes out of the closet, then put them back. Then he would sit on the couch and watch television and his mind would drift. He thought about a framed photograph he had left on his office desk. Holly had taken it, and it showed Moylan and Meredith and Erin at a Yankees game in July. It was cap day, and they were all wearing Yankees caps. He doubted he could ever find the negative. Then he thought about all the people who didn't get to say good-buy to their families.

Friday, September 14, was his twenty-sixth wedding anniversary, and on that morning he got dressed and he laced up his Souconys, and he opened up his front door. He looked outside, into the darkness. Then he closed the door and went back inside.

The Funny Sense

It is late spring, nearly five years later, and he is looking at the space where the World Trade Center once stood. It is the first time he has been back here. He says he's surprised that the footprints of the two towers aren't more clearly marked. He's disappointed that the twisted cross of metal that became the focus of so many Christians is no longer on the site.

He gazes into the sky.

"When I came out," he says, "it was on this level. I had a view—right in this area, the bodies were already falling. I could look up and see the people hanging out the windows. The news footage, you just saw smoke. From down here, it was like looking up from the bottom of a grill. I remember seeing how ungodly hot it was—there was an orange glow."

Moylan is a handsome man, square-jawed, gray-haired, hazel-eyed. He is six feet, a solid 190, on his way, he says, back to 180. he wears a blue suit and a pin of the twin towers and an American flag, and he looks like a soap-opera actor or the Air force pilot he might have been. If this were a different place, he might appear to be just a tourist searching the New York City skyline for wonders.

He turns from the ghost buildings and looks toward the bank of the river, at the benches where he used to unpack his peanut butter and jelly sandwiches or his yogurt cup. "This place was my luxury suite for lunch in the summertime.…I used to come out here on the bench and just dream."

In the weeks after the attack, Moylan studied a *New York Times* article about the sequence of events and realized that had he taken two or three minutes longer to get his coffee with Steidel at Starbucks, he still would have been in the elevator on the way to his office when the plane hit and he wouldn't have survived.

Moylan turns back east, away from the water. Reflection can be healing, but he has work to do. He needs to get back to his office, five miles north in Midtown. "The funny sense that I get being here," he says, "is, life goes on. It's continuing."

"I Don't Remember That"

It is early spring, dusk in Orange County, New York, and Moylan and Holly and their oldest daughter, Meredith, are driving the back roads of Warwick. Holly points out a place where George Washington slept. Meredith points out a dairy farm and creamery. We drive through the gaggle of geese and past the granite memorial to the people from Warwick who dies on 9/11.

At dinner, we talk about past races, about what running meant to Moylan before 9/11. Meredith talks about watching her father finish one marathon on an ocean boardwalk, yelling, "That's my daddy and he loves me," and years later joining him in center field of San Francisco's Candlestick Park for the end of a 5-K run. Holly and Meredith talk about how they enjoy staying up watching *Gilmore Girls* and chatting when John goes to sleep. Holly wonders aloud why her husband—or any man—needs one hundred T-shirts, and Moylan speaks mournfully of the "boxes and boxes" of his T-shirts she donated to charity.

I ask Holly and Meredith how long it took for them to get over the shock of seeing Moylan walk in the door, how they dealt with the hours of uncertainty.

"I wasn't uncertain," Holly says. "When we were watching the coverage on television, I told Meredith, 'Dad will be fine. He's a runner and he'll run right out of there. Besides, he called us from Hoboken, before he got on the train.'"

Moylan blinks, shakes his head.

"No, I didn't call you. I didn't have my phone."

"You definitely called us," Holly says. "You borrowed a phone and called us to let us know you were coming home."

Moylan blinks again. "I don't remember that," he says.

"Yeah, Dad," Meredith says, "You called from Hoboken. To let us know you were all right."

Storytellers

Harold Kudler, MD, is an associate clinical professor of psychiatry at Duke University and a nationally recognized expert on post-traumatic stress disorder (PTSD). He hears part of John Moylan's post-9/11 story and say, "It's quite common for people in the middle of an acute stress response to have disassociative phenomena."

To Dr. Kudler, Moylan's elaborate memory of his family being traumatized as a result of not hearing from him makes psychological sense. "Sometimes," Dr. Kudler says, "the effort to create meaning and to create a meaningful narrative about what has happened to you actually becomes more important than the actual memory and might replace it. This story about coming home as a ghost and having everyone else scared might be a way to say, 'Boy, was I scared. I felt like a ghost in my own life. I wasn't even sure when I got home if I had survived that.'"

Moylan's responses during and after the attacks—his vivid recollection of details, his construction of false memories, his nightmares, his long avoidance of the WTC site, his difficulty running afterward—are entirely consistent with symptoms exhibited by people facing extreme trauma, even the most resilient people, according to Dr. Kudler.

"There's a tendency to medicalize or pathologize responses," Dr. Kudler says. "It might be better to think that here's someone who is faced with a new challenge that's so radically different than the one he faced a few days earlier.

"Think of it like mourning. When you're bereaved, you wouldn't be able to invest in yourself, because you'd feel overwhelmed, and you'd sort of lose your center. For a while you wouldn't be able to do the things that reminded you of who you were, of the thing you did for yourself."

And Moylan's inability to go for his normal run?

"Running for him was something he did for himself, was important to him, and he made a point of always doing this regardless of anything else. Great exercise, recreational, self-affirming. But in the context of the disaster, when people are overwhelmed and filled with doubt, it's easy to see why someone wouldn't do those self-affirming things."

"And if he was angry, that anger may have drowned out his capacity to enjoy a simple pleasure like running, and take that simple time for himself. That anger could have drowned out a lot of those normal, good impulses."

When I tell Moylan what Dr. Kudler said, he is silent for a few seconds.

"He nailed me," he says.

Perspective

He would wake in the middle of the night, certain that his house was under attack. He would dream that he was up in a tower and flames were licking at him. He would dream of having to make a terrible choice but not knowing what to do. He would dream of dying, "that I went through what those people went through." Noises startled him. "He was restless and jumpy and things would frighten him," Holly says. "If we were out somewhere and a child cried out, he'd jump, he'd be scared."

During the day, he thought of the people who had died. "I couldn't rationalize what had happened. People in the normal course of living, going to work, murdered. I thought about how they never got to say good-bye to anyone. I thought about my family, and about facing a decision to burn to death or to jump."

Every morning in the weeks after 9/11, he would get up and he would plan to run. But he never made it outside. He would make coffee, and sit on the couch, and sometimes watch television, and have his oatmeal, and when it was time to take his shower and catch his train, that's what he would do.

He couldn't' stop thinking about chance, and fate, and wondering why he had survived.

At his company's insistence, he had two conversations with Red Cross officials, once in a group, once alone. He talked about how angry he was that there had been an attack. He talked about how angry he was that he had survived while others had died. He talked about how angry he was that he couldn't run. "And that about covers it," he says.

He reported for work on September 13, in Kemper's New Jersey office. The company assured Moylan and his coworkers that they would be reassigned to a building in midtown Manhattan, on a lower floor. The morning they reported for work there, on the tenth floor of Rockefeller Center, was the day authorities discovered an envelope filled with anthrax addressed to Tom Brokaw in the same building. Some of the Kemper employees left and never came back. Moylan stayed. The nightmares continued. He kept jumping at the slightest noise. But Holly didn't say anything. "We had talked about counseling," she says, "and he just said, 'Let me see how things go.'" He knew that running would help him get over all his problems. So he got up every day, ready to run. But he couldn't do it.

Then one day, he could. Just like that. One of life's mysteries.

There were no grand pronouncements before he went to bed the night before, no stirring speeches at dinner. He was still angry. He was still scared. He still thought about the falling bodies. But on Columbus Day, almost exactly a month after the attack, he managed to get his shoes on, and to get out the door. He made it four miles, and every step was difficult. His legs were heavy. He had trouble breathing. But he made it.

His first race was a half-marathon in Pennsylvania the next April. It was a clear day, warm, "almost like September 11," he says. "I remember that for the first time in a long time, I smelled grass, could smell flowers."

A few months later, in October, at a half-marathon not far from his home, he happened to overhear one of the runners mention that he was a firefighter. Moylan approached him. "He said he wasn't there, but he knew people who were. I told him I was in tower one. We both had similar feelings…about losing people. It was the first time I had verification that I wasn't the only person who felt like I did."

He ran the New York City Marathon in 2002 and 2003. He ran more marathons, more half-marathons. The nightmares faded away, as did his preoccupation with death and the randomness of fate. (He still jumps at the slightest noise, something he never did before 9/11.) Three years ago, Todd Jennings, who lived near Moylan and who had just started running, spotted Moylan on the train "in his gray flannel suit and running shoes." Eventually, they started talking. About training regimens, and race strategy, and running in general. "No," Jennings says, "we never talked about 9/11."

Moylan and Jennings traveled to the Boilermaker 15-K in Utica, New York, in 2005, and the night before the race they went out for a pasta dinner. "He told me," Jennings says, "'I want to be remembered on my tombstone as a runner. Running is who I am.'"

There are things you can't control, no matter how much you worry and plan. Terrible things happen, and there's nothing you can do to stop them. Those are lessons that will change a man. For better or for worse.

After eighteen years, Moylan left Kemper Insurance in 2002 to go to work for Greater New York Insurance. He doesn't worry about what others think about his blue suit/white running shoes combination in Midtown anymore. He ran a 3.22 marathon in 1982 and a 4:50 marathon in 2003.

He still wants to get back to a four-hour time, "but I don't worry so much about time anymore." He is training for this fall's New York City Marathon. He still thinks about retirement and paying for his daughters' education, but it doesn't eat at him quite as much as it used to. He still calculates risk and calibrates the likelihood of disaster and does his best to protect himself and his family, but he knows there are some things beyond a man's control, and to worry about them is to waste precious energy.

When he finds himself irritated or impatient, he thinks of a terrible choice he never had to make, and he is grateful. Every morning, as he steps out his door, he is grateful.

"I told my wife, I should have a new birthday," Moylan says. "My new life started on 9/11. The fact that I survived is a gift. I know quite a few people who didn't. I made a promise to myself. I was going to live differently." He tries not to dwell on the past, or to look too very far into the future. But he has made one promise to himself. "Yeah, I'm going to go back to Iceland sometime. That's a plan now."

The Hills Beyond

Weekends, he treats himself. Friday and Saturday nights, he soaks a pot of steel-cut oats in water so he can have homemade oatmeal after he runs. He sleeps till 5:30, has a cup of coffee, "my luxury," and dawdles for a full hour before he heads out the door. September 11 falls on a Monday this year, so he won't run. But the day before, he'll step out of his front door just as the sun rises above Warwick. He'll pass the Mobil station and the silent cows and the mooing cows, but that day he'll go at least fifteen miles, so there will be other sights too. He'll run by the VFW hall where the old men always wave and the fire station in town where the guys always have a nice word to say. He might see a deer, or a porcupine, or even a bear. At mile seven, he'll run by a house where a snarling rottweiler is tied to a tree, and he'll grip his pepper spray a little more tightly.

Just past that house, Moylan will ascend a gentle hill, heading east, and no matter how hard the run, no matter how he slept the night before or how he's feeling, as he crests the little hill, he'll slow down. It's his favorite spot on the weekend run—his favorite spot of any of his runs. It's just a little hummock, but when a man reaches it, he can turn to the right and look south, and he can see an entire valley stretching before him, and beyond that valley, forests and hills all the way to the horizon. He will still have another seven miles to go, and then his homemade oatmeal, with the apples and bananas and raisins and cinnamon he allows himself on weekends. Then on Monday he'll think again about the day that changed his life, and on the day after that he'll catch the 6:42 train to Hoboken, and on the day after that he'll do it again. Or not. Who can really predict what will happen to a man, even a careful man, a man who takes precautions? That's another of life's mysteries.

Moylan will allow himself to walk a little bit on Sunday at the top of the gentle rise, to linger, to look at the valley and the forests and the looming hills beyond. He loves this spot.

"It's a nice place to get perspective," he says.

WHY ARE MOVIES SO BAD? OR, THE NUMBERS

Pauine Kael

Film critic Pauline Kael (1919–2001) is often regarded as one of the most important and influential film critics of all time. Roger Ebert said, "She has had a more positive influence on the climate for film in America than any other single person over the last three decades." Known for her witty and opinionated movie reviews and her strongly down-to-earth, colloquial writing, she also established a new style of film criticism, approaching movies from an emotional perspective.

Early in her career, Pauline Kael wrote for various magazines before joining *The New Yorker* as its movie reporter from 1968-1991. She also wrote thirteen books about film.

———

The movies have been so rank the last couple of years that when I see people lining up to buy tickets I sometimes think that the movies aren't drawing an audience—they're inheriting an audience. People just want to go to a movie. They're stung repeatedly, yet their desire for a good movie—for *any* movie—is so strong that all over the country they keep lining up. "There's one God for all creation, but there must be a separate God for the movies," a producer said. "How else can you explain their survival?" An atmosphere of hope develops before a big picture's release, and even after your friends tell you how bad it is, you can't quite believe it until you see for yourself. The lines (and the grosses) tell us only that people are going to the movies—not that they're having a good time. Financially, the industry is healthy, so among the people at the top there seems to be little recognition of what miserable shape movies are in. They think the grosses are proof that people are happy with what they're getting, just as TV executives think that the programs with the highest ratings are what TV viewers want, rather than what they settle for. (A number of new movie executives come from TV.) These new executives don't necessarily see many movies themselves, and they rarely go to a theatre. If for the last couple of years Hollywood couldn't seem to do anything right, it isn't that it was just a stretch of bad luck—it's the result of recent developments within the industry. And in all probability it will get worse, not better. There have been few recent American movies worth lining up for—last year there was chiefly *The Black Stallion*, and this year there is *The Empire Strikes Back*. The first was made under the aegis of Francis Ford Coppola; the second was financed by George Lucas, using his profits from *Star Wars* as a guarantee to obtain bank loans. One can say with fair confidence that neither *The Black Stallion* nor *The Empire Strikes Back* could have been made with such care for visual richness and imagination if it had been done under studio control. Even small films on traditional subjects are difficult to get financed at a studio if there are no parts for stars in them; Peter Yates, the director of *Breaking Away*—a graceful, unpredictable comedy that pleases and satisfies audiences—took the project to one studio after another for almost six years before he could get the backing for it.

There are direct results when conglomerates take over movie companies. At first, the heads of the conglomerates may be drawn into the movie business for the status implications—the opportunity to associate with world-famous celebrities. Some other conglomerate heads may be drawn in for the girls, but for them, too, a new social life beckons, and as they become socially involved, people with great names approach them as equals, and it gets them crazy. Famous stars and producers and writers and directors tell them about offers they've had from other studios and about ideas they have for pictures, and the conglomerate heads become indignant that the studios they control aren't in on these wonderful projects. The next day, they're on the phone raising hell with their studio bosses. Very soon, they're likely to be summoning directors and suggesting material to them, talking to actors, and telling the company executives what projects should be developed. How bad are the taste and judgment of the conglomerate heads? Very bad. They haven't grown up in a show-business milieu—they don't have the background, the instincts, the information of those who have lived and sweated movies for many years. (Neither do most of the current studio bosses.) The conglomerate heads may be business geniuses, but as far as movies are concerned they have virgin instincts; ideas that are new to them and take them by storm may have failed grotesquely dozens of times. But they feel that they are creative people—how else could they have made so much money and be in a position to advise artists what to do? Who is to tell them no? Within a very short time, they are in fact, though not in title, running the studio. They turn up compliant executives who will settle for the title and not fight for the authority or for their own tastes—if, in fact, they have any. The conglomerate heads find these compliant executives among lawyers and agents, among lawyer-agents, among television executives, and in the lower echelons of the companies they've taken over. Generally, these executives reserve all their enthusiasm for movies that have made money; those are the only movies they like. When a director or a writer talks to them and tries to suggest the kind of picture he has in mind by using a comparison, they may stare at him blankly. They are usually law-school or business-school graduates; they have no frame of reference. Worse, they have no shame about not knowing anything about movies. From their point of view, such knowledge is not essential to their work. Their talent is being able to anticipate their superiors' opinions; in meetings, they show a sixth sense for guessing what the most powerful person in the room wants to hear. And if they ever guess wrong, they know how to shift gears without a tremor. So the movie companies wind up with top production executives whose interest in movies rarely extends beyond the immediate selling possibilities; they could be selling neckties just as well as movies, except that they are drawn to glamour and power.

This does not prevent these executives from being universally treated as creative giants. If a studio considers eighty projects, and eventually twenty of them (the least risky) go into production, and two of them become runaway hits (or even one of them), the studio's top executive will be a hero to his company and the media, and will soon be quoted in the *Los Angeles Times* and *The New*

York Times talking about his secret for picking winners—his intuitive understanding, developed from his childhood experiences, that people want a strong, upbeat narrative, that they want to cheer the hero and hiss the villain. When *Alien* opened "big," Alan Ladd, Jr., president of the pictures division of Twentieth Century-Fox, was regarded as a demigod; it's the same way that Fred Silverman was a demigod. It has nothing to do with quality, only with the numbers. (Ladd and his team weren't admired for the small pictures they took chances on and the artists they stuck by.) The media now echo the kind of thinking that goes on in Hollywood, and spread it wide. Movie critics on TV discuss the relative grosses of the new releases; the grosses at this point relative to previous hits; which pictures will pass the others in a few weeks. It's like the Olympics—which will be the winners?

There are a lot of reasons that movies have been so bad during the last couple of years and probably won't be any better for the next couple of years. One big reason is that rotten pictures are making money—not necessarily wild amounts (though a few are), but sizable amounts. So if studio heads want nothing more than to make money and grab power, there is no reason for them to make better ones. Turning out better pictures might actually jeopardize their position. Originally, the studios were controlled by theatre chains—the chains opened the studios, operating without the protection of theatres, in order to have a source of supply. But the studios and the theatre chains were separated by a Supreme Court order in 1948 and subsequent lower-court rulings; after that, the studios have found a new kind of protection. They have discovered that they can get much more from the sale of movies to television than they had been getting, and that they can negotiate presale agreements with the networks for guaranteed amounts before they commit themselves to a production. Licensing fees to the networks now run between $3,000,000 and $4,000,000 for an average picture, and the studios negotiate in advance not only for network showings and later TV syndication (about $1,500,000 for an average picture), and for pay television (between $1,000,000 and $1,500,000), but for cable TV, the airlines, cassettes, and overseas television. And, of course, they still sell to foreign distributors and to exhibitors here, and much of that money is also committed in advance—sometimes even paid in advance. So if a film is budgeted at $8,500,000, the studio may have $14,000,000 guaranteed and—theoretically, at least—show a profit before shooting starts, even if $4,000,000 is allowed for marketing and advertising. And the studio still has the possibility of a big box-office hit and *really* big money. If a picture is a large-scale adventure story or has superstars, the licensing fee to the networks alone may be between $15,000,000 and $25,000,000, and the total advance guarantees may come to almost double the budget. Financially, the only danger in an arrangement like this is that if the film goes seriously over budget the studio can still lose money. That's why directors who have the reputation of always coming in on schedule are in steady demand even if they've had a long line of box-office failures and their work is consistently mediocre, and why directors who are perfectionists are shunned as if they are lepers—unless, like Hal Ashby, they've had some recent hits.

The studios no longer make movies primarily to attract and please moviegoers; they make movies in such a way as to get as much as possible from the prearranged and anticipated deals. Every picture (allowing for a few exceptions) is cast and planned in terms of those deals. Though the studio is very happy when it has a box-office hit, it isn't terribly concerned about the people who buy tickets and come out grumbling. They don't grumble very loudly anyway, because even the lumpiest pictures are generally an improvement over television; at least, they're always bigger. TV accustoms people to not expecting much, and because of the new prearranged deals they're not getting very much. There is a quid pro quo for a big advance sale to television and theatres: the project must be from a fat, dumb best-seller about an international jewel heist or a skyjacking that involves a planeload of the rich and famous, or be a thinly disguised show-business biography of someone who came to an appallingly wretched end, or have an easily paraphrasable theme—preferably something that can be done justice to in a sentence and brings to mind the hits of the past. How else could you entice buyers? Certainly not with something unfamiliar, original. They feel safe with big-star packages, with chase thrillers, with known ingredients. For a big overseas sale, you must have "international" stars—performers who are known all over, such as Sophia Loren, Richard Burton, Candice Bergen, Roger Moore, Clint Eastwood, Burt Reynolds, Alain Delon, Charles Bronson, Steve McQueen. And you should probably avoid complexities: much of the new overseas audience is sub-literate. For a big advance sale to worldwide television, a movie should also be innocuous: it shouldn't raise any hackles, either by strong language or by a controversial theme. And there must be stars, though not necessarily movie stars. It has recently been discovered that even many Americans are actually more interested in TV personalities than in movie ones, and may be roused from their TV-viewing to go see a film with John Denver or John Ritter. In countries where American TV series have become popular, our TV stars may be better known than our movie stars (especially the ones who appear infrequently). A 1979 Canadian film, *Running,* starring Michael Douglas, who has appeared in a TV series and was featured in *The China Syndrome,* cost $4,200,000; by the time it was completed, the various rights to it has been sold for over $6,000,000. The lawyer-financier who set up the production of *Foolin' Around,* which stars Gary Busey, said he would not have made the picture without the television insurance of a supporting cast that included Tony Randall, Cloris Leachman, and Eddie Albert. Nobody needs to have heard of these independently packaged pictures for them to be profitable, and, in some cases, if it were not contractually necessary to open the film in theatres in order to give it legitimacy as a movie, it would be cheaper not to, because the marketing and advertising costs may outstrip the box-office revenue (unless that, too, was guaranteed). On productions like these, the backers don't suffer the gamblers' anxieties that were part of film business in the fifties and sixties, and even in the early seventies. Of course, these backers don't experience the gamblers' highs, either. Movie executives now study the television Q ratings, which measure the public's familiarity with performers, and a performer with a high rating (which he attains if he's been in a long-running series or on a daytime quiz show) is offered plum movie roles—even if this means that the script will have to be completely rewritten for his narrow range or bland personality.

There is an even grimmer side to all this: because the studios have discovered how to take the risk out of moviemaking, they don't want to make any movies that they can't protect themselves on. Production and advertising costs have gone so high that there is genuine nervous panic about risky projects. If an executive finances what looks like a perfectly safe, stale piece of material and packs it with stars, and the production costs skyrocket way beyond the guarantees, and the picture loses many millions, *he* won't be blamed for it—he was playing the game by the same rules as everybody else. If, however, he takes a gamble on a small project that can't be sold in advance—something that a gifted director really wants to do, with a subtle, not easily summarized theme and no big names in the cast—and it loses just a little money, his neck is on the block. So to the executives a good script is a script that attracts a star, and they will make their deals and set the full machinery of a big production in motion and schedule the picture's release dates, even though the script problems have never been worked out and everyone (even the director) secretly knows that the film will be a confused mess, an embarrassment.

Another new factor makes a risky project still riskier; if a movie doesn't have an easily paraphrasable theme or big stars, it's hard to sell via a thirty-second TV commercial. (The networks pay a lot for movies, but they get much of it back directly from the movie industry, which increasingly relies on TV commercials to sell a film.) It's even hard for the studio advertising departments to figure out a campaign for newspapers and magazines. And so, faced with something unusual or original, the studio head generally says, "I don't know how to market it, and if I don't know how to market it, it will lose money." The new breed of studio head is not likely to say, "It's something I feel we should take a chance on. Let's see if there's somebody who might be able to figure out how to market it." Just about the only picture the studios made last year that the executives took a financial risk on was *Breaking Away*. And despite the fact that it cost what is now a pittance ($2,400,000) and received an Academy Award Best Picture nomination, Twentieth Century-Fox didn't give it a big theatrical re-release (the standard procedure for a nominated film) but sold it to NBC for immediate showing, for $5,000,000. So a couple of weeks after the Awards ceremony, just when many people had finally heard of *Breaking Away* and might have gone to a theatre to see it, it appeared, trashed in the usual manner, on television. The studio couldn't be sure how much more money might come in from box offices, and grabbed a sure thing. In order to accept the NBC offer, the studio even bypassed pay TV, where the picture could have been seen uncut. It was almost as if *Breaking Away* were being punished for not having stars and not having got a big advance TV sale. And the price was almost insulting: last year, Fox licensed *The Sound of Music* to NBC for $21,500,000, and licensed *Alien* to ABC for $12,000,000, with escalator clauses that could take the figure up to $15,000,000; Columbia licensed *Kramer vs. Kramer* to ABC for nearly $20,000,000, and United Artists got $20,000,000 for *Rocky II* from CBS. But then how do you summarize in a sentence the appeal of a calm, evenhanded film about fathers and sons, town boys and college boys, and growing up—a modest classic that never states its themes, that stirs the emotions by indirection, by the smallest of actions and the smallest exchanges of dialogue?

If a writer-director conceives a script for a fiery young actor—K., a young man with star potential who has not yet had a role that brought him to the consciousness of the public—and shapes the central character to bring out K.'s volatility and ardor, he is likely to be told by the studio head, "K. doesn't do anything to me." That rules out K., even if the studio head has never seen K. act (and chances are he wouldn't remember him if he had). The studio head doesn't care if K. could become a star in this part; he wants R., because he can get a $4,000,000 network sale with the impassive, logy R., a Robert Wagner type who was featured in a mini-series. And if the point is pressed, the studio head may cut off discussion with some variation of "I must know what I'm doing, or I wouldn't be in this job." If he is feeling expansive, he may go on with "I won't say that you can't make a good film with K., and some people—some critics and your friends—will like it. But a good picture to me is a successful picture—one that will make money." If the writer-director still persists, it's taken as a sign of stupidity. A finer-grained executive—one of the rare ones who loves movies—may put it to him this way: "I like K., I like you, I like the script. But I can't recommend it. It's an expensive picture, and the subject matter makes it a long shot. And if I back too may long shots that don't come in, I'm out on my ass." That's the distillation of executive timidity, and maybe it's better to get it from the coarser man: you can have the pleasure of hating him—you aren't made to sympathize with his plight. Since all the major studios basically play by the same rules, the writer-director will wind up with a picture that is crucially miscast and has a vacuum at its center. By the time it is released and falls by the wayside, and he is publicly humiliated, K., disgusted at not having got the part, may have accepted a dumb role in a TV series and become a hot new TV personality, whom all the movie studios are propositioning.

Chances are that even if the writer-director had been allowed to use K., he would have been completely enraged and demoralized by the time he started shooting, because the negotiating process can stretch on for years, and anyone who wants to make a movie is treated as a hustler and an adversary. "Studios!" said Billy Wilder, paraphrasing an old complaint about women. "You can't make pictures with 'em, and you can't make pictures without 'em." Everybody in the movie business has the power to say no, and the least secure executives protect themselves by saying no to just about anything that comes their way. Only those at the very top can say yes, and they protect themselves, too. They postpone decisions because they're fearful, and also because they don't mind keeping someone dangling while his creative excitement dries up and all the motor drive goes out of his proposal. They don't mind keeping people waiting, because it makes them feel more powerful. I'm describing trends; of course, there are exceptions—those who are known (and sometimes revered) for quick decisions, like David Picker in his United Artists days, and Daniel Melnick in his brief stints at M-G-M and Columbia, and David Begelman at Columbia and now at M-G-M. But most of the ones who could say yes don't; they consider it and string you along. (Hollywood is the only place where you can die of encouragement.) For the supplicant, it's a matter of weeks, months, years, waiting for meetings at which he can beg permission to do what he was, at the start, eager to do. And even when he's got a meeting, he has to catch the executive's attention and try to keep it; in general the higher the executive, the more cruelly short his attention span. (They're television babies. Thirty seconds is a long time to them.) In this atmosphere of bureaucratic indifference or contempt, things aren't really decided—they just happen, along bureaucratic lines. (Generally, it's only if a picture is a hit that executives talk about having given it the go-ahead. They all angle for credit in the media.) During the long wait, the director has lost the cinematographer he wanted and half the performers; in order to get them necessary approvals, he has agreed to actors he knows are wrong, and he has pared down the script to cut costs, chopping out the scenes that once meant the most to him but that he knows he can't get in the tight, ten-week shooting schedule he has been forced to accept. And then, at the last minute, a few days before shooting is to start, the studio is likely to slice the budget further—and he's down to a nine-week schedule, which means trimming the camera moves that were half the reason he'd been eager to work on the idea in the first place. Is it any wonder if the picture that comes out has a sour spirit?

It may just barely come out anyway. If there's an executive shakeup during production or after the film is completed (and shakeups take place every few months), the new studio head has nothing to gain if the film succeeds (he can't take credit for initiating it); he may find it to his strategic advantage for the film to fail. The executives—bed-hoppers, who go from one berth to another—have no particular loyalty to the studio, and there isn't the lower-echelon executive stability to launch a film initiated during the old regime with the same care as one initiated during the new regime. It all depends on the signals that come from the top.

If a big star and a big director show interest in a project, the executives will go along for a $14,000,000 or $15,000,000 budget even if, by the nature of the material, the picture should be small. And so what might have been a charming light entertainment that millions of people all over the world would enjoy is inflated, rewritten to enlarge the star's part, and over scaled. It makes money in advance and sends people out of theatres complaining and depressed. Often, when people leave theatres now they're bewildered by the anxious nervous construction of the film—by the feeling it gives them of having been pieced together out of parts that don't fit. Movies have gone to hell and amateurism. A third of the pictures being made by Hollywood this year are in the hands of first-time directors, who will receive almost no guidance or help. They're thrown right into a pressure-cooker situation, where any delay is costly. They may have come out of sitcoms, and their dialogue will sound forced, as if it were all recorded in a large, empty cave; they may have come out of nowhere and have never worked with actors before. Even if a director is highly experienced, he probably has certain characteristic weaknesses, such as a tendency to lose track of the story, or an ineptness with women characters; he's going to need watching. But who knows that, or cares enough to try to protect the picture? The executives may have hired the director after "looking at his work"—that is, running off every other reel of one of his films. They are busy people. Network executives who are offered a completed movie commonly save time by looking at a fifteen-minute selection from it—a précis of its highlights—which has been specially prepared for them. God forbid that they should have to sit through the whole thing.

What isn't generally understood is how much talent and hard work are wasted—enough, maybe, to supply the world with true entertainment. A writer who is commissioned to adapt a book and turns in a crackerjack script, acclaimed by the studio executives, who call him a genius, then stands helplessly by as the studio submits it to the ritual lists of stars and the directors whom they can get the biggest guarantees on. And as, one by one, the stars and directors who aren't right for the project anyway take months to read it and turn it down, the executives' confidence in the script drains away. If a star expresses tentative interest, contingent on a complete rewrite, they will throw out the snappy script and authorize a new script by a sodden writer who has just had a fluke hit, and when the star decides to do something else anyway, they will have a new script written for a different star, and another and another, until no one can remember why there was ever any interest in the project. It may be shelved then, but so much money has already gone into it that in a couple of years some canny producer will think it should be brought back to life and reworded to fit a hot new teen-ager from television—who eventually will decide not to do it, and so on. To put it simply: A good script is a script to which Robert Redford will commit himself. A bad script is a script which Redford has turned down. A script that "needs work" is a script about which Redford has yet to make up his mind. It is possible to run a studio with this formula; it is even possible to run a studio *profitably* with this formula. But this world of real-politick that has replaced moviemaking has nothing to do with moviemaking. It's not just that the decisions made by the executives might have been made by anyone off the street—it's that the pictures themselves seem to have been made by anyone off the street.

The executives are managerial class with no real stake in the studio; they didn't build it, it's not part of them, and they're moving on—into a bigger job at another studio, or into independent production (where there's more money), or to form their own companies. The executives just try to hold things together for the short period that they're going to be around; there isn't even an elementary regard for the conservation of talent. And, as in any chaotic bureaucracy, the personalities and goals of those at the top set the tone for all the day-to-day decisions; the top executives' apathy about the quality of movies infects the studio right down the line. The younger executives who are pushing their way up don't want to waste their time considering scripts that may not attract a star. For them, too, a good picture is a picture that makes money, and so after *The China Syndrome* clicked at box offices, they could be heard talking about what a wonderful craftsman its director, James Bridges, was, and after *The Amityville Horror,* with its unbelievably clunky script, by Sandor Stern, showed big grosses, they wanted to sign up Stern as a writer-director. At the bottom as at the top, the executives want to score; they want a hit, not just for the money but for the personal pleasure of the kill.

Part of what has deranged American life in this past decade is the change in book publishing and in magazines and newspapers and in the movies as they have passed out of the control of those whose lives were bound up in them and into the control of conglomerates, financiers, and managers who treat them as ordinary commodities. This isn't a reversible process; even if there were Supreme Court rulings that split some of these holding from the conglomerates, the traditions that developed inside many of those businesses have been ruptured. And the continuity is gone. In earlier eras, when a writer made a book agreement with a publisher, he expected to be working with the people he signed up with; now those people may be replaced the next day, or the whole firm may be bought up and turned into a subdivision of a textbook-publishing house or a leisure-activities company. The new people in the job aren't going to worry about guiding a writer slowly; they're not going to think about the book after this one. They want best-sellers. Their job is to find them or manufacture them. And just as the studios have been hiring writers to work on screenplays, they are now beginning to hire writers to work on novels, which the publishers, with the help of studio money, will then attempt to promote to best-sellerdom at the same time that they are being made into movies. The writer Avery Corman has suggested "the horrifying prospect of a novelist being fired from his own book." It won't horrify the people who are commissioning these new book—pre-novelizations.

There are certain kinds of business in which the public interest is more of a factor than it is in the manufacture of neckties. Book publishing, magazines and newspapers, movies and television and live theatre—these are businesses, of course, but traditionally the people who work in them have felt privileged (by birth or ability or talent or luck, or by a combination of those factors). That has been true not only of the actors and journalists but of the entrepreneurs and the managers. There have always been a few businessmen in these fields who had the sensibility of artists (without the talent or the drive); if they had a good critical sense and a generous nature, they were appreciators of artists and didn't resent them. And so they became great producers in the theatre and movies, or great book and magazine editors. Contemporary variants of these people insist on being celebrity-artists themselves, and right now they all seem to be writing and directing movies.

In movies, the balance between art and business has always been precarious, with business outweighing art, but the business was, at least, in the hands of businessmen who loved movies. As popular entertainment, movies need something of what the vulgarian moguls had—zest, a belief in their own instincts, a sentimental dedication to producing pictures that would make their country proud of their contribution, a respect for quality, and the biggest thing: a willingness to take chances. The cool managerial sharks don't have that; neither do the academics. But the vulgarians also did more than their share of damage, and they're gone forever anyway. They were part of a different America. They were, more often than not, men who paid only lip service to high ideals, while gouging everyone for profits. The big change in the country is reflected in the fact that people in the movie business no longer feel it necessary to talk about principles at all. They operate on the same assumptions as the newspapers that make heroes of the executives who have a hit and don't raise questions about its quality.

When the numbers games takes over a country, artists who work in a popular medium, such as movies, lose their bearings fast. There's a pecking order in filmmaking, and the director is at the top—he's the authority figure. A man who was never particularly attractive to women now finds that he's the padrone: everyone is waiting on his word, and women are his for the nod. The constant, unlimited opportunities for sex can be insidious; so is the limitless flattery of college students who turn directors into gurus. Directors are easily seduced. They mainline admiration. Recently, a screenwriter now directing his first picture was talking about his inability to find a producer who would take some of the burden off him; he said he needed a clone—someone who would know what was in his mind and be able to handle a million details for him. But anyone observing this writer-director would know that he needs a real producer, and for a much more important reason: to provide the sense of judgment he has already lost. Nobody really controls a production now; the director is on his own, even if he's insecure, careless, or nuts. There has always been a megalomaniac potential in moviemaking, and in this period of stupor, when values have been so thoroughly undermined that even the finest directors and the ones with the most freedom aren't sure what they want to do, they often become obsessive and grandiloquent—like mad royalty. Perpetually dissatisfied with the footage they're compulsively piling up, they keep shooting—adding rooms to the palace. Megalomania and art become the same thing to them. But the disorder isn't just in their heads, and a lot of people around them are deeply impressed by megalomania. What our directors need most of all, probably, is a sense of purpose and a subject that they can think their way through. Filmmakers want big themes, and where are the kinds of themes that they would fight the studios to express? It's no accident that the two best recent American movies are both fantasy fairy tales—childish in the fullest, deepest sense. Working inside a magical structure, Carroll Ballard in *The Black Stallion* and Irvin Kershner in *The Empire Strikes Back* didn't have to deal with the modem world; they were free to use the medium luxuriantly, without guilt. You can feel the love of moviemaking—almost a revelry in moviemaking—in their films, as you can also in Walter Hill's *The Long Riders,* despite its narrative weaknesses and a slight remoteness. But we don't go to the movies just for great fairy tales and myths of the old West; we also hope for something that connects directly with where we are. Part of the widespread anticipation of *Apocalypse Now* was, I think, our readiness for a visionary, climatic, summing-up movie. We felt that the terrible rehash of pop culture couldn't go on, mustn't go on—that something new was needed. Coppola must have felt that, too, but he couldn't supply it. His film was posited on great thoughts arriving at the end—a confrontation and a revelation. And when they weren't there, people slunk out of the theatres, or tried to comfort themselves with chatter about the psychedelic imagery. Trying to say something big, Coppola got tied up in a big knot of American self-hatred and guilt, and what the picture boiled down to was: White man—he devil. Since then, I think, people have expected less of movies and have been willing to settle for less. Some have even been willing to settle for *Kramer vs. Kramer* and other pictures that seem to be made for an audience of over-age flower children. These pictures express the belief that if a man cares about anything besides being at home with the kids, he's corrupt. Parenting ennobles Dustin Hoffman and makes him a better person in every way, while in *The Seduction of Joe Tynan* we can see that Alan Alda is a weak, corruptible fellow because he wants to be President of the United States more than he wants to stay at home communing with his daughter about her adolescent miseries. Pictures like these should all end with the fathers and the children sitting at home watching TV together.

The major studios have found the temporary final solution for movies: in technique and in destiny, their films *are* television. And there's no possibility of a big breakthrough in movies—a new release of energy, like the French New Wave, which moved from country to country and resulted in an international cross-fertilization—when movies are financed only if they fall into stale categories of past successes. But once the groups that are now subsidizing studio-made films begin to weary of getting TV shows when they thought they were buying movies, there should be a chance for some real moviemaking. And when the writers and directors have confidence in what they want to express, if they can't find backing from the studios they ought to be able to find backers outside the industry who will gamble on the money to be made from a good picture, once it is completed. It's easier to make money on movies now: there are more markets, and we know now that the films themselves have a much longer commercial life than early moviemakers could have guessed. The studios may find that they need great moviemakers more than the moviemakers need them. Billy Wilder may be right that you can't make pictures with 'em, but of course he's wrong that you can't make pictures without 'em. There are problems both ways, but there may be fewer problems without them, and less rage.

It would be very convincing to say that there's no hope for movies—that audiences have been so corrupted by television and have become so jaded that all they want are noisy thrills and dumb jokes and images that move along in an undemanding way, so they can sit and react at the simplest motor level. And there's plenty of evidence, such as the success of *Alien*. This was a haunted-house-with-gorilla picture set in outer space. It reached out, grabbed you, and squeezed your stomach; it was more gripping than entertaining, but a lot of people didn't mind. They thought it was terrific, because at least they'd felt something: they'd been brutalized. It was like an entertainment contrived in Aldous Huxley's *Brave New World* by the Professor of Feelies in the College of Emotional Engineering. Yet there was also a backlash against *Alien*—many people were angry at how mechanically they'd been worked over. And when I saw *The Black Stallion* on a Saturday afternoon, there was proof that even children who have grown up with television and may never have been exposed to a good movie can respond to the real thing when they see it. It was a hushed, attentive audience, with no running up and down the aisles and no traffic to the popcorn counter, and even when the closing credits came on, the children sat quietly looking at the images behind the names. There may be a separate God for the movies, at that.

June 23, 1980

INDEX